Journal of Pentecostal Theology
Supplement Series
25

Editors
John Christopher Thomas
Rickie D. Moore
Steven J. Land

T&T Clark International
A Continuum imprint

Spirit of the

Last Days

Pentecostal Eschatology in Conversation

with Jürgen Moltmann

Peter Althouse

with a foreword by Jürgen Moltmann

T & T CLARK INTERNATIONAL
A Continuum imprint
LONDON • NEW YORK

Copyright © 2003 T&T Clark International
A Continuum imprint

Published by T&T Clark International
The Tower Building, 11 York Road, London SE1 7NX
15 East 26th Street, Suite 1703, New York, NY 10010

www.tandtclark.com

British Library Cataloguing-in-Publication Data
A catalogue record for this book is available from the British Library

Library of Congress Cataloging-in-Publication Data
A catalogue record for this book is available from the Library of Congress

Typeset by ISB Typesetting, Sheffield
Printed on acid-free paper in Great Britain by MPG Books Ltd, Bodmin, Cornwall

ISBN   0-8264-6914-0 (hardback)
        0-8264-6685-0 (paperback)

CONTENTS

A foreword is neither an afterword nor a review. A foreword is supposed to draw attention, to be an invitation to read a book. I am happy to write a foreword to this work of Peter Althouse, since I regard it as very important, and I recommend it to attentive readers. It is theologically significant, because it touches the heartbeat of the Pentecostal movements: Pentecostal movements are eschatological movements. In the expectation of the imminent coming of Christ the energies of the Holy Spirit are experienced, which according to Heb. 6.5 are 'the powers of a future world'. To demonstrate this, the author deals with the 'latter rain eschatology' of the early Pentecostal movement. Yet what kind of shape should the eschatological expectation of Christianity assume in order to experience such things?

This book is important not only to Pentecostal theology but also to the traditional Christian churches, for here the eschatological expectation likewise shapes the experience of the present and also the church's structure, even though this is mostly only a distant expectation. Tell me what you hope for, and I will tell you who you are! This study of Pentecostal eschatology has an eminent ecumenical significance. It can contribute to the embrace of the true Pentecostal spirit even by the traditional churches, by awakening within them a new eschatological hope.

Peter Althouse pursues both his aims by involving four Pentecostal theologians—Steven Land, Eldin Villafañe, Miroslav Volf and Frank Macchia —in dialogue with me and my eschatology. He deals with the theological path from the early 'pre-millennial dispensational eschatology' of the Pentecostal movement to a new 'transformational eschatology of the kingdom of God'. I welcome him on this path, since a successful outcome will lead to a fruitful liaison between the Pentecostal movement and liberation theology, and not just in Latin America, where it is badly needed.

My contribution in this foreword must be confined to my personal relationship with Pentecostal expectation and experience. For me, Christoph Blumhardt (1842–1919) in Bad Boll, Württemberg (an hour from Tübingen) is theologically the key figure. He was a master of hope and healing, an advocate of the sick and poor. Karl Barth called him 'a theologian of hope'. Christoph Blumhardt's roots lay in the revivalist movement of his father Johann Christoph Blumhardt, which began with a healing in Möttlingen in the Black Forest. The faith of his father manifested itself in the brief saying 'Jesus conquers'; the hope of his son in the equally short saying 'Jesus comes'. 'The Saviour is coming. He does not sit motionless in some place in eternity, waiting for a particular moment when he will suddenly arrive. Rather, he is coming. The future of Christ, then, is something to have always in front of us and to anticipate every day.'[1] The expectation of Jesus' *return* is therefore misleading in that it presupposes that Jesus is not here now, but will come again one day. In this way the present is emptied. But if Jesus is 'coming', then he steps each day out of his future into the present and each present has to open itself up to his arrival. 'Jesus is coming' means a future that is present without ceasing to be future. That can only mean a future that is not *futurum*, that is, something that is 'not yet', but at times will be and at times will be 'no more'. It is the *Advent*, that which 'comes to us' from God. Christoph Blumhardt did not hold to a futuristic eschatology, but an advent eschatology. If Jesus is embraced 'coming' then there is no problem of the 'delay of Christ's return'. The kingdom of God is then so 'near' that we can experience its healing and liberating effect. When Jesus proclaimed the 'presence' of the kingdom of God he did not mean a chronological moment, such as 'tomorrow at 12.30 pm', but a nearness that opens up to us our whole present. The healing and liberations that are experienced are not points in the past but messianic moments, experiences of what is coming, in which chronological time plays no part.

Blumhardt expects the kingdom of God *on earth* and nowhere else, 'so that we transfer the heavenly things to earth, so that we may at last see God on earth'. Hence he was attentive to the alienation of the modern world to nature and hoped for a 'harmony between humanity and nature'. It would be 'the solution to the social question'.

Blumhardt awaited the coming of Christ *within the history of the world*: he comes 'within the entire unfolding of time'. Thus he saw in the workers' movement of his day and in the liberation of peoples from European colonial power , 'signs of Christ', showing us where we should look for, and live, in solidarity with Christ.

I know that there is a considerable temporal and theological distance between the Pentecostalism of Blumhardt and that of America. I believe

---

1.   L. Ragaz, 'Der Kampft um das Reich Gottes', in C. Blumhardt, *Vater und Sohn—und weiter* (Zurich: Rotapfel Verlag, 1923), p. 148.

nevertheless that Christoph Blumhardt's eschatology of Christ 'coming' can be of help in overcoming a chronological dispensationalism through an eschatology of advent. It is not a question of speculation about the end of history, but of those expectations that allow us to experience healing and liberation, the awakening and the consolations of the living spirit of God.

The more that Pentecostal theology is broadened into a kingdom of God theology, the closer it comes to that liberation theology that, through the work of Jon Sobrino and Gustavo Gutiérrez, is nowadays also embedded in a kingdom of God theology. In a comprehensive kingdom of God theology the healing of the sick and the liberation of the poor are effected together. With the kingdom of God, which is 'coming' with Jesus, we gain not least apocalyptic counter-images to the state of this world and messianic counter-narratives to the increasing threats and dangers of 'this age'. Advent eschatology is always the eschatology of the divine alternative: 'Jesus is God's defiance against poverty, against sin and against all misery'.[2]

Peter Althouse's work has greatly stimulated me to think further about eschatology, and that is what I also wish for the readers of this book. To think eschatologically means to make the leap!

Tübingen
22nd June 2002
Jürgen Moltmann

2. Ragaz, 'Der Kampft', p. 60.

PREFACE

My journey has taken me in unexpected directions. I started out, in typical Pentecostal fashion, following a call of God on my life, but I was uncertain what this call would entail. I simply knew that I wanted to be faithful to God and enrolled in the local Pentecostal Bible College. Near the end of college, though, I realized that God was leading me along a different path.

While working on my undergraduate degree in sociology, studying the critical theories of Marx, Weber and Durkheim, I grew increasingly suspicious that Marx's positivistic theories of Communism were a secular version of Jewish-Christian eschatology and ethics. Marx argued that religion, as an element of culture, was a product of materialist socio-economic conditions. However, he also saw revolutionary potential within Christianity for overcoming socio-economic alienation. Thus while traditional Christianity maintained the status quo, radical forms of Christianity could potentially bring about a just society. Having grown up in a city that was influenced by the politics of social democracy, I wondered if there was a way of integrating Pentecostal theology and social justice, an element I saw lacking in contemporary Pentecostalism.

I enrolled at Wycliffe College with the intention of integrating my sociology background with my Pentecostal heritage in an effort to construct an authentic and responsible Pentecostal theology. It was not until I pursued my doctoral studies, however, that the pieces of the puzzle started to fit together. Serendipitiously, I registered for a course on Moltmann's theology. I knew very little of Moltmann and ended up in the course due to a scheduling conflict. Happily, I found Moltmann's work both fascinating and challenging. His writings introduced me to new theological issues. Although Moltmann's theology was somewhat alien to me, it resonated with some of my Pentecostal beliefs and concerns for social justice. Initially, my interest was in Moltmann's eschatology and pneumatology, but I soon realized that his participation in the Christian–Marxist dialogue also suggested ways for developing a social ethic. At the same time, I picked up Steven Land's newly published book *Pentecostal Spirituality*,[1] hoping to find an existential interpretation of the movement. I was intrigued with his work and it moved me in a different theological direction. In Land I saw an innovative approach to Pentecostal spirituality and similarities to Moltmann's theology.

Another piece of the puzzle fell into place while I was sitting in David Reed's Pentecostal and Charismatic theology course. I had assumed that Pentecostal eschatology was basically fundamentalist in structure with seven dispensations, the Rapture and the Millennial kingdom. I had even given a couple of lectures to that effect. However, it dawned on me that early Pentecostal theology of the latter rain was suggesting something different than fundamentalism's cataclysmic apocalyptic eschatology. Although still employing a dispensational pattern, latter rain eschatology foresaw a glorious end-time fulfilment of the Spirit's presence in the world immediately preceding the coming of Christ. Tongues, divine healing and other miraculous gifts were proleptic signs of the last days, but so were social concerns for racial peace, gender equality and justice. Within early Pentecostal theology were the seeds for a fully-fledged social ethic that circumvented the escapist attitude of fundamentalist dispensationalism that Pentecostals were later to adopt. In short, Pentecostal eschatology that saw the already/not-yet of the kingdom as transformation offered a theological framework that strengthened the inclusion of history and creation in the eschatological kingdom. This seemed to me more in line with the belief in the transforming presence of the Spirit in the world—embodied in the belief that Spirit baptism with the sign of tongues is empowerment for service—than the fundamentalist attitude of escapism. My Pentecostal dialogue partners are all addressing these issues and revisioning Pentecostal theology from their own perspectives, and Moltmann has proved to be an important voice in that process.

I hope the reader finds my attempt to construct a Pentecostal ethic more open to history and creation invigorating and helpful. The implications of a transformational eschatology go beyond the scope of my work here. Not only are there ecumenical implications, but I believe hermeneutical ones as well, rooted in a revision of latter rain theology. Traditional hermeneutics oscillates between the past (biblical, Jewish-Christian and apostolic) and the present. However, a trilectic hermeneutic that oscillates between past, present and future advent suggests a method for incorporating the

---

1. *Pentecostal Spirituality: A Passion for the Kingdom* (JPTSup, 1; Sheffield: Sheffield Academic Press, 1993).

coming kingdom into a thoroughly trinitarian hermeneutic. This discussion will have to wait for another time, however.

As with any work of this magnitude, a number of people have helped and supported me in this project. My deepest appreciation goes to David Reed, who taught me to think critically and thoughtfully about my Pentecostal tradition, and to Harold Wells, who exposed me to the theological insights of Moltmann. I would like to thank Reg Stackhouse for taking an interest in my ideas and encouraging me to pursue doctoral studies. I also want to thank my dialogue partners: Steven Land, Frank Macchia, Eldin Villafañe, Miroslav Volf and Jürgen Moltmann. Not only did I find their writings illuminating, but also a number were kind enough to update me on their latest publications. Frank Macchia was particularly helpful and sent me papers that were not yet in print. I want to express my appreciation to Jürgen Moltmann for kindly writing the Foreword. I have admired his theology for years and am pleased that he has found my work congenial. I also want to thank the staff at the Pentecostal Assemblies of Canada archives for access to materials needed at different stages in my research. Finally, both friends and family have supported me in this project in many different ways. I especially want to thank my wife Denise, who believed in me when I thought I would never see the end. Her love and faith make life all the more joyful.

ABBREVIATIONS

AJPS	Asian Journal of Pentecostal Studies
ASBFE	*Austin Seminary Bulletin Faculty Edition*
ATJ	*Asbury Theological Journal*
ATLA	American Theological Library Association
BQ	*Baptist Quarterly*
BUSPR	Boston University Studies in Philosophy and Religion
CC	*Christian Century*
ChrCr	*Christianity and Crisis*
CS	*Chicago Studies*
CT	*Christianity Today*
CTJ	*Calvin Theological Journal*
CTM	*Concordia Theological Monthly*
CurTM	*Currents in Theology and Mission*
DPCM	Stanley M. Burgess, Gary B. McGee and Patrick H. Alexander (eds.), *Dictionary of Pentecostal and Charismatic Movements* (Grand Rapids: Zonderman, 1988)
DukeR	*Duke Divinity School Review*
EJT	*European Journal of Theology*
EPTA	*European Pentecostal Theological Association*
ER	*The Ecumenical Review*
ERT	*Evangelical Review of Theology*
EvQ	*Evangelical Quarterly*
ExpTim	*Expository Times*
FH	*Fides et Historia*
GOTR	*Greek Orthodox Theological Review*
IICL	The 'Higher Christian Life': Sources for the Study of the Holiness, Pentecostal and Keswick Movements
HTR	*Harvard Theological Review*
IBMR	*International Bulletin of Missionary Research*
IHC	Studies in the Intercultural History of Christianity
IRM	*International Review of Missions*
JAH	*Journal of American History*
JCR	*Journal of Contemporary Religion*
JES	*Journal of Ecumenical Studies*
JETS	*Journal of the Evangelical Theological Society*

JITC	*Journal of the Interdenominational Theological Center*
JPT	*Journal of Pentecostal Theology*
JPTSup	*Journal of Pentecostal Theology*, Supplement Series
JSF	*Journal of Spiritual Formation*
JSNTSup	*Journal for the Study of the New Testament*, Supplement Series
JSSR	*Journal for the Scientific Study of Religion*
JTSA	*Journal of Theology for South Africa*
ModC	*Modern Churchman*
MoravianTsB	*Moravian Theological Seminary Bulletin*
MS	*Mission Studies*
MSJ	*Mater's Seminary Journal*
MT	*Modern Theology*
OC	*One in Christ*
PRS	*Perspectives in Religious Studies*
PSB	*Princeton Seminary Bulletin*
PSR	*Perspectives in Religious Studies*
PWS	Pietist and Wesleyan Studies
RelSRev	*Religious Studies Review*
ResQ	*Restoration Quarterly*
RevExp	*Review and Expositor*
RevRR	*Review of Religious Research*
RPW	*Reformed and Presbyterian World*
RST	*Religious Studies in Theology*
RW	*Reformed World*
SASP	Southern Anthropological Society Proceedings
ScotJRS	*Scottish Journal of Religious Studies*
SE	Studies in Evangelicalism
SewTR	*Sewanee Theological Review*
SJT	Scottish Journal of Theology
SL	*Studia Liturgica*
SP	*Synthesis Philosophica*
SPS	Society for Pentecostal Studies
SR	*Studies in Religion/Sciences religieuses*
SRS	Studies in Religion and Society
StVTQ	*Saint Vladimir's Theological Quarterly*
SWJT	*Southwestern Journal of Theology*
TE	*Theologica Evangelica*
TJ	*Trinity Journal*
TNN	*Theology, News and Notes*
TR	*Theology and Religion*
TS	*Theological Studies*
TSR	Texts and Studies in Religion
TTod	*Theology Today*

USQR	*Union Seminary Quarterly Review*
VE	*Vox Evangelica*
WesTJ	*Wesleyan Theological Journal*
WW	*Word and World*

INTRODUCTION

General Background

Eschatology has been of great importance to the Pentecostal movement. Being immersed in the millenarian culture of the late nineteenth century, early Pentecostals proclaimed the imminent return of Jesus Christ to establish the kingdom as a central doctrine of the 'full gospel'. Early Pentecostals developed their own brand of premillennial dispensational eschatology, arguing that the Pentecostal movement, with its manifestation of tongues, was the 'latter rain' outpouring of the Spirit. The 'former rain' was the outpouring of the Spirit on the day of Pentecost and the apostolic age. Believing that the gift of the Spirit had been withheld due to the church's apostasy, the restoration of the charismatic gifts was the latter rain outpouring intended to prepare the way for the final coming of Christ. Although Pentecostal eschatology was modified throughout the course of the twentieth century, eschatology has remained a prominent theme. The main difference was that, for early Pentecostals, the influx of charismatic activity through the latter rain outpouring of the Spirit was a sign that the people of God, and the world in which they lived, was being prepared and transformed for the imminent return of Christ to establish his kingdom. For many contemporary Pentecostals, however, the immediacy of the kingdom has become more distant, in part because Christ's return has been delayed. Today's Pentecostal has settled in the world, so needs to shift focus to develop a transformational ethic.

This shift has not been lost on contemporary Pentecostal theologians. At present, there is an ongoing revision[1] of Pentecostal eschatology, to develop a more transformative view of the kingdom, in an attempt to recover the prophetic elements of the early movement, which have been displaced by an apocalyptic vision of the world's destruction. Harvey Cox, for instance, a Harvard theologian sympathetic to the movement, argued that one of the

---

1. Revision in this book means to 're-envision' or create a new way of looking at something. At times it can function as a verb as well as a noun.

strengths of Pentecostalism has been its recovery of 'primal hope', an eschatological hope that envisioned spiritual and racial harmony through charismatic celebration.[2] The participants of Azusa Street, the initial locus of the Pentecostal movement, found 'a new and radically egalitarian spirituality. They also found a fellowship that foreshadowed the new heaven and new earth in which the insults and indignities of the present wicked world would be abolished or maybe even reversed.'[3] In other words, Cox believes that the primal hope of Pentecostal spirituality is transformative in scope.

In a similar vein, University of Tübingen theologian Jürgen Moltmann has been an important figure in bringing eschatology to the fore of theological discourse in the latter part of the twentieth century. Starting with *Theology of Hope* and continuing throughout his career, Moltmann has argued that eschatology needs to be transformative in character. For Moltmann, Christian faith is essentially and primarily Christian hope, 'forward looking and forward moving, and therefore also revolutionizing and transforming the present'.[4] The eschatological future, pictured in such concepts as the eschaton, the kingdom of God, the *parousia* and the new heaven and new earth, has the power to transform this present 'godforsaken' world, while providing hope for the future when God's glory and righteousness will be finally revealed. The future kingdom will be the divine consummation of what God has inaugurated in creation and in the Incarnation, death and resurrection of Jesus Christ. Creation itself will be transformed in the eschatological event. Moltmann's turn to eschatology is reflective of the eschatological focus of Pentecostalism.

To varying degrees in various authors, the revision of Pentecostal eschatology to include transformation into the kingdom of God has been influenced by Moltmann. The prominence of Moltmann's eschatological writings has been a focus of some emerging Pentecostal scholars, who have realized the importance of eschatology in their own theological heritage. It also may be that Moltmann himself was influenced by Pentecostals. Moltmann publicly noted the significance of Pentecostalism in the

---

2.   Harvey Cox, *Fire from Heaven: The Rise of Pentecostal Spirituality and the Reshaping of Religion in the Twenty-first Century* (Reading: Addison-Wesley, 1995), p. 82. Cox also included the recovery of 'primal speech' and 'primal piety' with 'primal hope', respectively related to the ecstatic speech of glossolalia and archetypal modes of worship such as dance or trances.

3.   Cox, *Fire from Heaven*, pp. 112-13.

4.   Jürgen Moltmann, *Theology of Hope: On the Ground and the Implications of a Christian Eschatology* (trans. James W. Leitch; London: SCM Press, 1967), p. 16.

Brighton Conference on World Evangelism and dialogued with them in 1994 over his *The Spirit of Life*[5] publication,[6] but revealed that Pentecostalism was not even in his mind while writing the book.[7] Moltmann later co-edited a 'Concilium' dialogue between a number of Pentecostal, Catholic, Protestant and Orthodox scholars.[8] However, the influence of Pentecostal theology on Moltmann may have come especially from one of his Pentecostal doctoral students, Miroslav Volf.

Four Pentecostal scholars have been selected as representative of Pentecostal revisionist thinking concerning eschatology: Church of God (Cleveland) theologian Steven Land; Gordon-Conwell Theological Seminary professor Eldin Villafañe, an Assemblies of God theologian with a special interest in developing a Hispanic Pentecostal theology, Yale Divinity School theologian Miroslav Volf, who is affiliated with the Evangelical Church of Croatia (Pentecostal), a member of the Presbyterian Church of the United States of America and presently worshipping in an Episcopal Church; and Assemblies of God theologian Frank Macchia, who teaches at Vanguard University, California. These scholars have been selected because they are all considered Pentecostal, they are all theologians (as opposed to historians or sociologists) and they all have at least one major scholarly publication related to Pentecostal eschatology. Land, Villafañe and Volf show varying degrees of influence from Moltmann. Macchia too has been partially influenced by Moltmann, but he has been influenced more by Wuerttemberg Pietism and Barthian theology. Macchia's inclusion will bring a sharper focus to the dialogue.

Steven Land's revisionist eschatology starts from the premise that Pentecostalism is better defined in terms of spirituality than systematic theology. Pentecostalism needs to be seen as an existential movement, with a concern for the trinitarian categories of orthodoxy (right beliefs), orthopraxy (right actions) and orthopathy (right affections), rooted in a

5.   Jürgen Moltmann, *The Spirit of Life: A Universal Affirmation* (trans. Margaret Kohl; Minneapolis: Fortress Press, 1992).

6.   Jürgen Moltmann, 'The Spirit Gives Life: Spirituality and Vitality', in Harold Hunter and Peter Hocken (eds.), *All Together in One Place: Theological Papers from the Brighton Conference on World Evangelization* (JPTSup, 4; Sheffield: Sheffield Academic Press, 1993), pp. 22-37.

7.   Jürgen Moltmann, 'A Response to my Pentecostal Dialogue Partners', *JPT* 4 (1994), pp. 59-70 (66).

8.   Jürgen Moltmann and Karl-Josef Kuschel (eds.), *Pentecostal Movements as an Ecumenical Challenge* (Concilium, 3; London: SCM Press, 1996).

proleptic eschatological vision of the kingdom of God.[9] Charismatic experiences, which define Pentecostal affections, need to be seen as a foretaste of the kingdom. God's kingdom is 'already' present through the
inauguration of Jesus Christ and the activity of the Spirit, but 'not yet'
fulfilled, as when the presence of God will be fully revealed. As such, the
vision of the future kingdom has transformative power in the present
world. Land adopts Moltmann's eschatological model and trinitarian
perspective to develop his revisionist eschatology.

Eldin Villafañe has constructed a Hispanic Pentecostal social ethic, and
done so in part through a revisionist eschatology. 'In order for the Hispanic Pentecostal Church to continue to minister *with* and *to* the poor and
oppressed', argues Villafañe, 'and thus to be true to the Gospel as a prophetic voice both as a church and by its message, and in order to preserve
its Hispanic cultural identity, it must construct a social ethic that affirms its
cultural heritage, and it must do so coming to terms with its social-status
as a minority-sect church in the U.S.A.'.[10] Villafañe has constructed a
social ethic that addresses the contextual realities of Hispanic Pentecostals
that looks not only to the joyful and life-affirming presence of the Spirit,
but also realities rooted in racial and socio-economic oppression. This
social ethic hinges on the eschatological 'reign of God', a reign already
present in Christ, but not yet fulfilled. The movement of history is part of
the movement of the Spirit urging creation towards its fulfilment in the
kingdom, a hard lesson for Pentecostals who have tended to adopt an ahistorical perspective. For Villafañe, salvation not only includes the personal
dimension of one's faith in Jesus Christ, but also a social dimension of
liberation from corrupt social systems.[11]

Miroslav Volf has also developed the social implications of a revisionist eschatology, one in which the kingdom of God will be the transformation of creation into the new heaven and new earth. Volf is significantly
influenced by Moltmann, who was Volf's dissertation director at Tübingen. Volf adopts Moltmann's eschatological model and argues that there
must be a continuity between the present world and the future kingdom.
The future kingdom will not see the annihilation of creation, but its total
transformation.[12] He then develops the social implications of such an

9. Land, *Pentecostal Spirituality*, p. 13.

10. Eldin Villafañe, *The Liberating Spirit: Toward an Hispanic American Pentecostal Social Ethic* (Grand Rapids: Eerdmans, 1993), p. xi.

11. Villafañe, *Liberating Spirit*, p. 186.

12. Miroslav Volf, 'On Loving with Hope: Eschatology and Social Responsibility',

eschatology, by constructing a theology of work based on the charismata of the Spirit, one in which the corporate achievements of human work will be transformed into the eschatological kingdom[13] and a social-political theology of reconciliation, one in which global conflicts and racial-ethnic disputes can be resolved through the embrace (or inclusion) of other cultural-ethnic peoples.[14] The embrace of 'the other' is reflective of the embrace of creation by God in the eschatological moment.

Frank Macchia has suggested an alternative revision of Pentecostal eschatology. Although he is the least influenced by Moltmann, Macchia has officially dialogued with Moltmann and translated one of his articles for the *Journal of Pentecostal Theology*.[15] Macchia argues that within the context of Wuerttemberg Pietism, the theologies of Johann Blumhardt and his son Christoph provide an important critique of Pentecostalism and the broader Evangelical culture. One can see similarities between Pentecostalism and the Blumhardts, for instance, in the struggle to combine revivalistic piety with responsible social commitment and in articulating a doctrine of healing as a material benefit of salvation.[16] The Blumhardts saw healing as a proleptic, visible manifestation of the kingdom of God, defined by Johann in terms of the Pentecost event of Acts 2 (rather than the future parousia) and by Christoph in terms of the christological/Incarnational event. This articulation of the kingdom allowed them to claim that history was the context through which God's kingdom was being manifested, both spiritually (Johann) and socially (Christoph). The fulfilment of the Spirit's work at

---

Transformation 7.3 (July–September 1990), pp. 28-31 (28); *idem*, 'Materiality of Salvation: An Investigation in the Soteriologies of Liberation and Pentecostal Theologies', *JES* 26.3 (1989), pp. 447-67.

13. Miroslav Volf, *Work in the Spirit: Toward a Theology of Work* (New York: Oxford University Press, 1991); *idem*, 'Human Work, Divine Spirit, and New Creation: Toward a Pneumatological Understanding of Work', *Pneuma* 9.2 (1987), pp. 173-93.

14. Miroslav Volf, *Exclusion and Embrace: A Theological Exploration of Identity, Otherness, and Reconciliation* (Nashville: Abingdon Press, 1996); *idem*, 'A Vision of Embrace: Theological Perspectives on Cultural Identity and Conflict', *ER* 47.2 (1995), pp. 195-205; *idem*, 'Exclusion and Embrace: Theological Reflections in the Wake of "Ethnic Cleansing"', *JES* 29.2 (1992), pp. 230-48.

15. Jürgen Moltmann, 'A Pentecostal Theology of Life' (trans. Frank D. Macchia), *JPT* 9 (1996), pp. 3-15.

16. Frank D. Macchia, *Spirituality and Social Liberation: The Message of the Blumhardts in the Light of Wuerttemberg Pietism* (PWS, 4; Metuchen: Scarecrow Press, 1993), p. 2.

Pentecost included history as significant in the unfolding of the kingdom.[17] The theology of the Blumhardts, argues Macchia, critiques Pentecostalism by de-emphasizing the Pentecostal tendency to stress the otherworldly/ supernatural and by incorporating the ecumenical significance of Pentecost, which emphasizes both the diversity and unity of peoples and language in tongues speech.[18] Macchia's subsequent research has shown an interesting influence of Blumhardt Pietism and understanding of the kingdom on his theology of glossolalia.[19]

The Purpose and Structure of this Book

A revisioning of Pentecostal eschatology is needed today in order to recover prophetic elements of early Pentecostalism that invite responsible social engagement in the world, and to overcome the 'fundamentalist' assumptions which have crept into Pentecostal theology in its middle years. To this end, I shall place the eschatological thought of selected Pentecostal theologians, and historic Pentecostal eschatology, into dialogue with the pneumatological eschatology of Jürgen Moltmann.

Chapter Outline
Chapter 1 examines the distinctiveness of Pentecostal eschatology, a distinctiveness that was encapsulated in the 'latter rain' doctrine. Early Pentecostals saw their movement as the restoration of the latter rain outpouring of the Spirit in preparation for the imminent coming of Christ. Pentecostal eschatology changed throughout the century, however, as a more fundamentalist eschatology insinuated itself into the movement and a schismatic revival known as the 'New Order of the Latter Rain' or 'Latter Rain Revival' used the same latter rain doctrine against established Pentecostal assemblies.

Chapter 2 examines the revisionist eschatologies of the four previously mentioned contemporary Pentecostal scholars—Steven Land, Eldin Villa-

---

17. Macchia, *Spirituality*, p. 161.
18. Macchia, *Spirituality*, p. 168.
19. Frank D. Macchia, 'God Present in a Confused Situation: The Mixed Influence of the Charismatic Movement on Classical Pentecostalism', *Pneuma* 18.1 (1996), pp. 33-54; *idem*, 'Sighs Too Deep for Words: Toward a Theology of Glossolalia', *JPT* 1 (1992), pp. 47-73; *idem*, 'Tongues as a Sign: Towards a Sacramental Understanding of Pentecostal Experience', *Pneuma* 15.1 (1993), pp. 61-76; *idem*, 'The Tongues of Pentecost: A Pentecostal Perspective on the Promise and Challenge of Pentecostal/ Roman Catholic Dialogue', *JES* 35.1 (1998), pp. 1-18.

fañe, Miroslav Volf and Frank Macchia—who have suggested revisions to Pentecostal eschatology, attempting to recover an authentic Pentecostal spirituality, which includes a mandate for social responsibility.

Chapter 3 examines Jürgen Moltmann's pneumatological eschatology, an eschatology that has had varying degrees of influence on contemporary Pentecostal scholars. It examines four areas in Moltmann's eschatology: the centrality of eschatology for Christian faith; the relationship between Jesus Christ, the Holy Spirit and the kingdom; the historical and political significance of eschatological hope; and cosmic eschatology as the transformation of creation.

Chapter 4 places Moltmann and the four Pentecostal theologians into dialogue. It examines the convergences and divergences between Moltmann and the revisionist eschatologies of Land, Villafañe, Volf and Macchia. While similarities can be ascertained between them, a number of differences between them emerge as well. Macchia's eschatological revision was the most dissimilar to Moltmann, and an important critique of Moltmann's eschatology.

Methodology

A descriptive-critical methodology is used throughout this book. The basic presupposition here is that one needs to comprehend what Pentecostalism has actually taught in order to assess its validity and evaluate it critically. The methodological criteria for this evaluation include: (1) a faithfulness to Scripture, with an awareness of its historical reception as canon and its hermeneutical application in the contemporary world; (2) a sensitivity to the various theological traditions; (3) the contextual appropriateness of theology as it relates to the cultural, social and political issues of today's world; and (4) its interaction with the social sciences. These presuppositions will be operative as they relate to Pentecostalism. To this end, Chapter 1 assesses Pentecostal eschatology by examining its theological history. Chapters 2 through 4 will be revisionist and dialogical, not only in assessing the revisionist eschatologies of Pentecostal scholarship and Moltmann's eschatology, but also with suggestions for further revisions.

Sources

The primary sources for the history and theology of the Pentecostal movement are pamphlets, periodicals, journals and writings of early Pentecostals. Unlike the historic churches, Pentecostals have not articulated, nor do they intend to articulate, a creed. The closest Pentecostals have come to a creed have been doctrinal statements affirmed by the respective Pentecostal denominations. Fortunately, many Pentecostal writings that were previously found only in scattered archives around the world can now be found in the 'Higher Christian Life' series.[20] Also, primary sources include the major pneumatological and eschatological volumes of Moltmann, and the substantial publications of the four selected Pentecostal theologians.

Limitations

There will be a number of limitations to this study. First, although the Oneness wing of Pentecostalism has been an interesting development within the movement, this book is restricted to the Holiness and Reformed wings of Pentecostalism. Secondly, while willing to connect with related disciplines such as history and the social sciences, this book is clearly theological. It attempts to give an internally authentic Pentecostal spirituality a strengthened theological framework. Finally, it has been commonplace for early Pentecostals to travel the world spreading their message, creating interesting and innovative Pentecostal developments worldwide. However, except for occasional reference to European Pentecostalism, the scope of this book is limited to the North American context.

---

20. Donald W. Dayton (ed.), *'The Higher Christian Life': Sources for the Study of Holiness, Pentecostal and Keswick Movements* (New York: Garland Publishing, 1985).

Chapter 1

PENTECOSTAL ESCHATOLOGY: THE STORY OF THE LATTER RAIN

In 1906, under the tutelage of African-American holiness preacher William J. Seymour, a revival broke out at Azusa Street, Los Angeles, California, which spread throughout the world in a relatively short time. This revival looked to the charismatic experiences of the apostolic church, commencing with the day of Pentecost, as normative for the modern church. Although Seymour had imbibed much of what was to become Pentecostal theology from Charles F. Parham, particularly the doctrine that the baptism of the Holy Spirit was evidenced by 'speaking in other tongues', it was the Azusa revival and its quest for spiritual and social renewal of the church in preparation for the imminent return of Jesus Christ that gave birth to the Pentecostal movement.

For the early Pentecostal, experience of the presence of God through the charismata of the Spirit was of utmost importance. One of the prominent features of the revival was the charismatic experience of glossolalia, which Pentecostals typically referred to as 'speaking in tongues'.[1] For the Pen-

---

1.   What Pentecostals identify as 'speaking in tongues' or glossolalia is technically defined as 'unintelligible vocalization' or 'miraculous use of language the speaker has never learned'. Robert Mapes Anderson, *Vision of the Disinherited: The Making of American Pentecostalism* (Oxford: Oxford University Press; Peabody, MA: Hendrickson, 1979), p. 16. Malony and Lovekin examine glossolalia from a behavioural science perspective through the anomalous, aberrant and extraordinary models. The anomalous model suggests that glossolalia functions as a focus for commitment to a religious group involving a reorientation of the personality or as a ritual that lifts the person above mundane existence. The aberrant model argues that glossolalia is connected to psychological or emotional disturbance and is often related to psychological problems. The extraordinary model suggests that glossolalia is atypical for either the individual or society. The primary question in this model is whether or not glossolalia occurs in an altered state of consciousness. See H. Newton Malony and A. Adams Lovekin, *Glossolalia: Behavioral Science Perspectives on Speaking in Tongues* (Oxford: Oxford University Press, 1985), pp. 8-9. Theologically, glossolalia can be seen as an encounter with the Spirit involving both natural and metaphysical elements.

tecostal, speaking in tongues was a sign that the believer had received the baptism of the Holy Spirit, an experience subsequent to conversion which was believed to empower the recipient for Christian service. Further glossolalic episodes were expected and encouraged. The Pentecostal believed, however, that Spirit baptism with the sign of tongues initiated the believer into further charismatic experiences and empowered the Christian for service.

Certainly Pentecostals identified themselves with the phenomenon of glossolalia as the restoration of one of the lost gifts of the Spirit for the church. Yet observers of the movement have focused predominantly on glossolalia to the exclusion of other features of the Pentecostal revival. For the early Pentecostal movement, speaking in tongues and other charismatic experiences were signs that God's Spirit was being poured out in the last days to prepare the way for Christ's imminent return, a theology known as the 'latter rain' outpouring of the Spirit. Thus a major thrust of the Pentecostal movement was its eschatological message, a message made real by the experiences of God's presence. Other aspects of Pentecostalism, such as its view of missions, ecclesiology, pastoral concerns, and so on, all stemmed from its eschatological vision.[2]

The following, then, will explore how charismatic experiences of the Spirit informed and were informed by the eschatological theology of the Pentecostal movement. Of course, one could look at how religious experiences common to early Pentecostals informed other theological views such as their ecclesiology or soteriology, but the longing for Christ's return was crucial for the early Pentecostal. Pentecostal eschatology was not uniform, however. Seymour's eschatological vision was different than that of Charles F. Parham, the Wesleyan Holiness preacher who first articulated the theological position that the sign of the baptism of the Holy Spirit was speaking in tongues.[3] Furthermore, the eschatology of Pentecostalism changed

---

2.   Early Pentecostal biographer Frank Bartleman summed up the Pentecostal message when he said: 'But here we are the restoration of the very experience of "Pentecost", with the "latter rain", a restoration of power, in greater glory, to finish up the work begun. We shall again be lifted to the church's former level, to complete the work, begin where they left off when failure overtook them, and speedily fulfilling the last great commission, open the way for the coming of the Christ' (Frank Bartleman, *Azusa Street* [S. Plainfield, NJ: Bridge Publishing, 1980], pp. 89-90). Also see D. William Faupel, 'The Function of "Models" in the Interpretation of Pentecostal Thought', *Pneuma* 2.1 (1980), pp. 51-71, for a sample of early Pentecostal eschatological thought.

3.   The official position of the Assemblies of God and other white Pentecostal denominations has been that 'speaking in tongues is the *initial evidence* of the baptism

throughout the century, as influences from other theological traditions and cultural variances made themselves felt.

After defining the various forms of the Pentecostal/Charismatic movement, this book explores the 'latter rain' eschatological articulations of William J. Seymour and Charles F. Parham, which were both restorationist and premillennial dispensational in orientation. Early Pentecostal eschatology was restorationist in looking back to the apostolic church with the day of Pentecost providing a powerful metaphor for the movement, and premillennial dispensationalist in looking forward to the imminent coming of Christ. It will then probe the reasons why the Pentecostal latter rain doctrine waned in the mid-twentieth century, reasons related to the growing influence of fundamentalist dispensational eschatology in Pentecostalism and the appropriation of latter rain theology by a schismatic movement known as 'The New Order of the Latter Rain', to challenge the institutional authority of the mainstream Pentecostal denominations. However, although latter rain doctrine waned in mainstream Pentecostal churches, it was revised and re-directed into the Charismatic Renewal movement, and especially the Independent Charismatic movement.

of the Holy Spirit'. See Gary B. McGee, 'Popular Expositions of Initial Evidence in Pentecostalism', in *idem* (ed.), *Initial Evidence: Historical and Biblical Perspectives on the Pentecostal Doctrine of Spirit Baptism* (Peabody, MA: Hendrickson, 1991), pp. 119-30. However, the initial evidence doctrine was not uniformly proclaimed among early Pentecostals. Parham articulated the initial evidence doctrine, though he also believed that tongues enabled the believer to witness to foreigners in their own languages without prior knowledge of those languages (see below, pp. 25-28). While Seymour imbibed the initial evidence doctrine from Parham, he later changed his thinking to say that tongues was only one of the signs of Spirit baptism. In May 1907, Seymour's periodical, the *Apostolic Faith*, claimed that speaking in tongues was the evidence, 'the Bible evidence', of the baptism of the Holy Spirit. Yet Seymour wrote in September 1907 that '*Tongues are one of the signs* that go with every [Spirit-] baptized person'. See Cecil M. Robeck, 'William J. Seymour and "The Bible Evidence" ', in McGee (ed.), *Initial Evidence*, pp. 72-95 (80-81). Not only did Seymour alter his position to argue that any of the charismatic gifts could indicate Spirit baptism, but he started to question the terminology of evidence itself. This issue came to the fore in the Assemblies of God in 1918 when Fred F. Bosworth argued that tongues was but one of the gifts that indicated Spirit baptism, while Daniel W. Kerr argued that 'tongues only' was the initial evidence of Spirit baptism. The Assemblies of God was to adopt the latter position as its official doctrine. See McGee, 'Popular Expositions', p. 130 n. 2; see also Anderson, *Vision of the Disinherited*, pp. 163-64. Chapter 2 will address the issue of initial evidence and Spirit baptism in the theology of Frank Macchia.

Varieties of Pentecostalism

The term Pentecostal has been used with varying degrees of accuracy to describe movements of spiritual revival and reform, whole denominations or specific churches within non-Pentecostal denominations. Pentecostal has also been used in the typological sense to describe a spirituality that stresses the renewing power of the Holy Spirit.[4] Historically, however, there are two movements that are considered Pentecostal: Classical Pentecostalism and the Charismatic movement.

Classical Pentecostalism consists of those groups that stem from the Azusa Street revival at the beginning of the twentieth century. While at risk of oversimplification, Classical Pentecostalism can be categorized in three ways: Wesleyan Holiness Pentecostalism; Reformed Pentecostalism; and Oneness Pentecostalism. The Wesleyan Holiness Pentecostal stream teaches a 'three works of grace' soteriological pattern consisting of the experiences of conversion, entire sanctification for the perfection of the believer and the baptism of the Holy Spirit which empowers the believer for witness and service. The Reformed Pentecostal stream collapses conversion and sanctification into one 'finished work of Calvary' doctrine, in which sanctification has already been accomplished on the cross of Jesus Christ but not yet fully realized in the life of the believer. Baptism of the Holy Spirit is a subsequent infilling believed to empower the Pentecostal for ministry. The Oneness Pentecostal stream follows in the steps of the Reformed stream, but has a modalistic view of the Godhead.[5] Important

---

4.   Richard Lovelace suggests two historical models of spirituality: The 'ascetic model' incorporates Christians who sought disciplines (*askesis*) for Christian life, particularly in the process of sanctification. The 'Pentecostal model' incorporates the presence and renewing power of the Holy Spirit, where the gifts of the Spirit are manifested. Although the ascetic model dominated the church during the patristic and mediaeval eras, the Pentecostal model reached its prominence in the Protestant Evangelical awakenings. By seeing 'Pentecostal' as a model for spirituality, Lovelace argues that Pentecostalism is rooted in the 'tradition of renewing activism which runs from Patristic spirituality up through the Reformers' (Richard Lovelace, 'Baptism in the Holy Spirit and the Evangelical Tradition', *Pneuma* 7.2 [1985], pp. 101-124 [101-103]). Lovelace's thesis is suggestive, but by seeing 'Pentecostal' as a type describing the renewing power of the Spirit seems to stretch the term to the point of making it meaningless. Every spiritual movement contends that it includes some element of the Spirit's renewing presence and power, even if it conforms more to the ascetic model.

5.   Donald W. Dayton, *Theological Roots of Pentecostalism* (SE, 5; Metuchen: Scarecrow Press, 1987), p. 18.

for all three groups is the connection between the theological belief in an experience of the baptism of the Holy Spirit subsequent to conversion and the charismatic manifestation of glossolalia. However, only the first occurrence of glossolalia is linked to Spirit baptism. Subsequent manifestations of tongues are signs of the fullness of the Spirit that has been activated in Spirit baptism.

From a historical perspective, whether one believes the Pentecostal movement commenced in 1900 with Parham's doctrine that 'tongues is the sign of the baptism of the Holy Spirit' subsequent to conversion, or in 1906/1907 with Seymour's Azusa Street revival, where the consequence of the presence of the Holy Spirit was a reconciled community of all races, classes and genders, the initial thrust of the movement was Wesleyan Holiness in orientation. The experiences of conversion and the 'second blessing' of sanctification, that perfects the believer through the grace of God, are considered two separate acts of grace to which the baptism of the Holy Spirit is added as a third. Reformed-minded Pentecostals accepted the Wesleyan context in the early years, but in 1910, William H. Durham, an Azusa Street preacher and friend of Seymour, preached a message entitled 'The Finished Work of Calvary'. In this message, Durham claimed that no second work of grace for the purpose of perfection was necessary. Instead, perfection was already realized in the historical reality of the cross. Because Christ had offered a perfect, atoning sacrifice on the cross, the believer was imputed with Christ's righteousness. The believer was perfected in faith by accepting the work Christ had already accomplished. Sanctification did not mean that there was a change in one's nature, as was argued in the Wesleyan doctrine of sanctification, but that one had been consecrated and set apart for God's service.[6] For Durham, sanctification was realized in the finished work of Calvary, but involved the believer's vigilance in crucifying the old nature. 'God expects them to live a clean, holy, separated life', stated Durham, 'to crucify the flesh in the Spirit'.[7] For Durham, sanctification was a daily process of renewing one's life before God, to become Christ-like in holiness, but perfection itself was already attained in the atoning work of Jesus Christ. Although Durham died in 1912,

6.   D. William Faupel, *The Everlasting Gospel: The Significance of Eschatology in the Development of Pentecostal Thought* (JPTSup, 10; Sheffield: Sheffield Academic Press, 1996), p. 67.

7.   William H. Durham, 'Some Other Phases of Sanctification', *Pentecostal Testimony* in *Pentecostal Testimony Files* (Assemblies of God Archives, Springfield, MO), p. 10.

Reformed-minded Pentecostals who agreed with his 'Finished Work' doctrine gathered together and in 1914 formed their own denomination, the Assemblies of God.

At the same time, a potentially schismatic movement known as the 'New Issue' or 'Oneness Pentecostals', claimed that the Lukan formula for water baptism (Acts 2.38), in which the believer was 'baptized in the name of Jesus only', was considered more pristine and therefore more correct than the Matthean trinitarian formula (Mt. 28.19).[8] While the two groups tried to co-exist in the first two years of the Assemblies' history, the aggressiveness of Oneness Pentecostals in proselytizing people to their position and the equally aggressive response by trinitarian-minded Pentecostals finally clashed in 1916, resulting in the Oneness Pentecostals being voted out of the denomination.

Secondly, in the 1960s the Charismatic Renewal movement arose with spiritual emphases similar to Classical Pentecostalism, especially practices of glossolalia. There were two streams in the Charismatic movement: one that encouraged renewal within the denominations; and another that sought independence from denominational ties. Adherents to the denominational group remained within their own denominations, effecting spiritual and liturgical changes within their own traditions. Although most Charismatics have adopted the Classical Pentecostal terminology of baptism of the Holy Spirit and associated it with speaking tongues, Charismatics have generally not accepted the Classical Pentecostal position that tongues was the 'only' evidence of Spirit baptism. Charismatics generally preferred to believe that any of the charismatic gifts[9] could indicate Spirit baptism and/ or that tongues was a personal prayer language. Charismatics of the liturgical-sacramental traditions have also been uncomfortable with the idea of a subsequent baptism, believing that there was to be only one baptism commencing with salvation. Nevertheless, Charismatics believed that the language of baptism of the Holy Spirit was important and continued to use it, even though it posed some difficult theological questions.[10] Further-

8.   D.A. Reed, 'Oneness Pentecostalism', in *DPCM*, pp. 644-51.

9.   Charismatics as a movement will be identified with the upper case 'C', while charismatic as a description of the manifestation of the Spirit's gifts will be identified with the lower case 'c'.

10.   Peter Hocken, 'Charismatic Movement', in *DPCM*, pp. 130-60 (158). The issue of a baptism of the Spirit subsequent to conversion is a subject of debate between James D.G. Dunn, *Baptism of the Holy Spirit: A Re-Examination of the New Testament Teaching on the Gift of the Spirit in Relation to Pentecostalism Today* (London: SCM Press, 1970), and Robert P. Menzies, *Empowered for Witness: The Spirit in Luke–Acts*

more, a distinction must be made here between 'Charismatic' as a spiritual renewal movement and 'charismatic' referring to the operation of the Spirit in the believer as the believer was gifted by the Spirit. In the latter sense all Christians were charismatic, but in the former sense only those Christians of the specific spiritual movement from the 1960s on were considered Charismatics.

During the 1960s and 1970s, Charismatics tended to stay within their own denominations, but in the 1980s and 1990s there was a trend for Charismatics who were frustrated with denominational limitations to form non-denominational assemblies. These newer assemblies made up a subsection of the Charismatic movement and have been labelled the Independent Charismatic movement. Independent Charismatics were considered charismatic because they insisted on experiences of the Spirit subsequent to conversion. However, the Independent Charismatic movement was diverse and difficult to classify. Pentecostal/Charismatic statistician David Barrett identifies the Independent Charismatic movement as those churches 'which either have separated from the charismatic renewal in parent mainline denominations...or have recently been founded independently (though from out of the same milieux), all being either independent congregations or in loose networks, and all being mainly or predominantly white membership...'[11] For now it can be stated that the Independent Charismatic movement consists of Charismatics who prefer to remain independent of denominational structures.

Pentecostalism in this book is narrowly defined as those people identified as Classical Pentecostal, stemming from the Azusa Street revival. While Pentecostals and Charismatics both had hope in the imminence of

---

(JPTSup, 6; Sheffield: Sheffield Academic Press, 1994). Dunn argues that the Pentecostal theology of a baptism of the Spirit subsequent to initiation-conversion (whether activated in infant baptism or voluntary conversion) is contrary to scriptural evidence. Arguing from a Reformed theological perspective, Dunn claims that the gift of the Spirit is soteriological in character and therefore cannot be separated from initiation-conversion. Interestingly, Dunn, on the one hand, argues that the Pentecostal belief of a subsequent action of the Spirit in the life of the believer stems from the Catholic belief of a subsequent act of the Spirit in confirmation, delineated through Anglican and Wesleyan sources (*Baptism of the Holy Spirit*, p. 226). Menzies, on the other hand, argues that Lukan sources separate the gift of the Spirit from initiation-conversion, though Pauline sources tie them together. Luke consistently portrays the Spirit as the source of prophetic inspiration and must be distinguished from Paul's conversion-initiation view. Menzies, *Empowered for Witness*, p. 238.

11.   D.B. Barrett, 'Statistics, Global', in *DPCM*, pp. 810-29 (827). Barrett provides a partial list.

the end-time *parousia*, Pentecostals had an eschatology different from the Charismatics. Pentecostals generally adopted a premillennial dispensational eschatology, while Charismatics rarely adopted the dispensational model.[12] The Independent Charismatic groups have tended to be premillennial, but without a doctrine of a Rapture or Tribulation. However, the church must be perfected in preparation before Christ's return, a theology developed from latter rain restorationism.

The Latter Rain Eschatology of Early Pentecostalism

In his seminal work on the historical formulation of Pentecostal theology, Donald Dayton shows that in the diverse beliefs that comprise the Pentecostal movement a common fourfold theological pattern emerged. While there is also a fivefold pattern, which sees sanctification as a crisis experience, Dayton argues that it is the fourfold pattern that better expresses the inner logic of the movement. This pattern, which Pentecostals subsumed under the rubric of the 'full gospel', emphasizes the doctrines of Christ as saviour, sanctifier, baptizer in the Holy Spirit, healer and soon-coming king.[13] The reason for the fourfold or fivefold conflict, which revolved around distinctions between the Calvinist and Wesleyan streams in Pentecostalism, focused on whether sanctification was an accomplishment of an instantaneous 'second blessing' experience or whether sanctification was a progressive work, 'already' judiciously realized in Christ's atonement, but progressively seeking the 'not yet' of the perfecting holiness of God. Be that as it may, all early Pentecostals had an urgent sense of the nearness of Christ's return. Whether they adopted a fourfold or fivefold pattern, this urgent expectation of Christ's coming nourished the other elements of the 'full gospel' rubric. Thus the urgency of salvation with an emphasis on evangelistic and missionary zeal, the insistence that both the baptism of the Holy Spirit with the sign of tongues and the work of sanctification

---

12. Hocken, 'Charismatic Movement', pp. 155-56. Premillennialism generally asserts that there will be a millennial period of Christ's bodily presence and reign of complete peace, righteousness and justice on the earth. Postmillennialism asserts that the kingdom of God is a present reality as the rule of Christ in human hearts that will lead to a long period of peace on earth identified as the millennium. Postmillennialists are not literalistic about the length of the millennium, nor do they expect a bodily return of Christ. See Millard J. Erickson, *Contemporary Options in Eschatology: A Study of the Millennium* (Grand Rapids: Baker Book House, 1977), pp. 91-92, 55-56.

13. Dayton, *Theological Roots*, pp. 19-22, 173.

would make the believer a more effective witness of the gospel, and the insistence on healing as an outflow of the charismatic presence of the Spirit of God in the latter days, were all heightened by the Pentecostal eschatological expectation.

While early Pentecostals were influenced by the Evangelical milieu of the time and generally adopted a premillennial dispensational eschatology with a sense of the immediacy of Christ's return,[14] they had their own version of premillennial dispensationalism. The key to understanding Pentecostal eschatology, though, is to understand what they meant by the 'latter rain' or the 'apostolic faith', names Pentecostals used to identify themselves.[15] This linkage was evident in Charles Parham's description of

14.   Evangelicalism is a difficult term to define. Donald Dayton, e.g., argues there have been three differing and unconnected ways in which the term Evangelical has been used. Sixteenth-century Reformational theology, eighteenth-century Pietism and twentieth-century fundamentalism all formed subsets of Evangelicalism. Consequently, Dayton believes the term Evangelical has become meaningless. Donald W. Dayton, 'Some Doubts about the Usefulness of the Category "Evangelical" ', in Donald W. Dayton and Robert K. Johnston (eds.), *The Variety of American Evangelicalism* (Downers Grove, IL: InterVarsity Press, 1991), pp. 245-51 (245). David Bebbington, however, offers a helpful, working definition of Evangelicalism consisting of those groups of Christians that emphasize conversion, activism, biblicism and crucentrism (focus on the cross). D.W. Bebbington, *Evangelicalism in Modern Britain: A History from the 1730s to the 1980s* (London: Unwin Hyman, 1989), pp. 2-3.

15.   Faupel explores five early Pentecostal theological motifs that can be developed into models. The 'full gospel' model sees Pentecostalism within the rubric of justification by faith, sanctification as a second blessing, healing, the premillennial return of Christ and baptism in the Holy Spirit evidenced by speaking in other tongues. The 'latter rain' model is a way in which Pentecostals interpret theology in light of their understanding of history. It argues that each dispensation is opened and closed by a move of God's Spirit. The 'apostolic faith' model asserts that Pentecostalism is a restoration of the apostolic church and doctrine in simplicity and unity. The 'Pentecostal movement' model is an experiential model, which argues that the movement is an inauguration of a new era of God's power and glory and that the Pentecostal narrative of Acts 2 is the pattern for experiential life in Christ. The 'everlasting gospel' model is eschatological and asserts the imminent, premillennial return of Christ which motivates evangelistic and missionary enterprises. In this model, the message of pending judgment is authenticated by signs and wonders and proclaimed through supernatural means. See Faupel, 'Function of "Models" ', pp. 53-63; also *idem, The Everlasting Gospel*, pp. 27-43. Although all five motifs were operative within early Pentecostalism, the latter rain is better able to connect eschatology to pneumatology, as the link between anticipation of the imminent return of Christ and the outpouring of the Spirit. In the latter rain motif, the outpouring of the Spirit occurs in the brief period prior to the final

the Pentecostal movement entitled, 'The Latter Rain: The Story of the Origin of the Original Apostolic or Pentecostal Movements'.[16]

The latter rain doctrine, expressed by D. Wesley Myland in *The Latter Rain Covenant and Pentecostal Power*, linked the Pentecost narrative of Acts 2 with the prophecy of Joel, which stated that in the 'latter days' the Spirit will be poured out on all flesh (Acts 2.1-22). Myland argued that the rainfall of Palestine came in two seasons: in the spring when planting occurred and in the fall as the crops ripened. Using the Palestinian climate as a metaphor for the outpouring of God's Spirit, he stated:

> If it is remembered that the climate of Palestine consisted of two seasons, the wet and the dry, and that the wet season was made up of the early and latter rain, it will help you to understand this [latter rain] covenant and the present workings of God's Spirit. For just as literal early and latter rain was poured out upon Palestine, so upon the church of the first century was poured out the spiritual early rain, and upon us today is being poured out the spiritual latter rain.[17]

The pattern of Palestinian rainfall provided a metaphorical image for Pentecostals, by which they understood their own relationship to the apostolic church and to the imminent end of the age.[18] Moreover, the doctrine of the latter rain is suggestive of a covenant theology, in which the diverse prophetic traditions of Israel were continued into the apostolic period through the event of Pentecost. Thus the promise of God to Israel is the promise of God to the church and the eschatological age, which extends from the time of Christ's Incarnation to his imminent coming.

---

inbreaking of the kingdom, and thus has transformative consequences on the present world. The transformative implication of eschatological hope is picked up by the four Pentecostal revisionists in dialogue with Moltmann, who expand the period of the last days to include the span of time from Christ's Incarnation and event of Pentecost through to the eschaton. The church is therefore in the last days and experiences the 'already' and 'not yet' of the kingdom.

16.   Dayton, *Theological Roots*, pp. 22-23.

17.   David Wesley Myland, *The Latter Rain Covenant and Pentecostal Power* (Chicago, IL: The Evangel Publishing House, 1910), p. 1, in Donald W. Dayton (ed.), *Three Early Pentecostal Tracts* (HCL, 14; New York: Garland Publishing, 1985); cf. Edith L. Blumhofer, *The Assemblies of God: A Chapter in the Story of American Pentecostalism.* I. *To 1941* (Springfield: Gospel Publishing House, 1989), pp. 150-51.

18.   Dayton, *Theological Roots*, p. 27; also D. William Faupel, 'The Everlasting Gospel: The Significance of Eschatology in the Development of Pentecostal Thought', (unpublished PhD dissertation; University of Birmingham, UK, 1989), p. 53.

The latter rain doctrine was later displaced by the intrusion of fundamentalist dispensational doctrine (a subject to be addressed in the next section), but the 'latter rain' was crucial for understanding the logic of early Pentecostalism. The movement saw itself as having a key role in the climax of history as the 'bride' of Christ, namely, the Christian faithful, as it prepared itself for Christ's return. This doctrine explained the rise of charismatic experiences[19] in the late nineteenth and early twentieth centuries and it also explained why there was such a 'drought' of charismatic experiences throughout the history of the church in the post-apostolic period. Just as the rains of Palestine fell in the spring during planting and in the fall during harvest, the Spirit of God was poured out when the apostolic church was birthed and in the last days when there would be a 'final harvest of souls'. Thus argues Dayton:

> These 'signs and wonders' not only tie the eschatological themes into the whole complex of the four-square gospel, but the Latter Rain framework makes the great apologetic problem of Pentecostalism into a major apologetic asset. The long drought from post-apostolic times to the present is seen to be a part of God's dispensational plan for the ages. What seemed to make the movement most illegitimate—its discontinuity with classical forms of Christianity—has become its greatest legitimation.[20]

The latter rain doctrine was not unique to Pentecostal thought. For instance, Phoebe Palmer, a Wesleyan Holiness preacher in the mid-nineteenth century, used the latter rain doctrine to defend the ministry of women in the church. She did this by linking the office of preaching (once in the sole possession of men) to prophecy. Using the Joel quotation in Acts 2, Palmer argued that since both men and women would prophesy in the latter days, so both men and women were called to preach the gospel.[21] Pentecostals later used this argument to justify the role of women in ministry[22] and the Pentecostals' call to preach, even when they were at best

19. Early Pentecostals spoke of the experiences of the Spirit as supernatural, rather than charismatic. The term charismatic was an influence of the Charismatic movement which tried to explain these experiences in light of church tradition and theology. However, 'charismatic' has greater theological validity, for it identifies these experiences as continually evident in the history of the church, without adopting the modernist assumptions when using the term supernatural.

20. Dayton, *Theological Roots*, p. 28.

21. Dayton, *Theological Roots*, p. 88.

22. For example, of the elders at Seymour's Azusa Street mission five were men and seven women. Iain MacRobert, *The Black Roots and White Racism of Early Pentecostalism in the USA* (New York: St Martin's Press, 1988), p. 56. Women's leadership

ignored or at worst despised and ostracized by most of the historic Christian churches.

For the Pentecostal movement, the Acts 2 narrative of the day of Pentecost provided an important link to the apostolic church, a link that made the movement restorationist in orientation. Pentecostal historian Edith Blumhofer asserts that seeing Pentecostalism as a restorationist movement bridges the tendency to split it into Wesleyan and non-Wesleyan components, while giving due importance to the various holiness movements, German Pietism, premillennialism and 'Higher Life' teachings inherent in Pentecostalism. The restorationist thesis also provides a basis for including Oneness Pentecostals in the broad context of Pentecostalism, as a group more thoroughgoing restorationist than its trinitarian counterparts. It gives due importance to the role African-Americans and racial minorities had in the early history of Pentecostalism, based on a restorationist view that 'all are one in Christ' (Gal. 3.21), a view justifying racial harmony.[23]

She also states that there are four ways in which the restorationist motif influenced the rise of Pentecostalism. First, restorationism was closely related to the perfectionist hope for personal and religious reform. Late nineteenth-century America was optimistic in its own progress and betterment. Restorationism contradicted this belief by advocating a return to earlier norms. Being essentially ahistorical, restoration called for a purification of religious norms and practices that had been 'polluted' by historical development. Personal perfection and religious reform could only be achieved by returning to the patterns of New Testament Christianity. Second, restorationism contributed to assumptions about Christian unity and simplicity, especially with reference to church structure and doctrine. Restorationists ignored the diversity that existed in the early church and espoused its unity. The belief was that the simplicity of the early church before the advent of doctrinal disputes was the pattern for unity in the church today. Third, restorationism accompanied eschatological themes, as evident in the latter rain doctrine. Restorationism reinforced assumptions about the former and latter rain outpouring of the Spirit, the former being the apostolic pattern, the latter being the restoration of this pattern and precipitous to the coming eschatological reign of Christ. Fourth, restorationism supported Pentecostalism's antidenominational attitudes, for Pente-

was prominent in the early Pentecostal movement in such roles as preaching, pastoring, evangelism and missions—the most prominent being Amiee Semple McPherson and Maria B. Woodworth-Etter.

   23.   Blumhofer, *Assemblies of God*, I, p. 15.

costals tended to find submission to church authority intolerable, both in terms of traditions and creeds as well as ecclesial power structures.[24] Thus Pentecostals called for the restoration of apostolic Christianity, a restoration that started with the Reformers' doctrine of justification by faith, Wesley's doctrine of sanctification and the Pentecostal doctrine of Spirit baptism with tongues and the gifts of the Spirit. (The Latter Rain Revival and Independent Charismatics added the restoration of prophets and apostles, as will be seen.)

While Dayton argues that the eschatological hope of Christ's return was one factor in the fourfold gospel, Wagner College professor, Robert Mapes Anderson, and Asbury Seminary historian, D. William Faupel, argue that the eschatological expectation was the primary thrust of the movement upon which other beliefs hinged. Anderson, who adopts a sociological deprivation model to explain the rise of Pentecostalism, argues that glossolalia was not only regarded as a sign of the baptism of the Holy Spirit (restoration), but also was a sign of a second Pentecost of the church and more importantly a sign of the imminent return of Christ (latter rain).[25] Because early Pentecostals regarded both church and state as being corrupt, they abstained from political activity aimed at social or ecclesial change. Instead, their hope for change was in the imminent coming of Christ, who would right the injustices and oppression in the church and the world.[26]

Likewise, Faupel argues that the primary thrust of the Pentecostal movement was its eschatological message and that it emerged as a paradigm shift in the millenarian belief system of nineteenth-century perfectionism.[27]

---

24. Blumhofer, *Assemblies of God*, I, pp. 18-19. Blumhofer's thesis critiques the earlier theses of Dayton, *Theological Roots*, pp. 173-79, and Vinson Synan, *The Holiness-Pentecostal Movement in the United States* (Grand Rapids: Eerdmans, 1971), p. 8, who assert that Pentecostalism was a schismatic movement within the Wesleyan Holiness movements and Anderson, *Vision of the Disinherited*, pp. 40-43, who asserts that Pentecostalism was Reformed/fundamentalist. Although Blumhofer believes that restorationism bridges Wesleyan/ Reformed distinctions, she then argues that Reformed sources of Keswick and American revivalist theologies better explain the rise of the Assemblies of God, thereby weakening her own thesis. Blumhofer, *Assemblies of God*, I, p. 15.

25. Anderson, *Vision of the Disinherited*, p. 4. Anderson's deprivation model is sociologically sound, but it is theologically shallow and does not look at the depth and significance of Pentecostalism.

26. Anderson, *Vision of the Disinherited*, p. 5.

27. Faupel, 'Everlasting Gospel', p. 17.

However, Faupel's definition of eschatology is too narrow. He argues that eschatology is a belief system in which 'the conviction that history is about to come to an immediate, turbulent end and that it will be replaced by a new, perfect society'.[28] Faupel's definition represents an apocalyptic type eschatology, typical of Pentecostal eschatological thought, but there have been other eschatologies that do not predict a 'turbulent end' to the world. For instance, we will see below that Moltmann's eschatology does not envision the destruction of the world in the eschaton, but its transformation into the new creation and that a number of contemporary Pentecostals are revisioning Pentecostal eschatology to reflect an eschatology of transformation rather than one of world destruction.

Pentecostals hold a 'Christ against culture' attitude, to put it in terms of H. Richard Neibuhr's typology.[29] They see values of secular society as being sinfully corrupt, values that had supported slavery until 1875 and later oppression of African-Americans, values that had established a demeaning class structure and that minimized the role of women in society. Pentecostals believed that the historic church had wedded itself to those values of society and had therefore violated its calling. Thus by holding an anti-establishment attitude, Pentecostals could remould the church, and by extension society, according to what they believed was the biblical paradigm of Pentecost. Just as the church was together in one accord in the apostolic age, without respect to race, gender or class (Acts 2.1), so early Pentecostals envisioned the modern church in preparation for the return of Christ. This vision was especially true for Seymour's hope for a reconciled church, where all races would worship and work together as brothers and sisters.

Seymour's revolutionary thrust was fuelled by a mixture of prophetic and apocalyptic visions. Using prophetic and apocalyptic in a typological

28.   Faupel, 'Everlasting Gospel', pp. 35-36.

29.   H. Richard Niebuhr, *Christ and Culture* (New York: Harper Torchbooks, 1951), pp. 40-44. Niebuhr offers a fivefold typology: 'Christ against culture', in which the Christian commmunity stands in opposition to culture; 'Christ and culture', where the Christian community and culture are virtually identical; 'Christ above culture', similar to the second type but with a certain discontinuity between culture and the Christian ideal; 'Christ and culture in paradox', in which both the authority of Christ and the authority of culture are accepted as well as the opposition that exists between them; and 'Christ transforming culture', where Christ is seen as the converter of both humans and culture. Early Pentecostals exhibited a Christ against culture mentality. They preferred to withdraw from what they believed were 'sinful' social structures and attempted to create a counter-culture through a biblically based community structure.

sense, the prophetic vision critiques the religious and social order by means of religious sources, that is, Scripture, tradition, religious experience, and so on, in an effort to change the social world. The prophetic usually accepts, to some degree, the social and religious order and makes an effort to participate in the inbreaking of the kingdom of God through protest of the worldly order. In the prophetic, there is a dialectic tension between what society is really like in the present and what it should be like according to some religious ideal. The apocalyptic vision is a belief that the world is completely destitute of godliness and that it will come to some cataclysmic end precipitated by Christ's return. The apocalyptic vision rejects the world order and concentrates on religious concerns.[30] Only a Christian elite will persevere until the day of the Lord, often called in Pentecostal/ Charismatic circles the 'bride of Christ' or 'overcomers'. The apocalyptic often exhibits revolutionary potential. Early Pentecostalism exhibited the apocalyptic trend, especially in the eschatological theology of Parham. While Seymour's eschatology was also apocalyptic, it had prophetic implications for the church and society in terms of race and gender.[31]

Perhaps it is fair to say that much of Pentecostal eschatology is an innovation of premillennial dispensationalism inherited from one-time Anglican turned Plymouth Brethren, John Darby, whose theology made its way into Wesleyan Holiness thinking. Both Parham and Seymour, as Holiness preachers, imbibed this form of dispensationalism. The dispensational schemata asserted that salvation history was divided into different epochs and in each dispensation God dealt with humanity in a way unique to that epoch. Two basic dispensational models emerged. One was a sevenfold pattern which insisted that salvation history was divided into seven distinct epochs that ended in failure, conflict and divine judgment. These included: (1) the age of 'Innocence' that ended with the 'Fall'; (2) the age of 'Conscience' that ended with the 'Flood'; (3) 'Human Government' that ended

---

30. See Reginald Stackhouse, *The End of the World? A New Look at an Old Belief* (New York: Paulist Press, 1997), pp. 10-28. Stackhouse argues that the apocalyptic and prophetic forms two eschatological types. On the one hand, the apocalyptic is revolutionary, emphasizes the supernatural, appeals to the marginalized, believes that only the elect will see the kingdom of God, is counter-cultural and interprets Scripture literally. On the other hand, the prophetic is reformational in character, emphasizes the natural order, appeals to the middle class, is universal in scope, accommodates societal values and is more complex when interpreting Scripture.

31. Pentecostal eschatology has shifted from the apocalyptic type to a more prophetic one, as will be seen in its shift from a hope in Christ's soon return to a hope for the kingdom of God.

with 'Babel'; (4) the age of 'Promise' that ended in Egyptian captivity; (5) the age of the 'Law' that ended with the rejection of Christ; (6) the age of 'Grace' which will end with the return of Jesus Christ. Although the exact point of Christ's return was disputed between pre- and post-millenarians, and Tribulationists, God's divine judgment was expected to close the age of Grace before the final age; (7) Christ's kingdom reign.[32]

Darby's dispensational thought was slightly different in that he added a futuristic scenario. He believed there was an absolute separation of Israel and the church and, as a consequence, unfulfilled Old Testament prophecies applied only to the Jewish nation. Further, since many Old Testament prophecies remained unfulfilled, Darby argued that at the end of the church dispensation, there would be a period of time in which the Jewish nation would be restored, the divided kingdoms of Israel would unite and the Messiah would be accepted by the Jews. This would be the period of the Tribulation.[33] He was also unique in arguing that there would be a 'secret Rapture' when the church would be taken up into heaven to be with Christ before the time of Christ's Second Advent. Faupel notes:

> At the time of the Rapture, Darby contended, Christ would come invisibly *for* the Church. Seven years later, at the time of the Second Advent, He would appear visibly *with* the Church. Between these two events, Israel would be restored as a nation, the anti-Christ would be unveiled, and the great Tribulation would occur.[34]

What made Darby's eschatology appealing was that the 'secret Rapture' would restore God's prophetic time-clock. The embarrassing problem of predicting a precise time for Christ's return which would fail to happen as predicted was averted. For Darby, the Rapture would unpredictably occur, and then the unfulfilled prophecies of Scripture would subsequently unfold.[35]

Although some Pentecostals adopted a sevenfold dispensational pattern (notably Parham), their theology was more consistent with the threefold model. The sevenfold pattern was generally espoused by 'fundamentalism', an anti-modernist theological movement that emphasized dispensational millenarianism, biblical inerrancy and the cessation of the charismatic

---

32. George M. Marsden, *Fundamentalism and American Culture: The Shaping of Twentieth-Century Evangelicalism 1870–1925* (New York: Oxford University Press, 1980), pp. 65-66.

33. Faupel, 'Everlasting Gospel', pp. 166-67.

34. Faupel, 'Everlasting Gospel', p. 168.

35. Faupel, 'Everlasting Gospel', p. 68.

gifts of the Spirit after the canonization of Scripture.[36] Dayton rightly argues that although an intermingling between Pentecostalism and dispensationalism occurred in general, early Pentecostalism was more influenced by the tripartite dispensationalism of Wesleyan theologian John Fletcher. He divided salvation history into the dispensation of the Father, which looked to the manifestation of the Son, the dispensation of the Son, which looked to the promise of the Father for the effusion of the Son and the dispensation of the Spirit, which looked for the return of the Son. The dispensation of the Spirit was now in full force. Fletcher's dispensationalism had an inner logic distinct from fundamentalist dispensationalism. It was better able to connect pneumatology with eschatology by making Pentecost an eschatological event comparable to the coming of Christ.[37] Moreover, the threefold dispensational pattern allowed Pentecostals to apply many Old Testament prophecies to the church and appropriate biblical promises that dispensationalists relegated to the millennial kingdom.[38]

Charles F. Parham's Eschatology
Parham adopted a premillennial dispensational eschatology, but innovated it in a way that would later make it coherent to Pentecostal thinking. As has been mentioned, latter rain thinking asserted that the manner in which a dispensation opened was also the way a dispensation closed. So just as the apostolic church opened with widespread charismatic manifestations, the closing of the church dispensation would also exhibit these manifestations. Furthermore, as the church age closed, there would be an intense 'harvest of souls' never before seen.

Parham was fond of preaching eschatological themes at annual camp meetings. 'Though not substantially different from the premillennial themes preached by other Pentecostals', comments Parham historian James Goff, 'the messages were more in-depth and more speculative with regard to current world events'.[39] What made Parham's eschatological messages

36. Marsden, *Fundamentalism and American Culture*, pp. 4-5; idem, *Understanding Fundamentalism and Evangelicalism* (Grand Rapids: Eerdmans, 1991), pp. 1-4; also see Jon Ruthven, *On the Cessation of the Charismata: A Critique of the Protestant Polemic on Postbiblical Miracles* (JPTSup, 3; Sheffield: Sheffield Academic Press, 1993).
37. Dayton, *Theological Roots*, pp. 51-52, 149-53.
38. Dayton, *Theological Roots*, p. 145.
39. James R. Goff, *Fields White unto Harvest: Charles F. Parham and the Missionary Origins of Pentecostalism* (Fayetteville: University of Arkansas Press, 1988), p. 155. Goff's central thesis is that Parham, rather than Seymour, should be credited as

uniquely Pentecostal was that he claimed that the sign of the subsequent baptism of the Holy Spirit, the subject of subsequence having plagued Wesleyan Holiness thinkers who often spoke of a 'second blessing' experience of sanctification, was speaking in other tongues. For Parham, Spirit baptism was an experience of empowerment for Christian service, an event that would speed the final harvest before Christ's return. What made Parham's eschatology unique to early Pentecostals, but not to later ones, was that he believed speaking in tongues under the supernatural inspiration of the Holy Spirit allowed the Christian to speak a foreign language without having learned that language. This ability, he believed, would allow the Spirit-baptized Christian who had no formal language training to go into foreign mission fields to preach the gospel in the language of those indigenous groups. The belief was that because the time was short before Christ's return, the Holy Spirit made supernatural allowances to prepare for the coming kingdom.[40]

Parham believed that since the coming of Christ was going to occur in his lifetime, there was an urgent need to evangelize the world. The intensity of missions thinking, an intensity forged in the belief that preaching

---

founding the Pentecostal movement, because Parham first articulated the doctrine that speaking in tongues was the initial sign of the baptism of the Holy Spirit. Those who argue that Seymour should be considered the founder of the movement, scholars such as MacRobert, *Black Roots*, p. 60, and Cox, *Fire from Heaven*, pp. 55-64, do so by arguing that Seymour sought racial integration as the primary message of the movement. Seymour's priority should be rejected, according to Goff, because the racial integration Seymour envisioned quickly disintegrated, approximately from 1914 to 1921, as white Pentecostals distanced themselves from black Pentecostals. The problem with Goff's thesis is that defining Pentecostalism solely by the initial evidence doctrine is one-sided. The primary surgence of the movement came from the Azusa Street revival, where Seymour was the undisputed leader. Whether one locates the beginning of Pentecostalism with Seymour or Parham, the Azusa Street revival appears to take on symbolic significance in the birth of the movement.

40. Goff, *Fields*, p. 72. A technical distinction must be made between glossolalia, which is defined as fabricated speech in a strange tongue occurring in a state of ecstasy or altered state of consciousness, and xenoglossia, which is the utterance of a foreign language not previously known to the tongues speaker. Research has not been able to substantiate the occurrence of xenoglossia. See Malony and Lovekin, *Glossolalia*, pp. 18-20. However, the theory of cryptomnesia provides a possible explanation for xenoglossia. This theory argues that a person might be able to speak a previously unlearned foreign language, if that person has heard that language in the past. The tongues speaker is somehow able to access an unconscious part of the brain which has stored memories of that language and then verbally reconstruct it. Goff, *Fields*, p. 77.

the gospel to the whole world was the last requirement to be fulfilled before Christ would return, provided a utilitarian function for tongue speaking[41] as an empowerment for Christian service. Parham further believed that it was a 'sealing of the bride'.[42] In the end-time Tribulation, those 'sealed' by the Spirit would receive 'resurrection bodies' and 'like Jesus, have the power to appear and disappear... [and] to traverse the earth at will'.[43] During God's millennial reign, these 'overcomers' would serve in important government positions.[44] For Parham, then, Spirit baptism was a special seal of God's approval and an assurance of one's place in the new age.[45]

41. Goff, *Fields*, p. 78.

42. Blumhofer, *Assemblies of God*, I, p. 74. Blumhofer asserts that Parham did not see baptism of the Spirit as an enduement of power for service, but the fact that he believed it enabled one to speak foreign languages supernaturally for the purpose of evangelization belied this assessment.

43. See Charles F. Parham, *A Voice Crying in the Wilderness* (Baxter Springs, KS: Joplin Printing, 4th edn, 1944), in Donald W. Dayton (ed.), *The Sermons of Charles F. Parham* (HCL, 36), pp. 70-79; cf. Anderson, *Vision of the Disinherited*, p. 85. In a highly speculative eschatology, Parham made a distinction between 'the body of Christ', 'the bride of Christ', 'the Man-Child' and 'the Saints'. The body of Christ was the true church, at a time when the 'Antichrist' (i.e. a political leader of a one-world government described as the 'King of the South') and the 'False Prophet' (i.e. the Roman Catholic Pope whom Parham believed was the ruler of an apostate church) were already at work in the world. An elite band of 144,000 believers will be taken from the body of Christ to become the bride of Christ (i.e. those blessed with the Pentecostal baptism). The bride will then 'give birth' to another 144,000 believers who will constitute an elite band called the Man-Child (i.e. those who have attained the highest state of perfection possible for human beings). At the beginning of the Tribulation, the Man-Child will be taken up in the Rapture and the bride of Christ will flee into the 'wilderness'. In what Parham described as the last stage of 'Redemption' before Christ's millennial reign, those baptized by the Spirit will be 'sealed' against the wrath of the Antichrist because they will have 'resurrection bodies'. The bride of Christ will preach to the Saints during the Tribulation (i.e. those Christians who were saved and sanctified but remained on the earth during the Tribulation because they had not been looking for Christ's coming or been baptized in the Spirit), telling them that they must not receive the 'mark of the beast' and must accept martyrdom. The Antichrist will not be able to touch the bride of Christ or the Man-Child, because they have resurrection bodies, and so will turn his wrath against those who do not accept the mark of the beast. At the beginning of the millennial reign, the Man-Child will return with Christ and together with the body of Christ, bride of Christ and the resurrected martyrs, will be rewarded with positions of authority over the masses who did not know God. Anderson, *Vision of the Disinherited*, pp. 84-86.

44. Like Anderson, Goff portrayed Parham and the Pentecostal movement as 'fundamentalist'. While Parham may have been more fundamentalist than other early

Parham also believed in the annihilation of the wicked, a belief that was generally not accepted by other Pentecostals. Eternal life, argued Parham, was granted only to those who had received Christ's salvation. Those who rejected salvation would be punished in a literal burning of hell, but this punishment was momentary, for the unredeemed would be consumed and their existence ended.[46]

The Pentecostal eschatological hope had theological ramifications for Pentecostal beliefs. Anderson rightly argues that early Pentecostalism was a form of 'anti-establishment Protestantism that was anticlerical, antitheological, antiliturgical, antisacramental, antiecclesiastical, and indeed, in a sense, antireligious'.[47] Consequently, while Pentecostals regarded the church establishment as elitist, they were more often open to women in ministry, they had an ecumenical vision of one unified church with Spirit-baptized Christians acting as a spiritual vanguard leading the way until Christ's coming, and they envisioned a church that would be unified in terms of racial and class integration.[48] However, this was more the theological vision of Seymour than that of Parham.

The most interesting ramification of Parham's apocalyptic vision was that by focusing exclusively on spiritual concerns he and fellow Pentecos-

---

Pentecostals, he adopted a non-fundamentalist position on evolution. Asserting a doctrine known as the day-age theory, Parham argued that because a day is like 1000 years to God, the days of the Genesis creation story equate to 1000-year ages. He was wrong on two counts: the equation between one day and one 1000 years cannot be taken literally but must be seen figuratively and it takes much longer than 7000 years for evolutionary development to take place. Nevertheless, it shows that Parham cannot be lumped in with fundamentalists. Goff, *Fields*, p. 103.

45.   Goff, *Fields*, p. 78.
46.   Goff, *Fields*, p. 153.
47.   Anderson, *Vision of the Disinherited*, p. 214.
48.   While Pentecostals saw themselves as inclusive and sought a unified church, many of their Evangelical based beliefs resulted in exclusionary practices and resulted in early conflicts and schisms between white and black Pentecostals, trinitarian and Oneness Pentecostals, and Wesleyan and Reformed Pentecostals. Moreover, while Spirit baptism was an experience of peace and empowerment to be desired, it sometimes had the effect of excluding those who had not received the baptism of the Spirit from being fully accepted into the Pentecostal community. Pentecostals were also unwilling to accept the theological positions of non-Evangelical denominations. They believed in an ecumenism which would be achieved 'not by man-made organization, but by the direct leading of the Spirit in the creation of a fellowship of all believers'. However, unless denominational churches held 'full gospel' beliefs, Pentecostals were unwilling to include them. Anderson, *Vision of the Disinherited*, p. 84.

tals had little use for worldly concerns, that being the cultural, political and governmental affairs of the world. These anti-cultural views were exhibited in the holiness behavioural attitudes of Pentecostals. For the most part, they abstained from alcohol, refrained from worldly amusements (e.g. theatre, card-playing, reading non-religious literature), dressed modestly, refused to wear jewellery, and so on. Their suspicions of politics and government were not only directed towards civic issues but towards religious ones as well, making early Pentecostal eschatology apocalyptic in character.

Early Pentecostal unwillingness to seek change through political means was related to its eschatological view. According to Anderson:

> The Pentecostal belief in an imminent, apocalyptic return of Christ was itself part of a larger myth that provided a unified view of the past, present and future—a myth that derived its validity from its correspondence to the real life experiences of those who accepted it. From the Pentecostal perspective history seemed to be running downhill—at least, for the Pentecostals—and the world seemed to be at the point of collapse—their world, at any rate.[49]

Because early Pentecostals were bereft of social standing and acceptability —most were blue-collar workers, immigrants and ethnic minorities, oppressed African-Americans and disillusioned church folk—there was a definite view that the world was 'going to hell-in-a-hand-basket'.

George F. Taylor, an early leader in the Pentecostal Holiness Church and editor for the *Pentecostal Holiness Advocate*, exhibited this anti-establishment attitude when he criticized the ability of the democratic process to effect social change, though he did believe that the church should be governed democratically. He commented:

> The Spirit of antiChrist [*sic*] pervades the world today. It is that which is keeping things going as they are. There is not a government on earth that is not controlled by this spirit. It is useless to say that the Christian people should rise up by ballot and put such a spirit out. Such a thing is impossible. The spirit will continue to gain ascendancy until it culminates in the final Antichrist of the ages. All efforts to put it down are fruitless. The only thing we can do is seek to save individuals from its power.[50]

Taylor's belief that changing the world through social activism was ultimately fruitless was held by many Pentecostals, and rooted in the belief that Christ was soon returning.

49. Anderson, *Vision of the Disinherited*, pp. 80-81.
50. *Pentecostal Holiness Advocate* (28 June 1917); as quoted by Anderson, *Vision of the Disinherited*, p. 208.

Parham held certain anti-capitalist and anti-American beliefs. He predicted that the second coming would be preceded by a violent class conflict, where the government, the rich and the mainline church which allied with the state would fight on one side and the masses would fight on the other. He argued in the style of classic Pentecostal rhetoric:

> Capital must exterminate and enslave the masses or be exterminated... In this death struggle...the rich will be killed like dogs... For a long time the voices of the masses have vainly sought for relief, by agitation and the ballot, but the governments of the world were in the hands of the rich, the nobles, and the plutocrats, who forestalled all legislative action in the interests of the masses, until the wage-slavery of the world became unbearable; until the worm, long ground under the iron heel of oppression, begins to burn with vindictive fire, under the inspiration of a new patriotism in the interests of the freedom of the working class. Therefore, would it be considered strange if the overzealous already begin to use the only means at hand for their liberty—by bombs and assassination to destroy the monsters of government and society that stand in the way of the realization of their hopes?... Ere long Justice with flaming sword, will step from behind the pleading form of Mercy, to punish a nation which has mingled the blood of thousands of human sacrifices upon the altar of her commercial and imperialistic expansion.[51]

Parham was obviously cynical about capitalism and social justice through governmental action. Although his rhetoric sounded similar to those of social gospellers who wanted to revolutionize the workplace, to alleviate poverty and give working-class people the dignity and respect they deserved, Parham was ambivalent towards the emerging unionist movements. The issue was not so much social justice as the oppressive conditions of the bureaucracies of institutional organizations. Parham remarked:

> While we are not personally a member of any lodge or union, neither have we aught against them, for if the church had done its duty in feeding the hungry and clothing the naked, these institutions would not have existed, *sapping the life of the church*... Upon the ascension to power of an Anti-Christ [sic], a worldwide union or protective association will be organized by the fanatical followers, and one will be compelled to subscribe to this union association, and receive a literal mark in the right hand or forehead, or he cannot buy or sell.[52]

---

51. Charles F. Parham, *The Everlasting Gospel* (Baxter Springs, KS: privately printed, 1942), pp. 28-30; as quoted by Anderson, *Vision of the Disinherited*, p. 209.

52. Parham, *Everlasting Gospel*, pp. 33-35; as quoted by Anderson, *Vision of the Disinherited*, p. 210.

Parham often used revolutionary rhetoric, which did not always translate into political activism. His ambivalence in regards to socialist causes was evident in one of his lectures entitled, 'Christianity vs. Socialism: He [Jesus?] is a Christian, not a Socialist, but graduated from a School of Socialism'. In it, Parham preached that the 'cry of socialism…is the heart-cry of Jesus'.[53]

A similar sentiment was echoed by James McAlister, a Pentecostal who pastored in Toronto, Ontario, for a period of time, though McAlister sympathized with the socialist cause:

> Whilst our sympathies are with every just claim of labor for shorter hours and better wages, and whilst we support all that is good in Socialism as against the greed of capital and the crime of profiteering, we cannot but feel that Democracy [unionism?] is intoxicated with the wine of lawlessness, and is in danger of insensate deeds of violence which will bring rivers of blood and a rain of tears.[54]

Parham clearly connected the unionist movement with the mark of the beast, which would establish Antichrist's rule during the Tribulation. McAlister's reference to 'rivers of blood' suggested a connection between the violence of the unionist movement and the battle of Armageddon. Thus Pentecostal anti-establishment attitudes stemmed from their apocalyptic eschatological beliefs.

Anderson argues that all millenarian movements exhibit progressive-revolutionary potential, which criticizes the status quo with a vision of a new social order that condemns the present order and seeks to change it. Pentecostalism certainly contained these revolutionary tendencies, but socially conservative elements eventually infiltrated and triumphed over revolutionary and progressive ones.[55] This revolutionary tendency resided in the Pentecostal apocalyptic vision, but contrary to Anderson's view, who views the movement as one faction of early twentieth-century fundamentalism, the fundamentalist programme crept into the movement in the 1930s to 1950s. Admittedly, there were early Pentecostals who were fundamentalist in orientation, but other religious perspectives were represented as well. Most prominent were Wesleyan Holiness and Keswick theologies. Before examining this issue, however, we need to consider Seymour's apocalyptic eschatology. It was similar to Parham's eschatology because

53. Goff, *Fields*, p. 156.
54. *Pentecostal Evangel* (10 July 1920), p. 1; as quoted by Anderson, *Vision of the Disinherited*, p. 210.
55. Anderson, *Vision of the Disinherited*, p. 195.

Seymour was socialized in the same Evangelical culture of Wesleyan Holiness, but he also had certain prophetic qualities, primarily due to his African-American heritage. Using the same Pentecostal narrative of 'when all were together in one accord', Seymour envisioned a social and racial integration within the church unseen since the time of the apostolic church, an integration that would occur in the latter days in preparation for Christ's return.

William J. Seymour's Eschatology
Iain MacRobert argues, against Goff and Anderson, that Seymour should be considered the founder of the Pentecostal movement, not only because he was the leader of the Azusa Street revival, but also because he envisioned a world in which blacks and whites, men and women, would live and work together in harmony as equals. The difference between black and white Christianity was that, while whites were anticipating the Second Advent, blacks were seeking a solution to American inequality. The appeal of the Pentecostal movement was that it promised a fulfilment of both dreams.[56]

According to MacRobert, what Seymour brought to the Pentecostal movement was a synthesis of Western theology and West African spirituality. 'The black understanding and practice of Christianity', argues MacRobert, 'which developed in the crucible of New World slavery was a syncretism of Western theology and West African religious belief and practice'. Black spirituality saw no distinction between the seen and unseen worlds; it made no distinction between the sacred and profane,[57] and it sought a psychological integration of mind, body and emotion in worship.[58] Western Christianity, which had adopted many of the assumptions of Enlightenment rationality, had not only made a distinction between the natural and metaphysical, but also had in many ways paid only lip-service to the belief that the presence of God is manifested in the world through the Spirit in more than scriptural illumination.[59] Pentecostals

---

56. MacRobert, *Black Roots*, p. 34.

57. MacRobert, *Black Roots*, pp. 2-3. MacRobert's thesis that Pentecostalism is a syncretism of West African spirituality and Western theology is provocative and suggestive, but is not demonstrated. He fails to show any connections to African spirituality, or how this syncretism occurs.

58. MacRobert, *Black Roots*, p. 34.

59. Jon Ruthven argues that Reformed Protestants generally, and more specifically B.B. Warfield, the subject of Ruthven's study, tended to restrict miracles and charismatic phenomena to the apostolic era. More importantly, Warfield restricted revelation

typically made distinctions between the natural and the supernatural, and believed that manifestations of the Spirit, such as tongues, healing, tongues and interpretation, singing in the Spirit,[60] and so on, were supernatural infusions of the Spirit in the physical world. They also believed that these manifestations proved to the sceptics that God not only existed but was actively operative in the world. Pentecostals would not, however, have understood that the natural/supernatural dichotomy was modernist in orientation.

Seymour sought racial integration in the church, based on a restoration-ist view of the Pentecostal account of Acts 2. In the United States, at the turn of the twentieth century, slavery had been eliminated so that blacks were free but not at all 'equal'. Racism was institutionalized in policies that denied blacks the vote, segregated them from whites, kept them from rising in social standing and ensured their continued subjugation. As a result, the black tradition in which Seymour was socialized included not only the study of the Bible but also a 'black folk Christianity' which included themes of freedom, equality and community. Thus freedom from sin also meant freedom from slavery, oppression and injustice, as well as freedom for the entire person (mind, body and emotion) to express himself or herself in the power and presence of the Spirit. The bodily expressions of tongues—shakings, falling in the Spirit, shrieking, laughing, and so on—were just as valid as the rational, liturgical styles of Western Christianity. For black Christianity, the vertical relationship to God, which was a prominent feature of Evangelicalism, and the horizontal relationship with human beings, which MacRobert believes was lacking in Evangelicalism, were important foci of spirituality.[61] Consequently, Seymour's spirituality

to the Word of God (Christ) and Christian doctrine which was solidified in the comple-tion of the canon of Scripture. Ultimately, under Warfield's Reformed thinking, the action of the Spirit was limited to biblical illumination and the regeneration of the believer, but failed to address the Spirit's ongoing means of communicating that reve-lation, communication which included charismatic phenomena and miracles. Ruthven, *On the Cessation of the Charismata*, p. 194.

60.   Classical Pentecostal doctrine made a distinction between speaking in tongues, which was the initial evidence of the baptism of the Holy Spirit, patterned after the Acts 2 narrative of the day of Pentecost, and tongues which was followed by an interpretation, intended for the edification of the church, which was patterned after the Corinthian account of the operation of charismatic gifts. There was also the manifesta-tion of singing in the Spirit, where the congregation would spontaneously sing in tongues in a harmonious way.

61.   MacRobert, *Black Roots*, pp. 34-35. While Evangelicalism may have been

sought an integration of personal piety and community. He also believed that racial integration in the church would have ramifications for racial integration in the world.

Primary in Seymour's vision for racial integration was his apocalyptic eschatological expectations. 'The revolutionary desire for and expectation of the cataclysmic Second Advent of the Lord Jesus Christ to exalt the poor, the humble and downtrodden, put down the high and mighty and the oppressors and right every wrong'[62] made up Seymour's eschatological message.

Seymour's theological background forged his interracial attitudes. In Indianapolis, Seymour belonged to a black congregation in the predominantly white 'Methodist Episcopal Church', rather than the all black denomination 'Negro Bethel African Methodist Episcopal Church'. Later in Cincinnati, Ohio, Seymour was influenced by black evangelist Martin Well Knapp, who fervently preached the apocalyptic Second Advent of Christ, divine healing and the integration of blacks and whites. Even later, Seymour joined the interracial 'Evening Light Saints', a denomination that emphasized a final spiritual outpouring before the end of world history, holiness, divine healing, racial integration and the need for Christians to reject denominational divisions in favour of a unified church that encompassed all races.[63]

Then, in 1905, through an association with African-American Holiness pastor, Lucy F. Farrow, Seymour came under the influence of Parham, when he was allowed to listen to Parham's teaching of 'tongues as the sign of the baptism of the Holy Spirit'. However, since Parham did not have Seymour's racial sensitivities, Seymour was not allowed to join the all white class, but had to sit outside the classroom with the door ajar. While Seymour sought interracial integration, Parham held strong racist beliefs, so much so that when Parham travelled to Azusa Street to assume leadership of the revival—leadership that Seymour was willing to hand over— Parham was loathe to find 'black and whites intermingling against every accepted custom of American society'. 'To my utter surprise and astonishment', wrote Parham, 'I found conditions even worse than I had antici-

---

more individualistic in terms of personal piety and focused on a conversion of rational assert, the horizontal relationship of the Christian community was important in almost all forms of Evangelical Christian expression.

62. MacRobert, *Black Roots*, p. 35.
63. MacRobert, *Black Roots*, pp. 48-50.

pated'.[64] Condemning Seymour and the Azusa revival ultimately ended Parham's prominence in the Pentecostal movement. While he continued to preach the Pentecostal message, he slipped into anonymity.

MacRobert argues that it was this link between adventist eschatology and racial integration which made Pentecostalism revolutionary. He comments:

> The early Pentecostal movement was also revolutionary, not only in terms of its ability to transcend the colour line, but also in terms of its adventism. The early Pentecostals anticipated the imminent cataclysmic end of the age to be brought about by the Second Advent of Christ. Although God was perceived as the prime mover in this eschatological event, Pentecostals saw themselves as agents of the forthcoming revolution. The arrival of the Kingdom could be hastened by them fulfilling the preconditions for the Lord's return by preaching the gospel in all the world. They believed glossolalia—or more correctly xenoglossia—to be God's means of communicating the message of salvation through them to the heathen of other lands in their native languages.[65]

Seymour believed glossolalia was the sign that the Holy Spirit was breaking down racial, gender and national barriers. This belief was confirmed by the manifestation of glossolalia among all peoples, both at the Azusa revival and elsewhere. Blacks and whites, Americans and foreigners, men and women were reconciled together in love as the Spirit blessed them with tongues.[66]

Like Parham, Seymour believed that speaking in tongues was not simply a prayer language or an existential/mystical experience of the Spirit, but the ability to speak other earthly languages to facilitate preaching the gospel to the entire world in preparation for Christ's return. Early Pentecostals believed that the Spirit would supernaturally infuse the believer with this ability because the time for Christ's return was so near. Of course, xenolalia was a short-lived doctrine because a number of missionaries failed miserably when they tried to speak foreign languages in this way. Consequently, speaking in tongues was later interpreted to be heavenly languages, intended either for the believer's own edification or for the church when tongues was combined with the gift of interpretation.

---

64. MacRobert, *Black Roots*, p. 60. MacRobert is correct, unfortunately, in his assessment that racism on the part of white Pentecostals ultimately fractured Seymour's experiment of an interracial church.

65. MacRobert, *Black Roots*, p. 80.

66. Jean-Jacques Suurmond, *Word and Spirit at Play: Towards a Charismatic Theology* (Grand Rapids: Eerdmans, 1994), pp. 5-6.

Anderson points out, however, that the early Pentecostals revised rather than rejected the belief that speaking in tongues gave one the ability to preach in an unknown foreign language. 'Only the *permanent* gift of preaching in a foreign language *at will* was repudiated.'[67] Pentecostals continue to believe, even to this day, that there are times when, in God's sovereign will, the Spirit speaks through the tongues speaker to someone of a different language. Of course, God could have spoken to that third party without the tongues speaker, but to do so miraculously was evidence, at least to the Pentecostal, that God was present in the modern world in supernatural or miraculous ways. It was also evidence that God was alive, a reaction to the atheistic worldview emerging widely at the turn of the century.

Thus both Parham and Seymour held their own forms of premillennial dispensationalism in which the baptism of the Holy Spirit with the sign of tongues, as well as other charismatic gifts, provided the impetus for the greatest end-time revival. The connection between Pentecostal pneumatological beliefs and eschatology, as well as restorationist sentiments, was expressed in the doctrine of the latter rain. The former rain looked back to the outpouring of the Spirit in the apostolic age as the dispensation of the church began. The latter rain also saw an outpouring of the Spirit, but at the end of the present dispensation as God prepared the world for his second coming. However, the latter rain doctrine lost its prominence in Pentecostal thinking as fundamentalist dispensationalism infiltrated the movement. The proverbial nail in the coffin was struck when 'The New Order of the Latter Rain' arose, using the same latter rain doctrine to challenge the institutional authority of mainstream Pentecostalism.

The Waning of the Latter Rain

Fundamentalist Influence
Emmanuel College (Toronto) Old Testament professor, Gerald Sheppard, writing from a Pentecostal Holiness perspective, argues that Pentecostals did not generally hold a dispensational fundamentalist eschatology in the early history of the movement. Over time, however, Pentecostals embraced a fundamentalist version of dispensational eschatology with such tenets as a pretribulation 'secret' Rapture. By adopting the fundamentalist eschatology, Pentecostals created hermeneutical, sociological and political problems

---

67. Anderson, *Vision of the Disinherited*, p. 91.

for the inner logic of their belief system. Arguments used by Pentecostals to defend the fundamentalist eschatology were inconsistent when applied to their ecclesiology, and fundamentalist eschatology created problems for the basic Pentecostal understanding of Acts 2.[68]

Sheppard focuses on the Assemblies of God, the largest Reformed Pentecostal denomination in the United States, though he believes the results of his analysis are applicable to other Pentecostal denominations. The ministers who formed the Assemblies of God had no intention of formulating a creed when they assembled for their first convention in Hot Springs, Arkansas, in 1914. Yet in 1916 they formulated 'The Statement of Fundamental Truths' in response to a fractious movement of Pentecostals, known as the 'New Issue' or 'Oneness Pentecostals', who claimed that a more pristine formula for water baptism should be used.[69] The 'Oneness Pentecostals' asserted that water baptism should be performed in the 'name of Jesus' following the Acts narrative, rather than according to the trinitarian formula of Matthew.[70]

The Oneness controversy notwithstanding, 'The Statement of Fundamental Truths' lacked a specifically fundamentalist focus. 'Only sixteen in number', argues Sheppard, 'the abbreviated affirmations were obviously not systematic or comprehensive, lacking any specific confession, for instance of the virgin birth, substitutionary atonement, or the bodily resurrection of Jesus Christ'.[71] The statements regarding eschatology may have implied the belief in a secret Rapture prior to a Tribulation, but such a position was not explicitly stated. The following included reference to the imminent coming of the Lord, the resurrection of the dead and the millennial reign of Christ on earth:

---

68. Gerald T. Sheppard, 'Pentecostalism and the Hermeneutics of Dispensationalism: The Anatomy of an Uneasy Relationship', *Pneuma* 2.2 (1984), pp. 5-34 (5). Sheppard's thesis is sound. However, while some Pentecostals see themselves dissociated with fundamentalism, others are comfortable in the fundamentalist camp. See Cox, *Fire from Heaven*, p. 310. Moreover, while Sheppard is able to show the shift to fundamentalist eschatology through the analogical connections of selected writings of a few Pentecostal leaders, showing historical connections would help to substantiate his thesis.

69. Sheppard, 'Pentecostalism and the Hermeneutics of Dispensationalism', p. 8.

70. One should note, though, that trinitarianism in Matthew is implicit rather than explicit. For a brief summary see Reed, 'Oneness Pentecostalism', pp. 644-51.

71. Sheppard, 'Pentecostalism and the Hermeneutics of Dispensationalism', p. 8.

THE BLESSED HOPE
The resurrection of those who have fallen asleep in Christ and their transla-
tion together with those who are alive and remain unto the coming of the
Lord is the imminent and blessed hope of the Church. 1 Thess. 4:16, 17;
Romans 8:23; Titus 2:18; 1 Cor. 15:51, 52.

THE MILLENNIAL REIGN OF JESUS
The revelation of the Lord Jesus Christ from heaven, the salvation of national
Israel, and the millennial reign of Christ on earth are the Scriptural prom-
ises and the world's hope. 2 Thess. 1:17; Rev. 19:11-14; Romans 11:26, 27;
Rev. 20:1-7.[72]

The emphasis in Pentecostal eschatology was the sense of 'a final glorious
revelation and outpouring of the Spirit in the last days', not the fundamentalist notion of a 'dark prospect of impending destruction for those not
suddenly taken out of this world'.[73]

From about the 1930s onwards, Pentecostals started adopting a more
fundamentalist–dispensational eschatology, yet it was an uneasy relationship. In 1935, the Executive Presbytery of the Assemblies of God officially enforced a pretribulation Rapture doctrine in response to a group of
ministers who were teaching a posttribulation Rapture.[74] The aspect of
dispensational thought that Pentecostals were generally unwilling to accept
was, however, the absolute dichotomy between the church and Israel. In
dispensational thought, Jesus' ministry was generally relegated to the
Jewish dispensation and, as such, the Sermon on the Mount and other
kerygmatic events were not believed to be applicable to the church.

Both Myer Pearlman's *Knowing the Doctrines of the Bible* (1937) and
B. Ralph M. Riggs's, *The Path of Prophecy* (1937) accepted fundamentalist
dispensational themes in regard to eschatology, but not when examining the
foundation of the church. Pearlman, who was an instructor at the Assembly
of God's Central Bible Institute, had more in common with Reformed
theology than dispensationalism.[75] C.P.C. Nelson's *Bible Doctrines* (1948)
argued that the doctrine of the Blessed Hope in 'The Statement of Fundamental Truths' (see above) assumed that 'imminence' supported a pretribulation Rapture doctrine. E.E.S. Williams, the General Superintendent during
the pretribulation controversy of the 1930s, back-peddled from a strict

73.   Sheppard, 'Pentecostalism and the Hermeneutics of Dispensationalism', p. 8.
73.   Sheppard, 'Pentecostalism and the Hermeneutics of Dispensationalism', p. 9.
74.   Sheppard, 'Pentecostalism and the Hermeneutics of Dispensationalism', p. 11.
75.   Sheppard, 'Pentecostalism and the Hermeneutics of Dispensationalism', pp.
11-15.

dispensational position in *Systematic Theology* (1953). While accepting a pretribulation Rapture doctrine, he was unwilling to accept the dispensational system when dealing with ecclesial issues. Specifically, Williams refused to accept that Jesus' ministry was relegated to the Jewish dispensation and not applicable to the church, but he argued that the church and the spiritual kingdom were one. Thus the Sermon on the Mount and Jesus' ministry were applicable to the church.[76] The move to fundamentalist dispensational theology was completed in the 1950s, however, evident when Frank M. Boyd accepted fully the dispensational system, including the dichotomy between Israel and the church.[77]

Peter E. Prosser, professor of church history and Christian doctrine at Regent University, Virginia Beach, Virginia, also argues that early Pentecostals were not, as a whole, fundamentalists.[78] Prosser locates the emergence of Pentecostalism in the Wesleyan Holiness revivals, rather than the Reformed/fundamentalist tradition. As such, Pentecostalism can be broadly traced to the mystical tradition of Anglicanism and primitive Methodism with its emphasis on an Arminian view of free-will, not the rationalist tradition of fundamentalism with its concern for the Baconian ideal of deducing general principles from the perceived facts of Scripture.[79] Although there was 'no exact connection' between early Pentecostalism and dispensationalism, fundamentalism quickly influenced the fledgling movement, so that Pentecostals soon wholeheartedly accepted the dispensational system. The prophetic system of fundamentalism was so close to early Pentecostal ideas of the latter rain that in order to gain credibility Pentecostals adopted the fundamentalist system uncritically.[80]

Yet Prosser points out that early Pentecostals were not in agreement or unity over the pretribulation Rapture doctrine. Dispensational doctrines were not affirmed in the 1920 handbook of the Church of God in Christ, nor in the statements of faith by the Church of God, Cleveland, Tennessee, nor the Pentecostal Holiness Church.[81] Prosser therefore challenges Pente-

---

76. Sheppard, 'Pentecostalism and the Hermeneutics of Dispensationalism', pp. 18-19.

77. Sheppard, 'Pentecostalism and the Hermeneutics of Dispensationalism', pp. 20-21.

78. Peter E. Prosser, *Dispensational Eschatology and its Influence on American and British Religious Movements* (TSR, 82; Queenston, ON: Edwin Mellen Press, 1999), p. xi.

79. Prosser, *Dispensational Eschatology*, p. 55.

80. Prosser, *Dispensational Eschatology*, p. 253.

81. Prosser, *Dispensational Eschatology*, pp. 286-87.

costals to think critically about the fundamentalist dispensational system they have adopted. He states:

> Until now, Pentecostalism has not affected these latter movements. Instead they have taken over Pentecostalism and made it lose its moorings. The fundamentalists major on doctrine and preservation of the status quo. Pentecostalism seems largely to be going in the direction of experience and emotion.[82]

The implication is that early Pentecostalism's prophetic critique of society has been muted by its acceptance of fundamentalism's preservation of the status quo.

The research of Douglas Jacobsen, Messiah College professor of church history and theology, Pennsylvania, supports Sheppard's thesis. Jacobsen suggests, however, that the influence of fundamentalism on Pentecostalism in the mid-twentieth century was not as strong as first believed. Studying the scholastic period of second generation Pentecostals of the Assemblies of God (1930–55), Jacobsen argues that the theological texts written and used by the Pentecostal educators at this time

> were not driven by the sense of threatened orthodoxy that spawned funda-mentalism… Pentecostal scholastics rarely quoted from fundamentalist authors, and they certainly were not part of the fundamentalist social club. Although Pentecostal scholastics clearly intended to be orthodox in their views, and in that sense cannot by the furthest stretch of the imagination be called modernist or liberal, their orthodox orientation does not mean that they were therefore fundamentalist by default.[83]

E.E.S. Williams referred to only one fundamentalist author, specifically C.I. Scofield and his *Scofield Reference Bible*. Yet Scofield's dispensa-tional and eschatological opinions were not emphasized. Williams's use of Scofield's Bible was for general biblical background information, rather than any specific theological opinion. In fact, Williams was critical of Scofield's views. M. Pearlman was more willing to refer to fundamentalist (William Evans, three times; Lewis Sperry Chafer, twice, and the Scofield Bible once) and protofundamentalist authors (A.J. Gordon, three times; Hodges, twice; and A.T. Pierson, once), but he more often referred to

---

82. Prosser, *Dispensational Eschatology*, p. 276.

83. Douglas Jacobsen, 'Knowing the Doctrines of Pentecostals: The Scholastic Theology of the Assemblies of God, 1930–55', in Edith L. Blumhofer, Russell P. Spittler and Grant A. Wacker (eds.), *Pentecostal Currents in American Protestantism* (Chicago: University of Illinois Press, 1999), pp. 90-107 (91).

British progressive Evangelicals and moderate liberals (A.B. Bruce, James Denny, Marcus Dods, George Smeaton and H.B. Swete). Jacobsen concludes that Pearlman was not tied to any specific theological party. Williams and Pearlman were more likely to refer to moderate liberal or mildly progressive theologians. Only later were Assemblies of God leaders willing to assume that they were Evangelicals or fundamentalists with an energized spiritual experience and revisioned their history accordingly.[84]

Nevertheless, the acceptance of fundamentalist dispensational theology was the result of historical pressures. Certainly there were Pentecostals who were fundamentalist in orientation in the early history of the movement, but early Pentecostals were drawn from a variety of theological traditions. Fundamentalism formed only one group. Second, there was a general shift in American religious culture towards fundamentalist themes during the twentieth century as the pressures of secularization were felt. Third, those Pentecostals who moved towards fundamentalism tended to be white. African-American Pentecostals were less willing to accept fundamentalist doctrines. Most importantly, though, Pentecostal sensitivities were closer to fundamentalism than other theologies. Yet, while Pentecostals and fundamentalists had some theological commonalities, fundamentalists were 'estranged from the [Pentecostal] movement by the fundamentalists' abhorrence for their tongue speaking and reputation for emotional extravagance'.[85] While Duke Divinity historian George Marsden includes Pentecostals in the fundamentalist camp, he notes that the Pentecostal emphasis on the experience of glossolalia and emotionalism creates certain affinities between Pentecostals and liberal strategies of experience.[86]

More recently, Faupel suggests that early Pentecostalism had more in common with the emphasis on experience in nineteenth-century liberal theology than originally believed. Faupel agrees with Missouri Synod Lutheran George Fry, 'that Liberalism and Pentecostalism are in fact

---

84. Jacobsen, 'Knowing the Doctrines', pp. 95-101.

85. Joel A. Carpenter, 'From Fundamentalism to the New Evangelical Coalition', in George M. Marsden (ed.), *Evangelicalism and Modern America* (Grand Rapids: Eerdmans, 1984), pp. 3-16 (14); also see Grant A. Wacker, 'Travail of a Broken Family: Radical Evangelical Responses to the Emergence of Pentecostalism in America, 1906-16', in Edith L. Blumhofer, Russell P. Spittler and Grant A. Wacker (eds.), *Pentecostal Currents in American Protestantism* (Chicago: University of Chicago Press, 1999), pp. 23-49, which examines the rhetoric fundamentalists used against early Pentecostals.

86. Marsden, *Understanding Fundamentalism and Evangelicalism*, pp. 42-43.

fraternal twins', that 'Pentecostalism is the logical end of Liberalism'.[87]
Taking the theology of Charles Augustus Briggs as an example of liberal
theology in the nineteenth century, Faupel suggests that the thrust of the
Pentecostal critique was not against liberalism but against fundamentalism.
Theological liberalism was not even in the consciousness of early Pentecostalism.[88] For Faupel, the connection between theological liberalism and
Pentecostalism revolved around the Pentecostal desire for an experiential
reality of faith in the personal, corporate and global dimensions of God's
call to faith.[89] The Pentecostal complained that 'head' knowledge had
replaced 'heart' knowledge in the reality of faith, in which 'A relationship
to the living God was substituted with a simple adherence to "man-made
creeds"'.[90]

The differences between Pentecostalism and fundamentalism notwithstanding, in the 1940s Pentecostals were invited to participate in an alliance
of Evangelicals which eventually solidified in the National Association of
Evangelicals (NAE). Pentecostals were considered conservative enough to
be invited, but some fundamentalists objected. On the one hand, J. Elwin
Wright and Harold J. Ockenga solicited Pentecostal participation. On the
other hand, Donald Grey Barnhouse called for old-line denominational
leadership to 'counterbalance Pentecostal influence' while Carl McIntire
considered Pentecostal theology as 'a subtle, disruptive, pernicious thing'
and refused to participate until the NAE 'got rid of the radical Holiness,
tongue groups'.[91] Nevertheless, the Assemblies of God, the Church of God
(Cleveland) and other Holiness and Pentecostal denominations were invited to join. Assemblies of God delegates secretary-treasurer, J. Roswell
Flower, missionary secretary, Noel Perkins, Williams, Riggs (see above)

87.   D. William Faupel, 'Whither Pentecostalism? 22nd Presidential Address Society for Pentecostal Studies, November 7, 1992', *Pneuma* 15.1 (1993), pp. 9-27 (21-22).
88.   Faupel, 'Whither Pentecostalism?', p. 21. Faupel admits that his position is in
the minority of Pentecostal scholarship, but his assessment suggests areas for further
research. Cox notes that after this paper was presented at the 1992 Society for Pentecostal Studies conference, it created fierce debate among the Pentecostal leadership
(*Fire from Heaven*, p. 311).
89.   Faupel, 'Whither Pentecostalism?', p. 19.
90.   Faupel, 'Whither Pentecostalism?', p. 21. Faupel's articulation of liberalism is
of the Schleiermachian type, as articulated by Briggs, which believes that common to
all human beings is a religious disposition or 'feeling of absolute dependence'.
91.   Edith L. Blumhofer, *The Assemblies of God: A Chapter in the Story of American Pentecostalism*. II. *Since 1941* (Springfield: Gospel Publishing House, 1989),
pp. 25-29.

and Thomas F. Zimmerman, either participated in or observed the proceedings.[92] In fact, Zimmerman, who became the general superintendent of the Assemblies of God from 1959 to 1985, was the first Pentecostal to be elected president of the NAE.[93] The ramifications were that Pentecostals gained a newfound respect by other denominations within the alliance and since Pentecostals had not developed their own theology, they were more willing to ally with fundamentalist theology. In fact, in 1975 Zimmerman attributed the rise and success of the Pentecostal movement to its doctrines, such as the deity of Christ, the virgin birth, substitutionary atonement, the need for repentance, the importance of the supernatural gospel over the social gospel, the priority of Scripture, the need for holiness and evangelistic zeal. These doctrines were all fundamentalist in perspective. The two doctrines typically Pentecostal were exuberance in worship, and an articulation of eschatology that was implicitly 'latter rain' in orientation.[94]

The result of the growth of fundamentalist dispensationalism within Pentecostalism was that fundamentalist doctrines were read back into the early doctrines of the Pentecostal movement. Sheppard argues that the move towards fundamentalism did not come without problems. The cornerstone of the logic of the movement, that being the Joel prophecy in the Pentecost narrative of Acts 2, did not fit into the fundamentalist dispensational system in which the prophecies regarding the nation of Israel were suspended until the end of the church age. Pentecostals claimed that other Old Testament prophecies, Jesus' ministry and the Sermon on the Mount were applicable to the present age.[95] Furthermore, the latter rain dispensational system of early Pentecostalism was displaced by fundamentalist dispensationalism. Although early Pentecostals operated with both a threefold and a sevenfold dispensational framework, particularly in Parham's theology, perhaps it is not too bold to say that early Pentecostal theology was more compatible with the threefold framework. Nevertheless, the fundamentalist sevenfold dispensational pattern with its conspiratorial theories identifying historical persons and/or nations as the Antichrist

92. Blumhofer, *Assemblies of God*, II, p. 24.

93. S.M. Burgess, 'Zimmerman, Thomas Fletcher', in *DPCM*, pp. 910-11.

94. Thomas F. Zimmerman, 'The Reason for the Rise of the Pentecostal Movement', in Vinson Synan (ed.), *Aspects of Pentecostal-Charismatic Origins* (Plainsfield, NJ: Logos International, 1975), pp. 5-13.

95. Sheppard, 'Pentecostalism and the Hermeneutics of Dispensationalism', pp. 23-25.

supplanted Pentecostalism's exciting hope of Christ's imminent return with fearmongering, associated with horrors of the Tribulation and the battle of Armageddon.

The New Order of the Latter Rain Schism
The second reason for the decline of latter rain doctrine and the rise of fundamentalist dispensationalism in Pentecostal eschatology was 'The New Order of the Latter Rain' or 'Latter Rain Revival',[96] a 1948 schismatic movement within Pentecostalism, which used the latter rain doctrine to challenge the authority of established Pentecostal denominations. The Latter Rain Revival started at Sharon Orphanage and Schools in North Battleford, Saskatchewan, under the leadership of George Hawtin. Hawtin was a Pentecostal Assemblies of Canada (PAOC) minister and principal of Bethel Bible Institute, Saskatoon. Although Hawtin pioneered Bethel as an independent school in 1935 and turned it over to the PAOC in 1942, he resigned from both the PAOC and the school over a dispute in which he decided to erect a new building without prior approval of the PAOC-controlled board. P.G. Hunt, a board member of Bethel, also resigned in sympathy with Hawtin.[97] Both Hawtin and Hunt joined Herrick Holt of the North Battleford Church of the Foursquare Gospel in an independent school that Holt had already established.

Just after this time, students of the school gathered in study of the Scriptures, fasting and prayer. One of the brethren received a 'word from God' to pray for another student and 'lay hands upon him'. Doing so in obedience, the brother received a 'revelation' concerning the student's life and ministry. Hawtin noted 'that all Heaven broke loose upon our souls and heaven above came down to greet us'.[98] The revival started to spread as people came to North Battleford to attend the camp meetings and conventions at Sharon.[99]

96.   Participants in the revival called it the 'Latter Rain Revival', a name often used for the Azusa Street revival, while opponents to the movement called it 'The New Order of the Latter Rain' to distinguish it from the early Pentecostal movement. For demarcation purposes, Latter Rain or Latter Rain Revival in the upper case will refer to the revival of 1948 and latter rain in the lower case will refer to the doctrine that was part of both early Pentecostalism and the Latter Rain Revival.

97.   Faupel, 'Everlasting Gospel', p. 400.

98.   G. Hawtin, 'The Church—Which Is His Body', *The Sharon Star* (1 March 1950), p. 2; as quoted by R.M. Riss, 'Latter Rain Movement', in *DPCM*, p. 532.

99.   Richard Riss, 'The Latter Rain Movement of 1948', *Pneuma* 4.1 (1982), pp. 32-45 (32).

The history of the revival is not as important here as much as its implications for latter rain eschatology. The doctrines of the Latter Rain Revival were not new. They had existed in one form or another in early Pentecostalism.[100] Like the early Pentecostal movement, the Latter Rain Revival saw itself as a restoration of biblical truths, especially in terms of the nature, mission, worship and authority of the church.[101] Like the early Pentecostal movement, the Latter Rain Revival emphasized healings and other charismatic phenomena, the imminence of Christ's return preceded by a latter rain outpouring of the Spirit and the occurrence of 'singing in the Spirit' in which the congregation broke out into a cacophony of singing in tongues. Even the Latter Rain Revival's practice of disparaging denominational organization was a belief held by early Pentecostals, particularly found in the writings of William H. Durham.[102] The difference was that the Latter Rain Revival focused its disparaging remarks on the Pentecostal denominations along with the mainline churches, a practice Classical Pentecostals were unwilling to tolerate.

The two most controversial doctrines for Classical Pentecostals, the impartation of the spiritual gifts through the laying on of hands and the restoration of apostles and prophets as an essential part of the fivefold ministries of Eph. 4.11, were also a part of early Pentecostal practice.[103] The difference was that the laying on of hands and the restoration of apostles and prophets were not dominant beliefs in early Pentecostalism. Laying on of hands was given greater theological weight by the Latter Rain Revival. In early Pentecostalism, the act of laying on of hands was incidental to the act of praying for another person. Early Pentecostals encouraged those seeking Spirit baptism or the spiritual gifts to 'tarry' on the Spirit. Those seeking were expected to wait and pray for extended periods of time before being blessed by the Spirit. The Latter Rain participants, however, believed that a spiritual leader could impart the spiritual gifts through the laying on of hands. Hawtin commented: 'Though the old-time tarrying meetings were still in evidence, God mightily used the ministry of laying on of hands. Those who had received this ministry were especially used of God so much that chronic seekers who had waited

---

100. Faupel, 'Everlasting Gospel', p. 422.

101. Faupel, 'Everlasting Gospel', p. 425.

102. Blumhofer, *Assemblies of God*, II, p. 58.

103. Riss, 'Latter Rain Movement', p. 532; *idem*, 'The Latter Rain Movement of 1948', pp. 36-38.

fifteen and twenty years were filled with the Spirit.'[104] The reception of the baptism of the Spirit or spiritual gifts was an act of faith similar to the reception of the gift of salvation. Although tarrying on God was still practised, it was unnecessary.[105]

Likewise, certain segments of the early Pentecostal movement believed that apostles and prophets were for the church today. The call for the restoration of the ministry of apostles and prophets was 'found in the Irvingite movement, in the teaching of John Alexander Dowie, in the Apostolic Faith Churches of William O. Hutchinson and in the teachings of early Pentecostal W. F. Carothers'.[106] Yet once again, the restoration of the fivefold ministries was not a dominant belief in early Pentecostalism.

In terms of eschatology, Hawtin adopted a more fundamentalist position with a premillennial, sevenfold dispensational pattern, but not a pretribulation Rapture. Hawtin declared that 'The Kingdom of Heaven, the seventh dispensation, is at hand—the great Sabbath of rest when we will reign with Christ for a thousand years'. However, Hawtin abandoned Darby's pretribulation belief and claimed that the 'overcomers' would suffer in the trials of the Tribulation to bring them into the new dispensation. 'The possessing of the Kingdom of Heaven by the saints of the most high', claimed Hawtin, 'is not going to be a mere "push-over" but through MUCH TRIBULATION we will enter it'.[107]

The Latter Rain Revival used the same latter rain doctrine as early Pentecostalism to explain the outpouring of the Spirit in the revival, innovating it slightly by using the image of the opened and closed door to distinguish it from the early Pentecostal version. Faupel notes:

104. George R. Hawtin, 'Editorial', *The Sharon Star* (1 August 1948), p. 2; as quoted by Richard M. Riss, *Latter Rain: The Latter Rain Movement of 1948 and the Mid-Twentieth Century Evangelical Awakening* (Mississauga, ON: Honeycomb Visual Productions, 1987), p. 73.

105. Riss, *Latter Rain*, pp. 58, 153-54 n. 53.

106. Peter Hocken, 'The Challenge of Non-Denominational Charismatic Christianity', in Jan A.B. Jongeneel (ed.), *Experiences of the Spirit: Conference on Pentecostal and Charismatic Research in Europe at Utrecht University, 1989* (IHC, 68; New York: Peter Lang, 1991), pp. 221-38 (225-26).

107. George R. Hawtin, 'Thy Kingdom Come', *The Sharon Star* (November–December 1951), p. 1; as quoted by Faupel, 'Everlasting Gospel', pp. 453-54. Curiously, Hawtin appeared to pick up an aspect of Parham's theology in the belief of 'overcomers', but it was a theology not generally accepted by the mainline Pentecostal denominations.

This image of a 'closed door' with a great revival on the other side became the 'key' to the Latter Rain understanding of worship. In the context of their roots, the community was waiting for renewal of the 'latter rain' that had fallen at the beginning of the century with the Pentecostal revival. The 'closed door' epitomized their conviction that the rain had ceased and the waters had evaporated leaving the Pentecostal soil hard and dry.[108]

The closed door depicted the conviction that access to the latter rain outpouring of the Spirit was limited. The closed door also explained why the revival outpouring of the Spirit at the beginning of the century had fizzled out. With the restoration of biblical truths, the Latter Rain Revival claimed to have the key for entry into God's outpouring presence.[109]

There were two main reasons why older Classical Pentecostal denominations rejected the Latter Rain Revival. One was the personal animosity between Hawtin and the institutional leaders of the Pentecostal Assemblies of Canada, the Assemblies of God and other Classical Pentecostal denominations. Admittedly, however, many Classical Pentecostals were impressed with the charismatic fervour of the revival. Assemblies of God minister Stanley Frodsham, for example, a participant of both the Azusa Street revival and the Latter Rain Revival, wrote in a letter to Faith Campbell that he approved of 'this new revival which God is so graciously sending, where so many souls are being transformed, where God is so graciously restoring the gifts of the Spirit'. In 1949, under pressure from the Assemblies of God, Frodsham retired from ministry and resigned as editor of the *Pentecostal Evangel*, the official magazine of the denomination.[110]

The second reason, and the greater threat to the major Pentecostal denominations, however, was that the Latter Rain Revival promoted a different model of ministry. Using latter rain eschatology, the Latter Rain Revival advocated the restoration of the ministries of prophets and apostles (Eph. 4.11). Prophets would roam from church to church, prophesying that the church was in a sinful state and offering personal prophecies to believers for guidance and instruction. This would often occur with the 'laying on of hands'. Criticizing the church on a corporate level while offering individual prophecies corresponded to the Latter Rain Revival's belief system that the denominational structures were corrupt. The emergence of the ministries of prophets and apostles proved threatening to Classical Pentecostal denominations, because they had developed presby-

108. Faupel, 'Everlasting Gospel', p. 455.
109. Faupel, 'Everlasting Gospel', p. 459.
110. Riss, 'Latter Rain Movement', p. 533.

terial/congregational structures.[111] While the local assemblies operated
with a congregational structure, where the assemblies chose their elders
(board-members) and pastors to make decisions regarding local ministry,
they established a voluntary association of like-minded churches with a
centralized presbyterial government to deal with large-scale ministry
issues. The Latter Rain Revival threatened this structure, by advocating
not only the disintegration of Pentecostal denominations, but also the fivefold model of ministry. Riss notes:

> The official policy of the Assemblies of God in this regard was that of
> 'voluntary co-operation'…'voluntary co-operation means that one of his
> own free will decides to become a co-operating member of the Assemblies
> of God, this co-operation becoming obligatory and not optional'. Some
> people had interpreted 'voluntary co-operation' to mean the co-operation
> was optional, and various evangelists of the Assemblies of God were hold-
> ing meetings in assemblies not endorsed by local assemblies and district
> officers of the Assemblies of God.[112]

Ultimately, the fivefold model of ministry proved too volatile for the
Assemblies of God and other Pentecostal denominations. They officially
denounced the beliefs and practices of the Latter Rain Revival, even
though many of those beliefs and practices were a part of their common
history.

Nevertheless, the established Pentecostal denominations opposed the
Latter Rain Revival. Not only did the officials of the Pentecostal Assemblies of Canada, Assemblies of God, several Holiness Pentecostal denominations and the Oneness organization the United Pentecostal Church reject
the Latter Rain Revival, but they downplayed the latter rain doctrine of the
early Pentecostal movement. Consequently, the fundamentalist dispensational eschatology, which had been making its way into Pentecostal
thought, was more readily accepted. By doing so, however, the established
Pentecostal denominations had rejected the distinctive eschatology of the
early Pentecostal movement. The emergence of the Latter Rain Revival
sounded the death knell for latter rain doctrine for many Classical Pentecostal denominations.

111. Sociologist Margaret M. Poloma argues that the way the Assemblies of God is
able to promote charismatic experiences among its assemblies is to emphasize a congregational government at the local church level and a presbyterian government at the
regional and national levels (*The Assemblies of God at the Crossroads: Charism and
Institutional Dilemmas* [Knoxville: University of Tennessee Press, 1989], p. 123).
112. Riss, *Latter Rain*, p. 127.

What Happened to the Latter Rain?

At first glance, the influence of the Latter Rain Revival on the major Pentecostal denominations appears to be insignificant. Both the Assemblies of God and the Pentecostal Holiness Church, the two largest Pentecostal denominations in the United States, officially denounced the beliefs and practices of the Latter Rain Revival. People involved with the Latter Rain Revival were quickly dropped from the membership roles of these Pentecostal denominations. In fact, the Assemblies of God was so confident that the Latter Rain Revival had little permanent influence that in 1961 Assemblies of God historian, Carl Brumback, stated that the Latter Rain had 'practically come to naught'.[113]

However, at a closer glance, the Latter Rain Revival was more significant in the development of Pentecostalism than first realized. The Apostolic Church, for instance, one of the early Pentecostal denominations founded in England in 1916 with close associations with W.O. Hutchinson's Apostolic Faith Church,[114] was significantly influenced by the Latter Rain Revival. Cecil Cousen, a pastor of the Apostolic Church in Hamilton, Ontario, and son of one of the founding members of the Apostolic Church,[115] along with George B. Evans, pastor of Toronto's Apostolic Church, visited Bethesda Missionary Temple in Detroit, Michigan, and later Elim Bible Institute in Hornell, New York (Elim later moved to Lima, New York). Both were centres for the Latter Rain Revival. Bethesda Missionary Temple became a centre for Latter Rain theology after its pastor, Mrs Myrtle D. Beall, attended revival meetings in Vancouver, BC, held by Hawtin and a number of other North Battleford leaders. Elim Bible Institute became a Latter Rain centre after its president, Ivan Q. Spenser, along with his son Carlton, visited Bethesda Missionary Temple in 1948.[116] Meanwhile, Cousen and Evans brought the Latter Rain message back to their respective churches. They later invited Dr Thomas Wyatt and Carlton Spenser, among others, to hold a convention in Toronto in 1950. After this meeting, many of the pastors of the Apostolic Church were invited to speak at Latter Rain meetings, including Cousen and Evans, Fred C. Poole, Frank

---

113. See Riss, *Latter Rain*, pp. 122-23.
114. D.W. Cartwright, 'Apostolic Church', in *DPCM*, p. 16.
115. P.D. Hocken, 'Cousen, Cecil', in *DPCM*, p. 228.
116. Riss, *Latter Rain*, p. 89.

Warburton and T. Kenneth Michell.[117] Eventually the Apostolic Church realized that it had to deal with the Latter Rain issue, because Latter Rain advocates within the Apostolic Church were questioning denominational ties. In 1952, the denomination required its pastors to reaffirm their allegiance to the denomination's constitution. All of them did so, except for James McKoewn and Cecil Cousen. Cousen was asked to surrender his ordination papers and was restricted from preaching in any Apostolic Church meeting. Nevertheless, Latter Rain beliefs and practices made their mark on the Apostolic Church, particularly the belief that apostles and prophets were restored to the church.[118]

The rift between Classical Pentecostal denominations and the Latter Rain Revival was further evident when Elim Missionary Fellowship, one of the founding members of the Pentecostal Fellowship of North America (PFNA), was dismissed for adopting Latter Rain beliefs. The PFNA was an ecumenical body of Pentecostal fellowships organized in 1948. Elim Missionary Fellowship was a constituent member. Latter Rain advocate, pastor for Elim Missionary Fellowship and president of Elim Bible Institute, Ivan Q. Spenser, was a member of the PFNA's Board of Administration. At the third annual convention in 1950, under strong opposition from non-Latter Rain board members and especially from the Assemblies of God, Spenser resigned his position. The opposition was specifically related to his Latter Rain beliefs.[119]

Latter Rain churches preferred to remain independent and autonomous at the local church level, despising the sectarian mentality they believed existed in the denominational churches. However, many Latter Rain churches formed a loose association under the International Independent Assemblies of God, a body that existed before the Latter Rain Revival, but one that became a Latter Rain organization. Likewise, Elim Missionary Assemblies, a fellowship of churches associated with Elim Bible Institute, embraced Latter Rain theology.

The real influence of the Latter Rain Revival, however, was on the Charismatic Renewal movement initially and later on the Independent Charismatic movement. Riss briefly noted some of the connections between the Latter Rain Revival and the Charismatic Renewal. One of the practices of

---

117. Riss, *Latter Rain*, pp. 105-108.

118. Riss, *Latter Rain*, p. 139. Cartwright notes that the church government by prophets and apostles was a distinctive feature of the Apostolic Church ('Apostolic Church', p. 16).

119. Riss, *Latter Rain*, pp. 123-24.

the Latter Rain Revival was to set Scripture to music. Ray Jackson brought the Latter Rain message to New Zealand, where he passed it on to David Schoch, Rob Wheeler and others. They in turn passed it on to David and Dale Garret. The Garrets then influenced the Charismatic movement with this same practice.

John Poole, the son of Apostolic Church pastor and Latter Rain advocate Fred C. Poole, became a prominent figure in the Charismatic Renewal. Not only did John Poole take over the pastorate of his father's church in Philadelphia, Pennsylvania, after his father's death, but also during the 1970s he was a frequent writer for the Charismatic periodical *New Wine*.

Similarly, Latter Rain centre Bethesda Missionary Temple, Detroit, played a role in the development of the Charismatic movement. James Lee Beall not only succeeded his mother Myrtle Beall as pastor of the church, but he was a frequent contributor to the widespread Charismatic periodical *Logos Journal*. In fact, *Logos Journal* grew out of the Latter Rain journal *Herald of Faith/Harvest Time*, edited by Joseph Mattson-Boze and Gerald Derstine. Both Mattson-Boze and Derstine had connections to the Latter Rain Revival. Mattson-Boze was part of the Latter Rain Revival and Derstine worked with Latter Rain advocate J. Preston Elby.

Carlton Spenser, president of Elim Bible Institute, was invited by Demos Shakarian to speak at a Full Gospel Businessmen's Fellowship (FGBF) convention in Washington. The FGBF was an important link between Classical Pentecostalism and the Charismatic movement. The fact that Spenser was a speaker at the FGBF indicated that the Latter Rain movement also had an influence on the Charismatic movement through this venue.

During the 1970s, H. David Edwards, the vice president of Elim Bible Institute at the time, was invited to be a speaker at the Charismatic event Jesus '76 in Mercer, Pennsylvania. Winston I. Nunes, pastor of Broadview Faith Temple, Toronto, and a leading exponent of the Latter Rain with close ties to Bethesda Missionary Temple,[120] was also a speaker at Jesus '76. Both Edwards and Nunes were prominent Latter Rain advocates, Nunes having represented both the International Independent Assemblies of God and Elim Missionary Fellowship at the World Pentecostal Conference in 1952.

Ern Baxter who was associated with healing evangelist William Branham, was a prominent leader of the Charismatic movement and closely associated with Christian Growth Ministries in Ft Lauderdale, Florida. Not

120. Riss, *Latter Rain*, p. 102.

only was Latter Rain writer George Warnock a secretary for Baxter for a couple of years, but in 1975 another of Baxter's secretaries recommended Warnock's book, *The Feast of Tabernacles*, as a 'Timothy, if you please'.[121]

Although these connections are diverse and at times tenuous, there appears to have been an influence of Latter Rain theology on the Charismatic Renewal. One can observe a commonality of beliefs and practices between the Latter Rain and the Charismatic Renewal. These include singing in the Spirit, dancing, the restoration of the fivefold ministries of Eph. 4.11, the laying on of hands as a foundational truth,[122] the feast of Tabernacles and tabernacle teachings.[123] Although sometimes divergent, the eschatological views of the Latter Rain were also adopted by the Charismatics. According to Riss, 'it would seem that an independent underground movement developed within the Charismatic Renewal, composed of individuals committed to various "end-time truths" that had arisen during the Latter Rain Revival'.[124]

Ultimately, however, Latter Rain theology was too restorationist and too antagonistic towards denominational polity to be wholeheartedly accepted by denominational Charismatics. Charismatics of the 1960s and 1970s were open to the moving of the Spirit and the restoration of spiritual gifts, but they were firmly rooted in the ecclesiastical structures of their respective denominations. Part of the problem may well have been that the Eph. 4.11 model of ministry, which included the ministries of prophets and apostles, conflicted with the episcopal, presbyterial and/or congregational models of mainline denominations. Although there was biblical support

121. Riss, *Latter Rain*, pp. 140-44.

122. In Latter Rain theology, the laying on of hands was considered a foundational practice of the church. Based in Heb. 6.1-2, Latter Rain participants believed that the laying on of hands was a 'foundational truth' of equal importance to water and Spirit baptism, resurrection of the dead and eternal life.

123. The Feast of Tabernacles and Tabernacle teachings were theological ideas articulated in George Warnock's publication *The Feast of Tabernacles*. At a 1948 Sharon camp meeting, Warnock, who had earlier been a personal secretary to Ern Baxter, heard James Watt casually mention 'that the third of Israel's great Feasts, the "Feast of Tabernacles", had not yet been fulfilled' (Riss, *Latter Rain*, pp. 73-74). Warnock used this idea to develop the premise that the Feast of Passover had been fulfilled in the death of Jesus Christ, the Feast of Pentecost had been fulfilled in the outpouring of the Spirit on the day of Pentecost, but that the Feast of Tabernacles was yet to be fulfilled. The Feast of Tabernacles would be a 'latter rain' outpouring of the Spirit upon the church. Riss, 'Latter Rain Movement', p. 533.

124. Riss, *Latter Rain*, pp. 141-43.

for the fivefold model of ministry, the authorities of the mainline denominations were committed to the structures already in place.[125]

A number of independent or non-denominational ministries with charismatic ties arose during the 1980s and 1990s which will be identified as the Independent Charismatic movement. Although a diverse group, they share certain commonalities that are rooted in the Latter Rain Revival. They are a diverse group, sometimes with common beliefs but often with conflicting ones. The Independent Charismatic movement is therefore a difficult movement to define.[126] Catholic Charismatic Peter Hocken defines the movement as follows:

> The Charismatic movement outside the historic churches is here called *non-denominational*, as a convenient label that is neither pejorative nor inaccurate. Non-denominational Charismatic Christianity refers here to all groups exhibiting Charismatic characteristics (practice of the spiritual gifts), and a post-conversion experience of the Spirit that have not yet acquired (and are often determined they will not acquire) the determinate structures of denominations.[127]

Hocken classifies the Independent Charismatic movement according to two categories: (1) assemblies with dynamic leaders who have no particular interest in fellowship with other churches; and (2) assemblies that have a concern for the corporate, covenantal character of their congregations.

---

125. Although not within the scope of this book, there are a number of ways in which the role and place of the ministries of prophets and apostles can be incorporated into present denominational structures. Moriarty, on the one hand, is sceptical that prophets and apostles should be incorporated into modern church structures at all (Michael Moriarty, *The New Charismatics: A Concerned Voice Responds to Dangerous New Trends* [Grand Rapids: Zondervan, 1992], p. 241). On the other hand, Charismatics such as Charles E. Hummel (*Fire in the Fireplace: Charismatic Renewal in the Nineties* [Downers Grove, IL: InterVarsity Press, 2nd edn, 1993], pp. 105-110); David Watson (*I Believe in the Church: The Revolutionary Potential of the Family of God* [London: Hodder & Stoughton, 2nd edn, 1983], p. 258); and Hocken ('Non-Denominational Charismatic Christianity', pp. 227-28), suggest interesting ways that the fivefold ministries can be incorporated into episcopal and presbyterial forms of government.

126. The difficulty in defining the Independent Charismatic movement is related to the lack of original source material, the speed at which the movement changes and the variety of opinions within the movement. See Nigel G. Wright, 'The Nature and Variety of Restorationism and the "House Church" Movement', in Stephen Hunt, Malcolm Hamilton and Tony Walter (eds.), *Charismatic Christianity: Sociological Perspectives* (New York: St Martin's Press, 1997), pp. 60-76 (60-61).

127. Hocken, 'Non-Denominational Charismatic Christianity', p. 221.

The emphasis is on developing a strong relationship with God and the church.

Sociologist Martin Percy offers an interesting and probably more workable definition of the Charismatic movement (including the Classical Pentecostal and Independent varieties). He describes it using the metaphor of 'a city on the beach'. Percy writes:

> I want to suggest at least for the moment, that we should think about neo-
> Pentecostalism at the end of the twentieth century as being like 'a city on the
> beach'… There is no question that neo-Pentecostalism is a major share-
> holder in the totality of Christian expression. But like a city, that expression
> is not monobehavioural: it is multifaceted, diverse and expansive, capable
> even of being at odds with itself. It has its own distinctive districts of belief
> and behaviour (for example, those who are 'pro-Toronto blessing', those
> who are anti, those who speak in tongues, those who don't, and so on), and
> also like a city it increasingly sprawls and expands.[128]

Percy continues to argue that while Charismatics like to describe the moving of the Spirit as waves of the Spirit, or of revival as the falling rain or of being drenched, soaked, washed and refreshed in the Spirit (note the latter rain imagery!), the same 'wave of the Spirit' frequently brings disaster to the Charismatic city by bringing division, erosion and schism to the community. The metaphorical city is expansive and diverse, but the waves can either bring spiritual revival, which allows the city to expand, or they can destabilize the city with schisms and controversy.[129]

If nothing else, Percy's definition reveals the difficulty in defining the diversity of the Charismatic landscape. Post-Charismatic critic Michael Moriarty prefers to divide the Charismatic movement into the 'old Charismatics' and the 'new Charismatics'. The old Charismatics consist of de-nominational Charismatics, but also include the Latter Rain Revival, faith healer William Branham, the Manifested Sons of God (an offshoot of the Latter Rain Revival), Oral Roberts and Gordon Lindsay. The new Charismatics consist of such diverse groups as kingdom of God (Earl Paulk), positive confession (Kenneth Hagin and Kenneth Copeland), the Vineyard's signs and wonders movement (John Wimber)—as well as Vineyard's offshoot the Toronto Blessing—and the present-truth movement (Dick Iverson

---

128. Martin Percy, 'The City on the Beach: Future Prospects for Charismatic Move-ments at the End of the Twentieth Century', in Hunt, Hamilton and Walter (eds.), *Charismatic Christianity*, pp. 205-228 (206-207).

129. Percy, 'City on the Beach', p. 207.

and Bill Hamon),[130] the present truth being the restoration of prophets and apostles.

Moriarty tends to be more rhetorical and reactionary than analytical in his assessment of the new charismatics and prone to generalizations. Nevertheless, he brings together many of the various strands that make up the Independent Charismatic movement. Moriarty insists that what connects the various strands is restorationism. He identifies seven common patterns adopted from the Latter Rain Revival all revolving around the belief in restoration: (1) restorationism—the belief that God has restored apostolic truth to the church; (2) fivefold ministry—the restoration of apostles and prophets in church leadership; (3) spiritual disciplines—disciplines such as casting out demons, fasting, laying on of hands as necessary aspects of the church's restoration; (4) prophecy—not only the practice of corporate prophecy for the edification of the church, but also the practice of personal prophecy for personal guidance and instruction; (5) recovery of true worship—the belief that God's presence will be manifested in a certain style of worship, often including singing, clapping, shouting, singing prophecies and dancing; (6) immortalization of the saints—although a minor belief in both the Latter Rain Revival and the new Charismatic movement, it insists that saints moving in latter rain restorational truth will attain immortalization before Christ's return; and (7) unity of faith—the belief that the church will attain spiritual unity and become triumphant before Christ's return.[131] One of Moriarty's concerns is that these beliefs sometimes lead to spiritual elitism, creating damage for other congregations.

Moriarty concludes that

> The doctrinal system driving the new charismatics is essentially a synthesis of various stands of teaching gleaned from Pentecostal, the neo-Pentecostal deliverance revival, the Latter Rain movement, the charismatic movement, the Manifested Sons of God, the positive confession movement…fashioned into a systematic doctrine centred around restorationism.[132]

Charismatic researcher Andrew Walker makes a similar claim in reference to England's House Church movement, a Charismatic group committed to

---

130. Moriarty, *New Charismatics*, pp. xii-xiii. Moriarty is inconsistent in where he places certain groups. Originally he places the positive confession movement with the new Charismatics, but later lumps them in with the old Charismatics, suggesting that Moriarty has difficulty classifying the Independent Charismatics.

131. Moriarty, *New Charismatics*, pp. 60-61.

132. Moriarty, *New Charismatics*, p. 109.

apostolic and prophetic leadership and 'shepherding', or the accountability of younger Christians to more mature Christians in order to develop certain Christian disciplines. Although this movement is a possible threat to Classical Pentecostalism and the Charismatic Renewal, primarily because the House Church viewed these groups as apostate and therefore fair game for proselytizing, Walker comments: 'Restorationism was not a new version of classical Pentecostalism as I mistakenly thought in 1985: it was a syncretistic amalgam of classical, renewalist and independent streams'.[133] Restoration was a common theme in early Pentecostalism and made its way throughout its various derivatives. It was a part of its eschatological belief of a latter rain outpouring of the Spirit to restore the church to its apostolic purity before Christ's soon return.

Andrew Walker argues that

> [House Church] Restorationists initially thought that their movement itself heralded the end of time. In this sense they were millennial and one might have expected them to be anti-modern. However, unlike both Irving and early Pentecostalism, Restorationists were optimistic about the future and were committed to the establishment of a powerful church before the thousand year reign of Christ.[134]

Walker's assessment of early Pentecostal eschatology does not account for the optimism of its latter rain doctrine, when the greatest outpouring of the Spirit and end-time revival since the apostolic church will occur. Only later did Classical Pentecostalism embrace the pessimistic eschatology of fundamentalism. Moreover, Walker ultimately rejects the notion that the 'frenzy' of Independent Charismatic spirituality is the result of eschatological expectation. Instead, the Charismatic movement follows the contours of secular modernity: it 'capitulated to the consumer and experiential hedonism of later modernity and [has] become commodified and corrupted'.[135] The pinnacle of this process is the Toronto Blessing, which emphasizes experiential spirituality but without the theological foundation of historic orthodoxy. Walker concludes that the theologian who best represents the Charismatic movement is not Jonathan Edwards, Charles Hodge, or even Charles Parham, for they were too biblicist, too rooted in historic

---

133. Andrew Walker, 'Thoroughly Modern: Sociological Reflections on the Charismatic Movement from the End of the Twentieth Century', in Hunt, Hamilton and Walter (eds.), *Charismatic Christianity*, pp. 17-42 (32).

134. Walker, 'Thoroughly Modern', p. 32.

135. Walker, 'Thoroughly Modern', p. 34.

orthodoxy. The true father of the movement will be the liberal theologian Schleiermacher, who rejected German rationalism and classical theology for a religion of experience and God consciousness.[136] Yet Walker fails to account for the importance of eschatological anticipation in creating the atmosphere for charismatic expression.

Nigel Wright argues that the House Church restorationist movement seeks the recovery of apostolic ministries and spiritual gifts and he agrees with Walker that the movement has a heightened eschatological awareness. However, in contradistinction to Walker, Wright incorrectly argues that its eschatology is a variation of postmillennialism. Wright comments:

> The concept that the process of divine restoration may be coming to a climax gave rise to a heightened eschatological awareness which saw Restorationism as potentially writing the last chapter of history. This was accompanied by a decisive rejection of the pessimistic pre-millennialism in which the majority of early leaders had been reared in favour of a form of post-millennialism which expected the restoring to the Church of its New Testament pattern to be accompanied by a massive and final revival as the immediate prelude to the coming of Christ... Restorationism was therefore seen in eschatological and almost apocalyptic terms, creating a sense of urgency which sometimes found expression in a ruthless condemnation of the historic churches as abandoned by God and in consequent proselytizing from them.[137]

House Church eschatology, however, still remains a form of premillennialism, but without a doctrine of the Rapture or the Tribulation. There is still an expectation that Christ will return to establish his kingdom reign. Nevertheless, House Church eschatology, which seeks the restoration of New Testament simplicity and unity accompanied by a massive end-time revival before Christ's return, sounds like latter rain restorationism.

Nigel Scotland, Field Chair of Religious Studies at Cheltenham and Gloucester College, England, makes similar observations of the House Church and Vineyard movements. While stress is placed on the end-times in the early stages of the denominational Charismatic movement and the Restoration House Churches, there was an eventual shift from a futuristic kingdom of God to regarding the kingdom as a reality in the present world. One of the reasons for this shift was that more than 30 years had passed from the beginning of the Charismatic movement to the present, frustrating the movement's anticipation of the coming of Christ. Vineyard

136. Walker, 'Thoroughly Modern', pp. 35-36.
137. Wright, 'Restorationism and the "House Church" Movement', p. 63.

leader John Wimber reinforced this shift by 'teaching that the Holy Spirit is moving now among the people of God to create a foretaste of the kingdom which Jesus will inaugurate at the end time'.[138] Admittedly, there is a nuanced difference between the view that Christians need to work to 'establish' the kingdom of God and the view that the spiritual gifts are a 'proleptic foretaste' of the kingdom.

Likewise, Earl Paulk's 'Dominion Theology' or 'Kingdom Now',[139] insists that the kingdom of God will not be manifested sometime in the future, but that it 'is always now'. Paulk believes that the doctrine of the Rapture is the 'Great Escape Theory!' Ultimately, the doctrine of the Rapture hinders the church from establishing the kingdom of God on the earth before Christ's return. Essentially, the Christian has been given the divine responsibility of participating in the establishment of the kingdom.[140] However, certain conditions need to be fulfilled to establish the kingdom of God. The church needs to be unified, in what Paulk calls the 'Manifested Sons of God',[141] and the saints need to be perfected. Both will be

138. Nigel Scotland, *Charismatics and the Next Millennium: Do They Have a Future?* (London: Hodder & Stoughton, 1995), p. 163.

139. Paulk is the pastor of Chapel Hill Harvest Church, Atlanta, and has a weekly television broadcast on the Trinity Broadcasting Network. H. Wayne House and Thomas Ice, *Dominion Theology: Blessing or Curse?* (Portland, OR: Multnomah Press, 1988), p. 378.

140. House and Ice, *Dominion Theology*, pp. 378-79.

141. Although a minor belief, the Manifested Sons of God was a term used by a number of Latter Rain Revivalists, who believed that if certain saints could reach a certain state of perfection through the restoration of the apostolic gifts and ministries, they would be immortalized. These 'overcomers' would receive 'redemptive bodies' and 'eternal life', which here meant eternal 'physical' life, so that the 'overcomers' would not die. See Blumhofer, *Assemblies of God*, II, p. 61. Initially it was believed that the Manifested Sons of God would be an army raised up by God to vanquish disease before Christ's return; it was transformed into a belief (albeit minor) in the immortalization of the body. See Riss, *Latter Rain*, p. 96. Moriarty traced the development of the Manifested Sons of God through the 1960s and 1970s. Under the leadership of John Robert Stevens, not only did the Manifested Sons of God teach the restoration of prophets and apostles, but 'They taught that a human being can become God, that a person can become perfect, and that he or she can become Christ... becoming "divine" and reaching "perfection" (separation from the world results in sinlessness) will result in "immortality" (becoming Christ)'. See Moriarty, *New Charismatics*, pp. 74-75. The Manifested Sons of God infiltrated the Independent Charismatic movement. For Moriarty, there is a clear connection to the Manifested Sons of God's 'immortalization' theory and the 'little gods' theory of present-truth restora-

accomplished through the restoration of the fivefold ministries. Paulk comments: 'The apostles, prophets, evangelists, pastors and teachers were given for the perfecting of the saints and unless that perfection is reached, the Kingdom of God cannot be established'.[142] Paulk makes little distinction between the church and the kingdom of God. In essence, the restored church is equated with the kingdom.

Although the actual form of eschatology varies between the early Pentecostal, Latter Rain Revival and Independent Charismatic movements, there is a logical coherence revolving around the latter rain doctrine. There is a consistent theme of latter rain restorationism through the evolution of the Pentecostal/Charismatic movements. Early Pentecostals sought to restore the apostolic gifts. Not only was the baptism of the Holy Spirit with the manifestation of tongues as depicted in the Pentecost account a gift to be restored, but it was also the key to the restoration of the Corinthian gifts. The Latter Rain Revival, Independent Charismatic and to some extent the denominational Charismatic movements sought to restore the ministries of apostles and prophets in an effort to implement more fully the fivefold ministries of Ephesians. Although this belief was expressed in early Pentecostalism, it was only a minor one. Nevertheless, it was a minor shift in thinking from the call for the restoration of prophecy, a common practice in early Pentecostalism, to call for the restoration of prophets and apostles. In all accounts, the restoration of apostolic Christianity was linked with the imminent coming of Jesus Christ.

Early Pentecostals believed that the restoration of Spirit baptism and the gifts of the Spirit would bring spiritual unity to the church. Denominational barriers and doctrinal differences would be curtailed as God's Spirit was poured out, because all would be in one accord. Early Pentecostals also believed that the restoration of the baptism of the Spirit and the spiritual gifts would empower the church to hold the greatest end-time revival, not seen since the apostolic era. The Latter Rain, Charismatic Renewal and Independent Charismatic movements also believed that the restoration of the gifts, as well as the fivefold ministries, would bring unity to the church. Many Independent Charismatics insisted that this unity was necessary for Christ to return to set up the kingdom. Many of the Independent Charismatics also believed that they needed to participate in this process through

---

tionists Hamon and Paulk. There also appears to be an indirect connection between the 'immortalization' and 'little gods' theories of Hamon and Paulk and the 'little gods' theory of positive confession as advocated by Copeland, Hagin, Tilton and others.

142. Earl Paulk; as quoted by House and Ice, *Dominion Theology*, p. 381.

the establishment of the fivefold ministries and the perfecting of the
church and that this would be accompanied by a great end-time revival.

A triumphalist theme in early Pentecostal, Latter Rain and Independent
Charismatic eschatology was also linked to latter rain restorationism. In a
positive sense, this triumphalism gave these Pentecostal/Charismatic groups
the optimism that they were a significant part of God's plan to prepare for
the kingdom, whether through a great latter day revival (early Pentecostal
and Latter Rain) or through a unified and perfected church that also proselytized (Independent Charismatic). The denominational Charismatics were
optimistic that they would renew the spirituality of their denominational
churches. In a negative sense, however, this revivalist mentality saw the
Christians of other churches as 'fair game', so early Pentecostal, Latter
Rain Revival and Independent Charismatic groups proselytized voraciously
from the so-called 'dead' churches, whether mainline denominations or
other Pentecostal/Charismatic churches. This triumphalism sometimes also
resulted in a type of elitism and/or exclusivism, both for individuals who
had acquired one of the apostolic gifts and for the entire church which saw
itself as truly apostolic and the harbinger of God's kingdom.

It seems, then, that certain elements within the Independent Charismatic
movement adopted some of the beliefs and practices of both Classical
Pentecostalism and the Latter Rain movement. Latter rain restorationism
provides the primary logic which connects these movements. The outpouring of the Spirit on the apostolic church was identified as the former rain
and the outpouring of the Spirit in the time of Classical Pentecostalism,
Latter Rain Revival and Independent Charismatic movements was seen as
the latter rain. The latter rain would bring about the unity of the church
and the greatest revival before the eschatological return of Christ. The
form of eschatology was different, though each remained millennial and
anticipated the return of Christ. Early Pentecostals were premillennial with
a latter rain perspective. Mid-century Pentecostals were pretribulation premillennialists, a perspective they adopted from fundamentalist eschatology.
Latter Rain Revivalists were posttribulation premillennialists and heirs to
the latter rain doctrine. Certain elements of the Independent Charismatic
movement were still premillennial, but without a Rapture or Tribulation.
Yet they too adopted latter rain restorationism. Apparently, the logic of the
latter rain doctrine is not related to millennialism, but to the restoration of
apostolic Christianity in connection to eschatological anticipation.

Chapter 2

REVISIONING PENTECOSTAL ESCHATOLOGY:
CONTEMPORARY PENTECOSTAL THEOLOGIANS
RETHINK THE KINGDOM OF GOD

The rise of fundamentalist dispensationalism and the waning of latter rain doctrine in Pentecostal eschatology tended to obscure the message at the heart of the early Pentecostal revival, the message that God's Spirit was relationally involved in the lives of God's people, not only in terms of personal redemption which included making the human being physically, spiritually and emotionally whole, but in terms of the end-time preparation of the church and world. Pentecostalism encouraged authentic experiences of the Spirit as a form of spirituality in all their charismatic and apostolic dimensions, experiences with both personal and social ramifications. Fundamentalism tended to quell the charismatic dimensions of Pentecostalism.

Pentecostal eschatology, therefore, needs to be reconsidered in light of its spiritual heritage and its contemporary situation. Neither a simple re-institution of the doctrines of the early movement, nor a wholesale abandoning of Pentecostal heritage is helpful, but rather a re-thinking of Pentecostal eschatology in a contemporary way which does justice to both.

Steven Land: Pentecostal Spirituality as Foretaste of the Kingdom

An interesting and fruitful revisionist approach to Pentecostal eschatology has been offered by Holiness Pentecostal theologian Steven Land. Land obtained his doctorate from Emory University, where he was influenced by the works of Wesleyan Holiness theologian Melvin Dieter as well as Jürgen Moltmann, 'both of whom made a lasting impression on me'.[1]

---

1.   Steven J. Land, 'The Triune Center: Wesleyans and Pentecostals Together in Mission', *WesTJ* 34.1 (1999), pp. 83-100 (84) (repr. in *Pneuma* 21.2 [1999], pp. 199-214).

Land is presently teaching at the Church of God School of Theology, Cleveland, Tennessee.

Land argues that developing a 'systematic' Pentecostal theology is a violation of the core of Pentecostal spirituality. 'The theological task', asserts Land,

> demands the ongoing integration of beliefs, affections and actions lest the spirituality and theology fragment into intellectualism, sentimentalism and activism respectively. When *theologia* is restored to its ancient meaning, the dichotomization that too often occurs or is perceived between theology and spirituality can be overcome.[2]

He therefore contends that Pentecostal theology needs to be articulated in terms of a 'spirituality' which seeks the consummation of the coming kingdom of God, a theology which must always be a prayerful enterprise.[3] Looking to an earlier Christian concept of the integration between theology and spirituality and looking to the eschatological kingdom of God is more compatible with the Pentecostal worldview of apostolic restoration and eschatological kingdom.

Land prefers to define Pentecostal spirituality as an integration of beliefs and practices, undergirded by orthodoxy (right praise and belief), orthopraxy (right practice) and orthopathy (right affections).[4] Land's stress on religious affections is not simply understood as experiences of God, nor is it understood as the emotive dimensions of human religious experience, but as an abiding disposition which is both objective and relational. Religious affections are not to be identified with Friedrich Schleiermacher's 'feeling of absolute dependence', a disposition centred in religious consciousness, but are the consequence of an encounter with God's grace in Jesus Christ through the power of the Holy Spirit. Land is concerned with the issue of pneumatic discernment which acknowledges the transformative work of the Spirit as an act of prayer.[5]

---

2.   Land, *Pentecostal Spirituality*, p. 41.

3.   At the 2001 Society of Pentecostal Studies in Tulsa, Oklahoma, Land claimed to have been influenced by Barth's theology of prayer. For Barth, prayer is a 'Thou' encounter that is dialogical and open to the eschatological horizon. Karl Barth, *Prayer* (ed. D.E. Saliers; trans. S. Terrien; Philadelphia: Westminster Press, 1985), pp. 17-19; as cited by Land, *Pentecostal Spirituality*, pp. 36-37.

4.   Land, *Pentecostal Spirituality*, p. 13.

5.   Ralph Del Colle, 'Pentecostalism and Apocalyptic Passion: A Review of Steven Land's *Pentecostal Spirituality: A Passion for the Kingdom*, A Catholic Response', *SPS Response*, Wycliffe College, Toronto, Ontario, 9 March 1996, pp. 4-8.

Land argues 'that the righteousness, holiness and power of God are correlated with distinctive apostolic affections which are the integrating core of Pentecostal spirituality. This spirituality is Christocentric precisely because it is pneumatic';[6] Jesus Christ is at the centre of the Spirit's activity, as the agent for the inbreaking of the kingdom in the world. Pentecostalism thus operates with a 'functional Christology, which emphasizes the present power of Christ to save, sanctify, heal, empower, direct, and enable the believer to participate in mission'.[7] Land insists, therefore, that Pentecostalism does not emphasize the Spirit to the exclusion of Christ, but emphasizes both in the charismatic experiences of the church. Land criticizes both Dayton and Faupel for arguing that in Pentecostalism there was a shift from Christology to pneumatology that emphasizes the Spirit over against Christ. Even though there was an eschatological shift in the Holiness movement from postmillennialism to premillennialism, there was not a corresponding shift from Christ to the Spirit, from love to power or from gradual to instantaneous transformation in the divine encounter. All are fused together in love.[8]

Land also believes that he is able to shift theology away from the fruitless dichotomy between reason and feelings to argue that Pentecostal religious affections are correlated with certain divine attributes, the kingdom of God and the act of testimony, suggesting a faith that is characterized by a crisis-development dialectic.[9] The crisis-development is seen in the biblical drama of creation, the call of Abraham, the coming of Christ and the outpouring of the Spirit. These crisis events depict the transformative effects of divine interaction with the world, but they are also part of the development of salvation-history that seeks its fulfilment in the kingdom. Certain crisis points such as conversion, sanctification, baptism of the Holy Spirit and healing are transformative events that provide a basis for further development in the Pentecostal's spiritual journey, one filled with both joy and sorrow, hope and pain, peace and despair, all qualities of human life. Consequently, Pentecostals no longer see themselves as victims, but as participants in the missionary movement of God towards the coming kingdom.[10]

---

6. Land, *Pentecostal Spirituality*, p. 23.
7. Land, 'The Triune Center', p. 86.
8. Land, *Pentecostal Spirituality*, p. 63.
9. Land, *Pentecostal Spirituality*, p. 13.
10. Steven J. Land, 'Praying in the Spirit: A Pentecostal Perspective', in Jürgen

Underlying Land's work is the premise that Christian faith is an existential task, though he fails to define what he means. He argues that 'Pentecostalism lived and lives in an apocalyptic existence made existentially palpable by the perseverance, manifestation and power of the Holy Spirit'.[11] Emphasis in Pentecostal circles is for the Christian to walk in right relationship with God,[12] an emphasis more compatible with the existentialist notion of subjectivity than the Reformed/fundamentalist notion of rational assent to church authority and doctrine. This existential appropriation and participation is made real, argues Land, in the Pentecostal emphasis on oral worship and testimony, in which the Holy Spirit's presence and moving is of central importance.[13] However, Land's notion of 'existentialism' remains vague and could as easily have been replaced by the term experience (and often is). Land may have been correct to argue that Pentecostal 'worship and spirituality' is 'existential', but he does not define what his understanding of existentialism is, nor does he back it up with evidence or argumentation.

Land rejects the fundamentalist interpretation of Pentecostal eschatology. Fundamentalist dispensationalism draws too sharp a distinction between the kingdom age and the church age, insists Land, but Pentecostals celebrate the inbreaking of the kingdom of God into the present age, in which all the charismatic gifts are operative[14] as the Spirit works towards the eschatological transformation of creation. He argues that Pentecostal eschatology needs to be reinterpreted as a spiritual passion for the coming kingdom of God, which is 'already' present in the Spirit's activity inside and outside the Christian community, but 'not yet' fulfilled in the kingdom of God.[15] He comments:

> This 'promise-fulfilment, already-not yet' is a tense dynamic which characterizes Christianity's eschatological passion. From time to time when the tension is resolved prematurely—either in the direction of an other-worldly, 'not yet' escapism or a this-worldly, 'already' accommodation—there arise movements of restoration, revival, awakening and renewal to remind the

Moltmann and Karl-Josef Kuschel (eds.), *Pentecostal Movements as an Ecumenical Challenge* (Concilium, 3; London: SCM Press, 1996), pp. 85-103 (86).

11. Land, *Pentecostal Spirituality*, pp. 65-66.
12. Land, *Pentecostal Spirituality*, p. 37.
13. Land, *Pentecostal Spirituality*, p. 35.
14. Land, *Pentecostal Spirituality*, p. 53.
15. Land, *Pentecostal Spirituality*, p. 55.

church that it is the 'eschatological mother' whose sons and daughters are meant to prophesy.[16]

Movements of spiritual awakening, revival and renewal, such as the Pentecostal movement, are the catalyst that kept the tension between the 'already' and 'not yet' from being resolved.

Although Land revisions Pentecostal eschatology as a passion for the transformation of creation into the kingdom of God, retaining the terminology of apocalyptic is important to him. The apocalypse is not an end-time cataclysmic event which sees the destruction of all creation, only to be re-created *ex nihilo* into a new creation or eschatological kingdom. Rather, apocalyptic is revisioned into a transformational inbreaking of the kingdom, that retains the intense eschatological yearnings of early Pentecostalism. As such, salvation is seen as a narrative journey of the inbreaking of the kingdom that includes worshipping, walking (ethics) and witnessing. It is a walk that lives out the cosmic drama, testifying of Christ and one's daily life within the eschatological community.[17] The story of Pentecost becomes a liturgical paradigm and the existential reality of the inbreaking kingdom.[18] Although Land argues for the primacy of grace over the historical process in the inbreaking of the kingdom,[19] implicit is the notion that history itself will be transformed in the kingdom. However, for Land history is included in the transformation of the kingdom, primarily because history is the context for human social/existential relationships with one another and with God. Institutional and systemic structures seem to be excluded, at least implicitly. The use of apocalyptic in reference to the eschatological transformation appears to include social history and creation, but not the social-structural aspects of history.

Nevertheless, the dialectic tension of the 'already-not yet' is a tension that Land argues cannot be resolved in some sort of Hegelian sense of Absolute Spirit (Geist). God is not dissolved in history, but 'history is in God…God works in history, in the world, for the good of those called according to his purpose'.[20] To resolve it in favour of the 'not yet' results in a form of escapism, where social issues are left unaddressed. To resolve it in favour of the 'already' results in social accommodation, where there

16. Land, *Pentecostal Spirituality*, p. 15.
17. Land, *Pentecostal Spirituality*, p. 183.
18. Land, *Pentecostal Spirituality*, p. 174. The paradigmatic importance of Pentecost is a notion that is developed more extensively by Frank Macchia (see below).
19. Land, *Pentecostal Spirituality*, p. 137.
20. Land, *Pentecostal Spirituality*, p. 198.

is little distinction between the beliefs and values of the world and those of the church. The eschatology of 'not yet' escapism ends in elitism and/or isolationism of the sectarian or cultic variety. The eschatology of 'already' accommodation fails to provide a prophetic critique of the injustices of the world.[21]

Land shifts Pentecostal eschatology from the fundamentalist vision of apocalyptic world destruction to the transformation of the world, and integrates the trinitarian framework of orthodoxy, orthopraxy and orthopathy into an authentic Pentecostal spirituality. In doing so, Land revisions an underemphasized element of early Pentecostalism that called for the prophetic critique of the social injustices of the world. Although Land does not explicitly develop the implications of social ethics in his theology, the structure is there for such a project.

Eldin Villafañe: Pentecostal Social Ethics and the Reign of God

Similarly, Eldin Villafañe, a Gordon-Conwell Theological Seminary theologian, professor of social ethics, and an Assemblies of God pastor, constructs a Pentecostal social ethic rooted in the religious ethos of Hispanic Pentecostals. Villafañe is in a unique position for developing a Pentecostal theology of liberation, in that he identifies himself as a Latino American Pentecostal and a minister to the poor and oppressed eminently influenced by the liberation theologies emerging out of Latin America.[22] Space does not permit a full exposition of Villafañe's theology, even though he offers an interesting analysis of the contextual place of Hispanic Pentecostalism and its experiences of suffering and oppression in history, as well as the distinctive cultural characteristics of Hispanics and how they are incorporated into Pentecostal faith. I will limit my discussion to the relationship between his social ethics and pneumatological eschatology.

Villafañe criticizes the tendency in Pentecostalism of defining spiritual experiences too individualistically. Instead, he proposes a more social understanding of Hispanic Pentecostal spirituality, starting with a more appropriate definition of the human being. Villafañe prefers the terminology of person over individual, because it conveys the socialness of the human being. The Enlightenment definition of the human being as an isolated individual entity is truncated. The human being must be considered a

    21. Land, *Pentecostal Spirituality*, p. 119.
    22. Eldin Villafañe, 'The Contours of a Pentecostal Social Ethic: A North American Hispanic Perspective', *Transformation* 33 (1994), pp. 6-10 (6).

'person-in-community', gaining personal identity from the communal context.[23] Quoting Peter Berger and Thomas Luckman approvingly, Villafañe writes: 'Solitary human being is being on the animal level... As soon as one observes phenomena that are specifically human, one enters the realm of the social. Man's [*sic*] specific humanity and his sociality are inextricably intertwined.'[24] By extension, human experience (religious or otherwise) cannot be defined in terms of isolated individual experience, but is something constructed through a dialectic of personal/interior and social/ exterior realities. Thus Villafañe argues that Pentecostal spirituality should have both an interior and exterior focus.[25]

The significance of a more social understanding of spirituality is that both sin and salvation are seen as social as well. While sin is generally viewed as individual reproach against God and/or human beings, Villafañe asserts that Hispanic Pentecostals are well suited to address the issues of social evil, because they have been the subject of socio-economic oppression. He proposes that the Pentecostal belief that Christians are in a cosmic struggle against 'the flesh, the world and the devil' needs a social correlate of the struggle against 'sinful social structures, the "world" (*kosmos*) and "principalities and powers"'.[26] Sin is not only personal attitudes or misdeeds that damage one's relationship with God, but corrupt social structures that dehumanize people.

Likewise, salvation is predominantly viewed as personal redemption, in which the individual is called by God to repent of sin, to accept God's gift of eternal life procured through Christ's crucifixion and resurrection (redemption) and to live a godly life (sanctification) until death or Christ's earthly return. However, Villafañe proposes that a social understanding of salvation is also required. Salvation must also include liberation from

---

23.   While not within the scope of this book, defining the human being as person rather than individual is a more biblical-patristic perspective which is closer to a trinitarian view of God.

24.   Peter L. Berger and Thomas Luckman, *The Social Construction of Reality: A Treatise in the Sociology of Knowledge* (New York: Anchor Books, 1967), p. 51; as quoted by Villafañe, *Liberating Spirit*, p. 134.

25.   Villafañe, *Liberating Spirit*, pp. 134, 171.

26.   Villafañe, *Liberating Spirit*, pp. 165. Villafañe notes that in Scripture, 'world' has both a positive and negative meaning. In a positive sense, world refers to God's created order, including nature and all peoples. In a negative sense, world (*kosmos*) takes its meaning from apocalyptic thought and 'represents the twisted values which threaten genuine human life'. Villafañe, *Liberating Spirit*, pp. 176-77. The problem is that he does not adequately define what Pentecostals meant by 'the world'.

those social structures that ultimately dehumanize people. Villafañe argues, then, that Hispanic Pentecostals need to develop a holistic spirituality with both 'personal transformation/ piety (prayer, mystic, [*sic*] contemplation, thus inner directed and vertical) and social transformation/ piety (justice, advocacy, social action, thus outward-directed and horizontal)'.[27]

With this social definition in mind, Villafañe constructs a theological system in which ethics is a function of pneumatology, rooted in the eschatological 'reign of God'. 'A Pentecostal social ethic', insists Villafañe, 'must give voice to the distinctive voice of the Spirit: Ethics as Pneumatology. Further it must be a liberating ethic consistent with a Liberating Spirit.'[28] Christian social ethics in the present must take their bearings from the future reign of God, because the reign of God is the Spirit's historical project.[29] In New Testament eschatology, the reign of God breaks into the world in the person of Jesus Christ. This reign was 'already' present in Christ, but awaits its final consummation in the 'not yet' future. Jesus Christ both 'proclaimed' and 'demonstrated' God's reign by preaching the 'good news' of the kingdom and then demonstrating it through miraculous deeds. Yet Christ was not alone in ushering in the kingdom, because Christ's life and mission was inaugurated and empowered by the Holy Spirit, so that Christ was rightly considered the 'Charismatic Christ'.[30] Thus the reign of God was 'particularized' in Jesus Christ and made efficacious through the cross, but it was through the Spirit that the reign was 'universalized' as the risen Christ was mediated to us.[31] The ramification is not only personal salvation through personal faith in Jesus Christ, but liberation from corrupt social systems as the reign of God permeates historical reality.[32]

The Holy Spirit has a political agenda in creation to bring about the reign of God. The 'politics of the Spirit' complements the 'politics of Jesus' to create a 'pneumatic political discipleship'.[33] However, Villafañe criticizes the 'politics of Jesus' theology for defining Christian social

27. Villafañe, *Liberating Spirit*, p. 165.
28. Villafañe, 'Contours', p. 6.
29. Villafañe, *Liberating Spirit*, p. 195.
30. Villafañe, *Liberating Spirit*, pp. 184-85.
31. Villafañe, *Liberating Spirit*, p. 195.
32. Villafañe, *Liberating Spirit*, p. 186.
33. Eldin Villafañe, 'The Politics of the Spirit: Reflections on a Theology of Social Transformation for the Twenty-First Century', *Pneuma* 18.2 (1996), pp. 161-70 (162). The 'politics of Jesus' is articulated by John Howard Yoder to argue that Jesus' message was highly political.

ethics too narrowly within the institution of the church. The church is not equivalent to the reign of God. The church is the 'most *visible expression* and most *faithful interpreter*' of the kingdom. The church '*embodies* the kingdom in its life and…mission'.[34] The church is the community of the Spirit, which not only reflects and gives witness to the values of the kingdom, but struggles against personal and systemic sin. The kingdom is destined to include the whole of creation, however, not simply the church.

Although the church is the 'premier political community formed by the life-giving Spirit', the Spirit challenges Christians to go beyond the church to embrace the totality of the social order and its institutions.[35]

> To participate in the reign of God means to participate in God's rule. It is to take seriously God's call as a church to be a community of the Spirit *in* the world and a community of the Spirit *for* the world, but not *of* the world. This participation implies that there is no area of life where the rule of God cannot be exercised.[36]

While struggling against dehumanizing elements within the world, the kingdom affirms the goodness of God's creation, including human culture and history. Therefore, '[t]he Reign of God, the Spirit's historical project, takes seriously the world—as humanity, creation and its culture. Present history is affirmed; for history is the arena of the obedience of faith of the reign of God. The clear teaching of Scripture also looks to that future in which all things are made new…in a renewed creation'.[37] Thus the kingdom, with the church as its vanguard, is not set to destroy creation in some apocalyptic fashion that would annihilate creation, but will renew creation through liberation from personal and corporate/systemic sin, when God embraces all of creation.

Nevertheless, the church is the community of the Spirit and the body of the pneumatic Christ. The reign of God is the 'Spirit's historical project', indicating that history itself is part of the realm of the Spirit. The church is part of the kingdom, but the kingdom surpasses the church. Thus Villafañe claims:

> To participate in the Reign of God is to participate in the power of the age to come that are [*sic*] present and available to the church by the Spirit. The

---

34. Orlando Costas, *The Integrity of Mission: The Inner Life and Outreach of the Church* (New York: Harper & Row, 1979), p. 8; as quoted by Villafañe, *Liberating Spirit*, p. 187.
35. Villafañe, 'Politics of the Spirit', p. 162.
36. Villafañe, 'Contours', p. 6.
37. Villafañe, *Liberating Spirit*, p. 191.

church must follow the Spirit as Christ… This participation implies that
there is no area of life where the rule of God cannot be exercised. While
God rules in the church through the pneumatic (risen) Christ, the church
must not see itself as the only *locus* of the Reign of God…'[the church
must] define itself as an instrument for the full realization of the Kingdom
of God and as a sign of a true yet still imperfect realization of the Kingdom
in the world'. The church is thus challenged not to see itself as an *end* but
as a means towards the building of God's Reign.[38]

Villafañe continues to argue that participation in the reign of God
requires Christians to participate in the political process, to affect change
in the world so that dehumanizing structures and powers may be
vanquished. 'Christian participation in the political process is predicated',
argues Villafañe, 'in the understanding that Christ is Lord of the Kingdom
of this world, too. Although the rule of Christ has not been fully manifested—awaiting the *eschaton*—his claim and dominion are to impact all
human relations, meaning, the political process.'[39] The implication for
Hispanic Pentecostals, as Christians who actively demonstrate the charismatic manifestations of the Spirit, is that they need to develop a more
responsible social and political ethic based on the charismata of the Spirit.

Villafañe is concerned that our 'pneumatic political discipleship' is
being co-opted by non-biblical political ideologies. Christian social ethics
and action must be guided by biblical teachings, stories and paradigms of
divine love, justice and peace. A pneumatic political discipleship is para-
bolic, hinging on a faithful and active response to Scripture and the contextual realities of the present world. It seeks liberation through the liberating
Spirit. Christian political action must demonstrate 'God's preferential option
for the poor' for the spiritually, politically, economically and socially oppressed, who need the Spirit's liberation.[40] All world politics must be
judged by the politics of the Spirit, which seeks reconciliation, justice,
peace and liberation.[41]

The strength of Villafañe's theological project is that it offers a way for
Hispanic Pentecostals to develop a social ethic reflective of the eschatological reign of God, of their own charismatic understanding of the Spirit
and of their experiences of oppression, socio-economic deprivation and
racism. Although Villafañe deals specifically with Hispanic Pentecostals,

38. Villafañe, *Liberating Spirit*, p. 196.
39. Villafañe, *Liberating Spirit*, p. 196.
40. Villafañe, 'Politics of the Spirit', pp. 167-68.
41. Villafañe, 'Politics of the Spirit', pp. 168-69.

it can be argued that a similar scenario will help other Pentecostals to develop this social ethic, because they too have experienced various forms of oppression, socio-economic deprivation and racism. The theological task, for Villafañe, is to offer a visionary and prophetic voice for the contextual struggles and joys of the Hispanic community in relation to the liberating power of the Spirit as God's reign breaks in among us.[42] Villafañe's theological project locates and develops a theology of the Spirit from the experiences of Hispanic Pentecostalism, defined by those contextual experiences. He believes that 'this relativizing of our different identities does not mean that they are unimportant, rather that they are submitted to Christ. What is indeed eliminated is the superiority of one over another and the possibility of imposing one identity on another.'[43]

Miroslav Volf: Eschatological Significance of Work and Embrace

A third Pentecostal who develops a transformationist eschatology is Yale Divinity theologian Miroslav Volf. Although he presently worships at an Episcopal church and is a member of the Presbyterian Church of the United States of America, he still holds membership with the Pentecostal denomination, the Evangelical Church of Croatia.[44] Volf studied under Moltmann at Tübingen where he wrote his dissertation on Karl Marx's understanding of work. Volf was also a draft editor of the 'Oxford Declaration on Christian Faith and Economics' (1990), a document emerging from the Oxford Conference on Faith and Economics, and the locus of his thinking for the theology of work.[45] Throughout his writings, one can see that Volf is influenced by his Pentecostal background.

Utilizing Moltmann's eschatological framework, Volf insists that '*it is both possible and wise to construct Christian social ethics within the framework of belief in the eschatological continuity between present and future creation*'.[46] He rightly notes that it is theologically inconsistent to assert a 'non-earthly eschatological existence' (i.e. an otherworldly heavenly existence devoid of materiality), 'while believing in the resurrection of the body… It [also makes] little sense to affirm the goodness of creation and

---

42. Eldin Villafañe, *Seek Peace in the City: Reflections on Urban Ministry* (Grand Rapids: Eerdmans, 1995), p. 7.
43. Villafañe, *Peace in the City*, pp. 49-50.
44. Miroslav Volf to Peter Althouse, email, July 2000.
45. Volf, *Work in the Spirit*, pp. vii-xi.
46. Volf, 'Loving with Hope', p. 28; also Volf, *Work in the Spirit*, p. 79.

at the same time expect its eschatological destruction.'[47] Volf rhetorically comments that 'what God will annihilate must be either so bad that it is not possible to redeem it, or so insignificant that it is not worth being redeemed'.[48] Akin to the Eastern Orthodox theology of recapitulation, Volf argues that the eschatological new creation will be a recapitulation of all of creation, incorporating the present creation into the new creation. 'For there can be no fullness of salvation for some without the fullness of salvation for all; nor can there be the fullness of salvation for human beings without the fullness of salvation for the entirety of created reality.'[49]

The eschatological transformation of the world into the new creation has significance for the wider enterprise of social ethics. For Volf, the eschatological new creation is the basis for constructing an ethic of human work. As an aspect of this present creation, human work will be perfected, transformed and incorporated in the new creation. While most objects of human work will decay long before the eschatological transformation, there will be a cumulative effect in which the corporate work of the human race will be eschatologically redeemed. Each generation builds on the work of previous generations, indicating that 'much human work leaves a permanent imprint on the material and social environment', becoming part of 'human personality and identity'.[50] For instance, Gutenberg's work in creating the printing press will likely be incorporated into the new kingdom, because it not only changed the social-cultural environment from an oral to a literary society, but changed the structure of human personality.[51] Volf argues that human work itself will be purified in eschatological transformation and integrated into the divine action of the new heaven and new earth. 'Through

47. Volf, 'Loving with Hope', p. 29.
48. Volf, 'Loving with Hope', p. 30.
49. Miroslav Volf, *After our Likeness: The Church as the Image of the Trinity* (Grand Rapids: Eerdmans, 1998), p. 267.
50. Volf, 'Loving with Hope', p. 31.
51. Volf is unclear about how the cumulative efforts of work are incorporated into human personality, but it is possible that the thesis of social anthropologist Clifford Geertz is in the background. Geertz argued that not only does the evolutionary development of the human being influence the development of culture, but also that the semiotic webs of culture reciprocally influence the evolutionary development of the human nervous system. See Clifford Geertz, 'The Growth of Culture and the Evolution of Mind', in *idem*, *The Interpretation of Cultures: Selected Essays* (New York: Basic Books, 1973), pp. 55-83; cf. Miroslav Volf, 'Theology, Meaning, and Power', in Carmen Krieg and Thomas Kucharz (eds.), *The Future of Theology: Essays in Honor of Jürgen Moltmann* (Grand Rapids: Eerdmans, 1996), pp. 98-113.

their work', asserts Volf, 'human beings contribute in their modest and broken way to God's new creation'.[52]

Volf further explicates his pneumatological understanding of the nature of work. A theology of work can be developed in relation to two theological models: protological creation or the eschatological new creation. A theology of work developed within the protological model starts from the premise of God's good creation. Although the Old Testament stresses the uniqueness of God's creative activity *ex nihilo*, it also stresses the relationship between God's work of creation and human work. Human beings are required to cooperate with God in the preservation of creation, connoting a relationship of mutual dependence.

Alternately, a theology of work developed within the eschatological model sees human work as proleptic cooperation with God in the eschatological transformation of the world into the new creation. Volf rightly rejects an apocalyptic annihilation of the world, not only because it devalues the goodness of original creation, but because it makes meaningless any effort by human beings in the here-and-now to bring about positive change. If the present world is to be destroyed, argues Volf, then 'our mundane work has only earthly significance for the well-being of the worker, the worker's community and posterity…[so that] in the final apocalyptic catastrophe, human work is devoid of ultimate significance'.[53] Volf opts for a transformative eschatological model. The protological model has the problem of justifying the status quo. Attempts to change the structure of work or to eliminate alienation within work are resisted because the protological model tends to support the belief that the preservation of creation must coincide with the preservation of the established order.[54] Moreover, the eschatological model is able to incorporate the positive elements of the protological model while critiquing the negative aspects of the present world. Thus 'The noble products of human ingenuity, "whatever is beautiful, true and good in human cultures", will be cleansed from impurity, perfected and transfigured to become part of God's new creation'.[55]

Volf qualifies his understanding of the eschatological transformation, however. First, human beings cannot simply bring in the new creation through their working efforts because sin has damaged creation. They can

---

52. Volf, 'Loving with Hope', p. 31.
53. Volf, 'Human Work', p. 175.
54. Volf, 'Human Work', p. 179.
55. Volf, 'Human Work', p. 175.

only contribute to the kingdom in a broken, creaturely way. Volf asserts that

> a theology of work cannot operate with an *evolutionist* understanding of social realities. The concept of the new creation precludes all naïve belief in the permanence of human moral progress. A truly *new* creation can never result from the action of intrahistorical forces pushing history toward ever-superior states. Although we must affirm the continuity between present and future orders, that affirmation should not deceive us into thinking that God's new creation will come about in linear development from the present order of things… Holding to the theological framework of the new creation allows us to perceive progress in certain aspects of social life or in certain historical periods, and it allows us at other times to share Luther's view that 'the world (as a whole, or a particular "world") is deteriorating from day to day'.[56]

In other words, the belief that human work will establish the kingdom through the progressive betterment of society must be rejected as false. Secondly, the coming eschatological kingdom must be seen primarily as a gift from God. As a gift, human beings must wait upon God in expectation for the new kingdom. The coming kingdom will be free of evil and will transcend anything human beings could possibly create. Thirdly, waiting for the kingdom does not mean that human beings should watch passively, but that they should actively participate through their works in service to the kingdom. ' "Kingdom-participation" is not contrary', insists Volf,

> rather it is complementary to 'Kingdom-expectation'. Placed in the context of kingdom-participation, mundane human work for worldly betterment becomes a contribution—a limited and imperfect one in need of divine perfection—to the eschatological kingdom which will come through God's action alone.[57]

Volf identifies a paradox of human involvement in the eschatological kingdom, a paradox in which humans must both wait and work, but it is a paradox rooted in Scripture itself.

With this eschatological framework in mind, Volf constructs a theology of work based on the charisms of the Spirit. It represents a paradigmatic shift from Luther's soteriological understanding of work as vocation to a pneumatological understanding of work rooted in charisms. Volf is critical of the vocational understanding. Although it addresses the issues of work in the feudal systems of the Reformation, it is unable to address the issues of work in industrial-informational societies of modernity. For Luther,

---

56. Volf, *Work in the Spirit*, p. 84.
57. Volf, 'Human Work', pp. 178-79.

every Christian had a vocation and every type of work was vocational, so the Christian who worked was fulfilling God's call. He made a further distinction between spiritual vocation and external vocation. Spiritual vocation was God's call to participate in the kingdom of God. External vocation was God's call to serve God and others in the world. The external vocation manifested itself in one's profession.

However, the vocational view of work in modernity has several problems: (1) It is unable to address the elements of alienation in certain kinds of work, because vocation is defined by the origin and purpose of work and not by its quality. The vocational view of work makes no distinction between humanizing and dehumanizing work. (2) Luther's nexus between vocation and calling ends up subsuming call into vocation and vocation into occupation. (3) It is ideologically misused when dehumanizing work is elevated to service to God. (4) The vocational understanding of work is unable to address the 'diachronic pluriformity' of work in modern industrial-informational societies. Change from one occupation to another relates more to the nature of modern work than to the individual's intentions, inaccurately suggesting unfaithfulness in one's vocational calling. (5) Finally, Luther's view of vocation implies a single occupation, but the reality of modernity is that work consists of a 'synchronic pluriformity of tasks'. People often need several occupations at one time to make ends meet.[58]

Because the vocational model has these problems, Volf argues that a theology of work is better constructed pneumatologically on the charisms of the Spirit. For Volf, charisms need to be qualified: (1) Charisms are not so broadly defined that they encompass all ethical activity, a definition that ultimately reduces charisms to ethics. Volf differentiates between fruit of the Spirit and gifts of the Spirit. Fruit designates the character of Christian ethical existence. Gifts are related to specific tasks God calls us to do. (2) Charisms are not so narrowly defined as to restrict them to ecclesiastical activities. The Spirit must not be restricted simply to Christian fellowship in the church, but must extend to fellowship with the world. (3) Charisms are not the sole possession of an elite group within Christian fellowship. No Christian is without a charism. (4) Charisms are not to be seen as only extraordinary, but must include both ordinary and extraordinary characteristics. In other words, administration is just as important as prophecy or tongues. Volf therefore defines the relationship between eschatology, calling, ethics and work as:

---

58. Volf, 'Human Work', pp. 179-82.

> the calling [soteriology] to enter the kingdom of God [eschatology] and to
> live a life that corresponds to the kingdom…expresses itself at the point of
> its individual appropriation in a call to bear the fruit of the Spirit which
> should characterize all Christians [ethics] and branches itself out in the gifts
> of the Spirit to each individual [work].[59]

Volf argues that a pneumatological theology of work based in the charisms of the Spirit has the following advantages over the vocational model:
(1) Work based on the charisms of the Spirit places work within the centre
of Christian faith, not only by enabling every Christian to perform tasks in
both the church and the world, but by eliminating a hierarchical valuation
of work. Every task is meaningful. (2) Work must be understood as cooperation with God. Under the power and direction of the Spirit, work is
enabled by the charismata of the Spirit. The Spirit's impartation of these
gifts is 'a guarantee' (2 Cor. 1.22) of the realization of the eschatological
kingdom. Jesus Christ as the giver of these gifts through the Spirit is present in their impartation. 'Through the gifts of the Spirit', comments Volf,
'Christ is realizing his eschatological rule in the world. Thus cooperation
with God in work through the empowerment and direction of the Spirit
should be interpreted as cooperation in the kingdom of God that "com-
pletes creation and renews heaven and earth".'[60] (3) A pneumatological
understanding of work overcomes the ambiguity in Luther's theology of
work between spiritual calling through the preaching of the kingdom and
external calling as one's place in society. (4) Work is seen as service to
others, because the function of the gifts is to serve others. (5) The pneumatological understanding of work can potentially overcome the alienating
aspects of certain kinds of work. Work enabled by the charismata of the
Spirit is transformative because it does not tolerate the tension between
alienating work and the character of human personality.[61] In other words,
there is a spiritual correspondence between the gift to enable one to
perform work and the character of work itself. (6) The pneumatological
view of work is potentially open to the same ideological misuse as the
vocational understanding of work. Nevertheless, elevating work to cooperation with God demands an obligation to overcome all forms of alienation and dehumanization in work. (7) This view of work is better able to
deal with the 'diachronic pluriformity of employment/jobs' in modern
societies (i.e. the succession of different kinds of employment), because

59. Volf, 'Human Work', p. 185.
60. Volf, 'Human Work', p. 186.
61. Volf, *Work in the Spirit*, p. 97.

Scripture tells us to seek multiple gifts of the Spirit. (8) It is also better able to deal with the 'synchronic pluriformity of jobs/employment' in modern societies (i.e. different kinds of employment at the same time), because a person may have more than one charism at a time.[62]

Volf's theology of work is constructed from a transformationist view of the kingdom of God in which the charismata of the Spirit enable all human beings to work according to their gift. It represents a social ethic in which work is liberated from the alienating and dehumanizing effects of a sinful world. It is part of the liberation of creation looking forward to the eschato-logical new creation. Volf's theology of work represents a theology of liberation. He reveals his sympathies for the theologies of liberation else-where when he argues that both liberation and Pentecostal theologies are alike in their materialist view of salvation. 'It is of ecumenical importance', argues Volf, 'for liberation and pentecostal [*sic*] theology to recognize each other as feuding family members'.[63] While classical Protestant theol-ogy maintains a radical distinction in salvation between inner spirituality and material well-being, liberation theology insists that salvation touches one's 'bodily human existence' by stressing the materiality of salvation through sociopolitical liberation. Pentecostals stress the materiality of salvation in their doctrine of divine healing.[64] Divine healing is not only provided in the atonement, but a partial realization of the reign of God in the here-and-now.[65] Although not explicitly stated, Volf implies that certain aspects of Pentecostalism represent a form of liberation similar to that of liberation theology, precisely because it stresses the material aspects of salvation. He concludes with a call to integrate 'the *personal-spiritual* aspects of salvation emphasized in classical Protestantism, the *individual-physical* aspects of salvation emphasized by Pentecostalists, and the *socioeconomic* aspects emphasized by liberation theologies'.[66]

However, Volf more recently notes the limitations of liberation as a theological category. The problem is that the distinctions of liberation and its corollary oppression are often blurred in the context of sociopolitical reality. Volf comments:

> These categories—especially the category of 'liberation'—are inadequate in dealing with cultural conflicts. The trouble is that in a sense they fit conflict-

62. Volf, 'Human Work', pp. 185-88.
63. Volf, 'Materiality', p. 449.
64. Volf, 'Materiality', p. 448.
65. Volf, 'Materiality', p. 457.
66. Volf, 'Materiality', p. 467.

situations too well: *both* Hutus and Tutsis, *both* Croats and Serbs see
themselves as oppressed and engaged in a struggle for liberation. The categories of 'oppression' and 'liberation' provide each with moral weapons that
make their battles so much deadlier. Moreover, in many situations of ethnic
conflict we do not have a clear perpetuator and a clear victim; both parties
have oppressed and both parties have suffered oppression, though often in
varying degrees and at different junctures in their common history.[67]

In many cases of world conflict there is not a clear oppressor and a clear
liberator; all sides experience oppression and all sides see themselves in a
struggle for liberation.[68]

   Volf constructs what he calls a theology of embrace. This theology of
embrace still exposes the evils of oppression and seeks liberation, but it
goes one step further to facilitate reconciliation between peoples and/or
groups in conflict. The categories of oppression and liberation are not replaced, but are inserted into 'a larger theological framework which will
preserve their strengths and curtail their weaknesses'.[69] As such, liberation
is not an end in itself, but one of the many factors in the process of reconciliation. Volf's theology of embrace is constructed in light of his eschatological model, a model he adopts from Moltmann. This present creation
will be embraced by God and transformed into the new creation. Embrace
between peoples and cultures is a correlate of God's embrace of creation.
'The end of the world is not violence', he argues, 'but a nonviolent embrace without end'.[70]

   Volf's theology of embrace employs the categories of 'otherness',
'distance and belonging', 'exclusion' and 'embrace'. For Volf, 'otherness
was integral to Christian ethnic and cultural identity'.[71] Jesus Christ came
into the world as a 'stranger', because there was a fundamental estrangement between God and the world, an estrangement that ultimately led to
the cross. The followers of Christ likewise inherited this estrangement
because they were not of this world but of God. Because Christians were
strangers in the world, they had good reason to embrace the otherness of
other peoples and/or cultures. The otherness of Christians in the world
allowed them to empathize with the otherness of different ethnic, gender
or religious peoples.[72]

   67.   Volf, 'Vision of Embrace', p. 200.
   68.   Also see Volf, *Exclusion and Embrace*, pp. 103-105.
   69.   Volf, 'Vision of Embrace', p. 201.
   70.   Volf, *Exclusion and Embrace*, p. 300.
   71.   Volf, 'Exclusion and Embrace', p. 236.
   72.   Volf, 'Exclusion and Embrace', p. 236.

The metaphor of stranger provides a balancing concept between distance and belonging. The otherness of the stranger 'cultivated the proper relationship between distance from the culture and belonging to the culture. The biblical metaphor "stranger", if properly understood, might help us achieve that balance.'[73] Christians are better able to address the issue of otherness, because they are of two worlds: the world in which they belong and the world from God above. However,

> Christians are not insiders who take flight to a new 'Christian culture' and become outsiders to their own culture; rather, when they have responded to the call of the gospel they have stepped, as it were, with one foot outside their own culture while the other remains firmly planted in it. Though they are not from the 'world', in an important sense they are 'from the culture' which has shaped them.[74]

Christians therefore experience both distance and belonging. They belong to the world but are distanced from it as well. Although distance and belonging are in a sense antithetical concepts, they are not to be secluded from each other. Volf points to the dangers of stressing one at the expense of the other:

> Belonging without distance destroys: I affirm my exclusive identity as Croatian and want to shape everyone in my own image or eliminate them from my world. Distance without belonging isolates: I deny my identity as Croatian and draw back from my own culture. But more often than not, I become trapped in the snares of counter-dependence... Distance from a culture must never degenerate into flight from that culture.[75]

Belonging must never turn into exclusivism and distance must never lead to isolationism.

Volf argues that there are good reasons for Christians to maintain cultural distance, reasons ultimately connected to the eschatological new creation. Distance from one's own culture is necessary because in the end Christians owe allegiance to God and the eschatological reign. Why should Christians maintain cultural distance, asks Volf? First of all, rebirth in the Spirit of the new creation means that a Christian is part of 'the rich and complex reality of the new creation', a complexity that makes space for all forms of otherness.[76] Through spiritual rebirth, the richness and diversity of the eschato-

---

73. Volf, 'Vision of Embrace', p. 197.
74. Volf, 'Vision of Embrace', p. 198.
75. Volf, 'Vision of Embrace', p. 198; *idem, Exclusion and Embrace*, p. 50.
76. Volf, 'Exclusion and Embrace', p. 237.

logical new creation is embodied in the new believer in an embryonic form. The embryonic embodiment of the new creation in the believer represents what Volf calls a 'catholic personality'. Volf states that

> the Spirit re-creates us and sets us on the road towards becoming what I call a 'catholic personality', a personal microcosm of the eschatological new creation. A catholic personality is a personality enriched by otherness, a personality which is what it is only because multiple others have been reflected in it in a particular way. The distance from one's own culture that results from being born of the Spirit creates a fissure in me through which others can come in.[77]

Catholic personality allows the Christian to embrace individual and cultural otherness. It avoids exclusivism because the Christian becomes 'a particular reflection of the totality of others…[which] transcends indifferent relativism. Each does not simply affirm the otherness as otherness but seeks to be enriched by it.'[78] Catholic personality also breaks through the boundaries of the church, because it anticipates the incorporation of the church into the new creation.[79]

A catholic personality presupposes a 'catholic community'. The church has taken root in many cultures, both shaping those cultures and being shaped by them. Therefore the church is as diverse as the plurality of cultures. At the same time, the church, as the body of Christ, is to be one in unity. It must reflect the triunity of God. Consequently, no one church is to isolate itself from other churches or other cultures. Every church is to allow itself to be open, both to the approval and criticism of other churches. According to Volf, the notion that the local church is part of the universal church needs the inverted corollary: in a profound but real sense, every local church is itself a catholic community, because all other churches are a part of that church; all other churches have had a part in shaping the local church's identity.[80]

In an analysis of Roman Catholic, Orthodox and Free Church ecclesiology through the theologies of Joseph Ratzinger, John D. Zizioulas and the first Baptist John Smyth respectively, Volf clarifies his view of catholicity. He argues that the local church is ascribed catholicity through 'anticipation' of the eschatological community of God.[81] In the new creation, the entire

---

77. Volf, 'Vision of Embrace', p. 199.
78. Volf, 'Exclusion and Embrace', pp. 237-38.
79. Volf, *Exclusion and Embrace*, p. 130.
80. Volf, 'Vision of Embrace', p. 199.
81. Volf, *After our Likeness*, p. 268.

people of God and the entire 'cosmos' will be a differentiated unity analogous to the differentiated unity of the trinitarian being of God. The relationships of persons in the local church and between churches must correspond to the trinitarian God. These relationships are eschatologically abiding. On the one hand, the relationship between local churches are historically determined and therefore transient. On the other hand, God 'indwells' the local church through the people who constitute the local churches. The local church is catholic insofar as it anticipates its eschatological catholicity.[82] Consequently:

> It is precisely as partially overlapping entities that both the local church and the universal church are constituted into the church through their common relation to the Spirit of Christ, who makes them both into the anticipation of the eschatological gathering of the entire people of God. This is why every local church can also be completely the church even though it encompasses only a part of the universal church.[83]

The local church's anticipation of the eschatological community means that any church in any given culture is a catholic community.

Cultural distance as shaped by the eschatological new creation entails '*judgment against a monochrome character of one's own culture and against evil in every culture*'. In an earlier article, Volf argues that 'catholic foreignness' is what gives Christians the ability to distance themselves from culture. He later modifies his argument to include the concept of the 'evangelical personality'. Catholic foreignness gives the Christian the ability to step outside of a given culture in order to critique it. Volf insists:

> Because everything belongs partly to a catholic personality, a person with catholic personality cannot belong totally to any one thing. The only way to belong is with distance. This distance from any particular reality, from any particular person or culture—which exists for the sake of transcending the exclusion of all other realities from that person's identity—might be called 'catholic foreignness'. Christians are not simply aliens to their own culture; they are aliens who are at home in every culture, because they are open to every culture.[84]

'Catholic foreignness' endows Christians with the ability to distance themselves and thus critique their own cultures, but their catholicity allows them to embrace the goodness of all cultures, precisely because of the universal relevance of Jesus Christ and the eschatological new creation.

82. Volf, *After our Likeness*, p. 203.
83. Volf, *After our Likeness*, p. 141.
84. Volf, 'Exclusion and Embrace', p. 237.

While the catholic personality is an enrichment by the multiplicity of otherness, it must discriminate between 'truth and falsehood, between justice and arbitrariness, between life and death'.[85] However, this discrimination has purpose, that purpose being the transformation of the world into the new creation. Just as the new believer is transformed into a catholic personality by the Spirit of the new creation, so the 'evangelical personality' entails the transformation of the world in anticipation of the eschatological new creation. In other words, the evangelical personality enables the Christian to work towards the transformation of creation, even though this transformation will be enacted by God. Moreover, just as the catholic personality needs a catholic community, so too the evangelical personality needs an 'ecumenical community'. The ecumenical community allows the Christian community to distance itself from its own cultural biases. The ability to distance itself is rooted in the demand for every church to hear the diverse voices of all other churches. By listening to the voices of other communities, the gospel of Jesus Christ is truly discerned.[86]

The miracle of Pentecost is a 'primal catholic event' and an example of embrace. Pentecost has been interpreted as a reverse of Babel, by Pentecostals and non-Pentecostals alike. According to Genesis, those human beings who were arrogant enough to believe they could attain equality with God by building a tower were punished by a confusion of language and a scattering of peoples. Pentecost, as a reversal of Babel, restores the unity of language, so that people from every nation and culture can speak and understand the language of faith.[87] Volf believes, however, that this interpretation is mistaken, because the Christians at Pentecost did not speak one uniform language, but were able to communicate through the use of different languages. Speaking only one language would have reverted to the uniformity of Babel,[88] whose construction of the tower was in fact an attempt to enforce uniformity. God's punishment was not the result of Babel's attempt to be equal with God, but for Babel's 'totalitarian project to centralize, homogenize, and control' and suppress the cultural differences by erasing those people who did not fit into its grand scheme.[89] The implication is that catholicity cannot enforce uniformity, but seeks unity in the differences that exist between peoples.

85. Volf, 'Vision of Embrace', p. 199.
86. Volf, 'Vision of Embrace', pp. 199-200.
87. Volf, *Exclusion and Embrace*, p. 226.
88. Volf, *After our Likeness*, p. 268.
89. Volf, *Exclusion and Embrace*, p. 226.

These concepts are all part of the main categories of exclusion and embrace. Exclusion takes many forms, but any form of exclusion is definitively sin. Exclusion is a form of evil based on individual or collective hatred of others. Exclusion took place in Nazi Germany when the obsession for racial purity led to the Holocaust. Exclusion took place in the Balkans when the Serbian obsession with territorial purity meant the expulsion and eventual killing of Croats residing in Serbian territory. Although these two examples are extreme forms of exclusion, it occurs in more subtle ways, even in Western countries. Volf comments that

> this type of debasement is being repeated today in many parts of the world: the 'others' are first dehumanized or demonized and then discriminated against, marginalized, driven out or destroyed. Even in western capitalist societies where explicit and public exclusion is forbidden by formal rules implicit and private exclusion still takes place, often in the form of unconscious but no less effectual aversion.[90]

Thus exclusion, whether explicit or implicit, needs to be identified as sin and placed in judgment.

A theology of embrace moves beyond the category of liberation: it seeks a reconciliation between conflicting peoples or groups, an acceptance of the otherness of others. Embrace includes forgiveness, even when forgiveness seems an impossibility. Embrace includes repentance, both of the offending and offended parties, because neither is truly innocent of sinfulness. Both parties need to repent for both parties to be forgiven. Forgiveness is the boundary between exclusion and embrace; it heals exclusionary acts and breaks down the walls of division. It creates distance between both parties that allows them the option of peacefully going their separate ways in a type of civilized exclusion, or to embrace the other. Embracing the other is acceptance of shared commonalities while also respecting differences.[91]

The image of embrace is a metaphor. The hug of an embrace resembles the peace that comes after conflicting individuals or groups repented of their exclusionary acts and both forgive and are forgiven by the other. Embrace makes space for the otherness of the other. It preserves both self-identity and the acceptance of others. Volf explains:

> An embrace always involves a double movement of *aperture* and *closure*. I open my arms to create space in myself and others. The open arms are a

---

90. Volf, 'Vision of Embrace', p. 201.
91. Volf, 'Exclusion and Embrace', pp. 246-47.

> sign both of discontent at being myself only and of desire to include the
> other… In an embrace I also close my arms around the other—not tightly,
> so as to crush her and assimilate her forcefully into myself—for that would
> not be an embrace but a concealed power-act of exclusion—but gently, so
> as to tell her that I do not want to be without her in her otherness. I want her
> to remain independent and true to her genuine self, to maintain her identity
> and, as such, to become part of me so that she can enrich me with what she
> has and I do not.[92]

Embrace is not forced, but a mutual enrichment that allows for self-expression.

A theology of embrace, then, does not seek isolation but openness to otherness, to be enriched by the differences of the other. It does not mean disintegration of personal or cultural boundaries, because without boundaries there is no life, only chaos. Embrace seeks to abolish 'the false boundaries which perverted an order that sustains and enriches life…'[93] A theology of embrace seeks to validate the uniqueness of cultural diversity, to cultivate different languages, to sustain traditions and nurture cultures, things that require boundaries. At the same time, boundaries need to remain porous to allow the otherness of other languages, traditions and cultures to enrich one's own culture. Boundaries are necessary for sustaining the life of diverse cultural matrices, but not so rigid that they enforce a uniformity.[94]

The significance of Volf's theology is, first of all, that it brings his Pentecostal heritage into the mainstream of academic theology. Developing a theology of work on the charismata of the Spirit in all probability stems from his inundation with the operation of the gifts of the Spirit in Pentecostal circles. Admittedly, there are other influences on Volf, and he modifies the traditional Pentecostal understanding of the charismatic gifts of the Spirit. Yet it is telling that a Pentecostal bases a theology of work on the gifts of the Spirit. Secondly, Volf's theology is a significant contribution to ecumenical and even interfaith dialogue. He not only includes all Christians but all persons as receptors of the Spirit's gifts, suggesting that God's Spirit moves beyond denominational and religious traditions. The significance of this fact is made sharper because Volf does not base his theology of work on a general revelation of creation, but on the eschatological transformation of the world, a subject usually related to redemption.

92. Volf, 'Exclusion and Embrace', p. 247.
93. Volf, 'Vision of Embrace', p. 203.
94. Volf, 'Vision of Embrace', pp. 203-204.

Likewise, Volf's theology of embrace upholds acceptance of otherness, an otherness that surely includes other denominational traditions *and* other religious faiths. Embracing other Christian traditions and other faiths does not mean a negation of the uniqueness of one's own faith, but that the other faiths enrich one's own, just as one's faith enriches the other's. Commonalities can be explored while differences are respected. A further advantage is that it incorporates the important socio-economic insights of theologies of liberation, but seeks more than just liberation: it seeks reconciliation, cultural enrichment, and above all peace.

Volf's theology of work and his theology of embrace are examples of a social ethic developed from the eschatological vision of a transformed new creation. This new creation will not be a new creation *ex nihilo* (out of nothing), coming after the apocalyptic destruction of the present world, but it will be built on the transformation of this present creation. It will include the cumulative cultural achievements of humanity, though purified, perfected and transfigured by God. Volf's eschatology is the groundwork for his subsequent work and a self-conscious appropriation of Moltmann's eschatology. However, his theology of work and his theology of embrace are groundbreaking contributions to Christian social ethics. Volf uses a transformationist eschatology to develop this social ethic, and does so from a Pentecostal perspective. It is not quite accurate to define Volf's work as a Pentecostal social ethic based on a transformationist eschatology of the new creation, but it is fair to claim that his work is one of the best examples of such an eschatological social ethic articulated by a Pentecostal.

Frank Macchia: Tongues of Pentecost as Sign of the Kingdom

Assemblies of God Pentecostal theologian Frank D. Macchia, professor at Vanguard University, California, likewise revisions Pentecostal eschatology and does so with a corresponding revision of the Pentecostal distinctive of speaking in tongues. Macchia is contextually situated within an Italian-American Pentecostal tradition; his grandmother, Antoinette Ipoledo-Macchia, is an important Pentecostal leader. Macchia's Italian background suggests a possible appreciation for Roman Catholicism, particularly in his development of a Pentecostal sacramental theology. We will see that Macchia is also strongly under the influence of Barthian theology and German Pietism.[95]

95. Macchia obtained his ThD from the University of Basel, under Jan Milic Lochman. Frank D. Macchia, 'Curriculum Vitae'.

Macchia convincingly argues that within the context of Wuerttemberg Pietism the kingdom of God theologies of Johann Blumhardt and his son Christoph provide an important critique of Pentecostalism. There are similarities between Pentecostalism and the Blumhardts' theological struggles to combine revivalistic piety with responsible social commitment and a doctrine of healing, articulated by the Blumhardts as the result of the radical inbreaking of the kingdom into the present world. The elder Blumhardt defined healing as deliverance from illness that was interpreted as being caused by demon possession, while the younger Blumhardt articulated healing along social lines, as the restoration of broken relationships and liberation from oppressive social conditions.[96] Macchia's interest is not in tracing the roots of Pentecostalism in Wuerttemberg Pietism per se, but in critiquing the Pentecostal/Evangelical tendency to split revivalistic spirituality from responsible social engagement and ethics.

Macchia's analysis of the Blumhardts focuses on the role that the eschatological kingdom had in the theology of Wuerttemberg Pietism. 'The single most important impulse in the spirituality of nineteenth-century Wuerttemberg pietism', claims Macchia, 'was the conviction that the Christian must live in the light of the coming kingdom of God'.[97] Healing was seen as a visible manifestation of the kingdom of God, defined by Johann in terms of the Pentecost event of Acts 2 rather than by the future parousia, and by Christoph in terms of the christological/ Incarnational event. This enabled them to claim that history was the context through which God's kingdom was being manifested, both spiritually (Johann) and socially (Christoph). The fulfilment of the Spirit's work in Pentecost meant that history itself was significant in the unfolding of the kingdom.[98]

Space does not permit a full description of Macchia's insightful analysis of Wuerttemberg Pietism, but he reveals an interesting interaction between apocalyptic, theosophical/mystical and prophetic/ethical kingdom of God eschatologies in the Blumhardts' theological background.[99] In brief, Macchia points to four theological shifts in the kingdom of God spirituality of nineteenth-century Wuerttemberg Pietism. One was a shift from a futuristic, apocalyptic spirituality to a focus on the inbreaking of the kingdom in present history. The second was a shift from the kingdom of God seen as a cosmic transformation of creation to a specific concern for the

96.   Macchia, *Spirituality*, p. 2.
97.   Macchia, *Spirituality*, p. 7.
98.   Macchia, *Spirituality*, p. 161.
99.   Macchia, *Spirituality*, p. 7.

liberation of the poor and sick. The third was a shift from the apocalyptic future outpouring of the Spirit to an association between the work of the kingdom and the universal outpouring of the Spirit in the present church age. The fourth was a tension between an expectation of the future fulfilment of the kingdom and an inbreaking of that kingdom in the present. One must both 'wait' and 'hurry' for the kingdom.[100] Johann Blumhardt (the elder) and Christoph Blumhardt (the younger) developed their kingdom of God eschatologies within the Wuerttemberg context.[101]

Johann Blumhardt's Theology

Although there is no space here to thoroughly explore the theologies of the Blumhardts, I will consider their contribution, mainly through the eyes of Macchia. After a two-year 'battle' to heal a woman named Gottlieben Dittus from evil spirits, which finally came when a voice roared through her sister that 'Christ is Victor', and a subsequent short-lived revival that was finally quashed by church authorities, Johann (1805–1880) started to think about the yearning for the kingdom and its realization in the liberation of the sick and the suffering.[102] The significance of the battle for Johann was that it exposed him to the helplessness of suffering, the power of darkness, and human bondage. It also convinced him that there was victory in Christ to heal the sick and suffering. The revival forged Johann's restorationist tendencies, because he concluded that the apostolic power of the Holy Spirit was lacking in the church of his day and that a new outpouring of the Spirit was needed to restore this power.

The Spirit of Pentecost and the kingdom were two important foci that converged in tension for Johann. Macchia comments:

> The Spirit of Pentecost and the kingdom of God were vehicles for Blumhardt of the presence of the living and personal God in the world. The roots of the Spirit/kingdom are the incarnation of the personal God in Christ. As the Lord was the incarnation of the personal God, so are the Spirit of Pentecost and the kingdom the 'personal entrance of the Lord'. This means that Blumhardt had a Christocentric understanding of the Spirit of Pentecost and the kingdom of God. The Holy Spirit represents Christ. Indeed Jesus is the one who inaugurates the kingdom, and he is the goal toward which we strive.[103]

---

100. Macchia, *Spirituality*, p. 42.
101. Macchia, *Spirituality*, pp. 62-63.
102. Macchia, *Spirituality*, pp. 64-69.
103. Macchia, *Spirituality*, p. 72.

The mediation of the presence of Christ and the kingdom was through the Pentecost event as an inbreaking of the kingdom that included signs of the future kingdom such as healing, signs and wonders, revivals and preaching.[104] Johann believed that the distance of the Spirit of Pentecost from the church of his day was due to disbelief and disobedience. In fact, he believed the Spirit of Pentecost was absent from the church. He made a distinction, however, between the Spirit of Pentecost and the Spirit of salvation. The Spirit of God was present 'with' us to effect salvation, but not directly or empirically 'in' us. The latter was the Spirit of Pentecost that would be universally present in the healing and liberation of creation.[105]

Johann began to focus on the liberation of the suffering and the sick. The victory of Jesus Christ on the cross was the basis for conquering suffering in the world, and indeed the liberation of all of creation. The outpouring of the Spirit in Pentecost was the means whereby the gifts of the Spirit were mediated to the children of God as direct help for victory. The absence of the gifts in history was a sign of the church's distance from Pentecost, a result of disbelief and disobedience. Johann therefore gained a new appreciation for the liberation of the suffering, the sick and the oppressed. 'The miserable and the poor are constantly oppressed', claimed Johann. 'All misery of which the Bible speaks is oppression from some source, and oppression is always the worst suffering.'[106] For Johann, the oppressed were those who were 'injured or attacked in their person or existence', 'the walked on', those made into 'nothing', 'while each person has a right as one in the image of God to be a somebody'.[107] The source of oppression was caused both by persons against other persons and universal suffering under the 'power of darkness'. The outpouring of the Spirit of Pentecost as an inbreaking of the kingdom was the means whereby the gifts of the Spirit were mediated to the children of God to bring victory over darkness. Healing and liberation provided a holistic view of salvation for both the soul and the body. Both bodily and spiritual suffering will be healed and fully liberated in the kingdom, but a foretaste of healing and liberation was present through the inbreaking of the kingdom in the Spirit of Pentecost.[108]

Curiously, though, Johann left the social-critical implications of his theology underdeveloped. The poor and the suffering were representative

---

104. Macchia, *Spirituality*, p. 73.
105. Macchia, *Spirituality*, p. 86.
106. Johann Blumhardt; as quoted by Macchia, *Spirituality*, pp. 76-77.
107. Macchia, *Spirituality*, p. 77.
108. Macchia, *Spirituality*, pp. 73-74.

of the general human condition under the bondage and oppression of sin. Johann was not interested in grand social change, preferring to leave this to the inbreaking of the kingdom in the outpouring of the Spirit.[109] Contrary to the Pietist spirituality of the previous generation, Johann believed that seeing the act of repentance as private and individual was a sign of our fallenness. Redemption must include the restoration of all things. Individual salvation was one aspect of the redemption of the whole of creation. Christ's resurrection will permeate all of creation to finally remove sin and death.[110]

From his uncle, Johann adopted the waiting/hurrying or passive/active tension concerning God's sovereignty to bring in the kingdom and human participation in the kingdom. On the one hand, Johann gave the impression that the kingdom and outpouring of the Spirit will break into the world supernaturally as a crisis event and sovereign act of grace. On the other hand, Johann stressed the role of human participation in the kingdom as the 'way', 'process' or 'nearing' of the kingdom. 'The kingdom of God has a history and a development', argued Johann, 'so that there is always something new that one can join to the old. The changing time periods always ensure new viewpoints, new explanations, interpretations, new forms, making new thoughts or those taken anew from Scriptures necessary.'[111] He rejected the apocalyptic destruction of the world.[112] The Pentecost/kingdom connection meant that the kingdom was breaking into history as an act of grace, but also demanded human participation to care for the sick and the suffering. The inbreaking of the kingdom at Pentecost meant that history itself was important in the development of the kingdom. Although he rejected an apocalyptic eschatology, the supernaturalistic aspects of Johann's theology tended to nullify the natural elements of liberation, ultimately making his theology more passive than active. Although Johann had a place for human responsibility in the inbreaking of the kingdom, it rarely went beyond the elements of groaning, prayer, faith and preaching.[113]

There was a convergence in Johann's thinking about the kingdom. These included an emphasis on the inbreaking of the kingdom to heal the sick, an emphasis on the outpouring of the Spirit upon the individual

---

109. Macchia, *Spirituality*, p. 78.
110. Macchia, *Spirituality*, pp. 82-83.
111. J. Blumhardt; as quoted by Macchia, *Spirituality*, p. 88.
112. Macchia, *Spirituality*, p. 90.
113. Macchia, *Spirituality*, pp. 95-96.

believer for revival and Christian empowerment, an assumption that there was a universal outpouring of the Spirit in history at Pentecost that was the basis for missionary activity, a dispensational view of history and a hope for the restoration of all creation through the resurrected Christ in a universal outpouring of the Spirit in the parousia. From this convergence, Johann sought the victory of the battle against darkness for all of creation. For Johann, the universal outpouring of the Spirit would occur 'in the latter days' before the parousia, in preparation for the coming Christ and the restoration of all of creation.[114]

Christoph Blumhardt's Theology

Johann's son, Christoph (1842–1919), took the kingdom message in more of a social-critical direction, albeit showing both continuity and discontinuity with his father's theology. He was ordained in 1866 and after ministering in a few different locations, finally joined his father at Bad Boll. Shortly before Johann's death in 1880, he charged Christoph with the words, 'I bless you for victory'.[115]

Christoph took up the cause of the poor and suffering from his father's message, but contextualized it, seeing the poor and suffering in the alienation of the factory worker, the plight of the farmer and the poisoning of the trees. Unfairly simplifying his father's message as being too spiritualistic, Chistoph believed that his father's message that the Spirit of Pentecost was absent from the world was wrongheaded. For Christoph, the universal outpouring of the Spirit stemmed from the incarnate and resurrected Christ for the transformation of creation in glory that ultimately relativized all ecclesiastical forms and traditions. Christoph secularized the message of the kingdom. For Christoph the kingdom radicalized all religious (both Christian and non-Christian), ecclesiastical and secular ideologies. Christoph did not abandon the notion of the uniqueness of the church entirely, but

> He understood the ambiguity of both religious and secular movements and institutions in bearing witness to the Kingdom of God in human redemption and liberation. He was more willing to find signposts of the coming messianic Kingdom in contexts beyond the church, both religious and secular, than he was within the church.[116]

114. Macchia, *Spirituality*, pp. 70-71.
115. Macchia, *Spirituality*, p. 112.
116. Frank D. Macchia, 'The Secular and the Religious under the Shadow of the Cross: Implications in Christoph Blumhardt's Kingdom Spirituality for a Christian

Christoph shifted the roots of the inbreaking kingdom from the Spirit of Pentecost to the Incarnation of Christ. There was also a shift from the absence of God in the world (in the Spirit of Pentecost) to the presence of God in the world in the Incarnation of Christ. For Christoph, the presence of God and the unfolding of the kingdom in universal redemption was the consequence of the Incarnation. Christoph still hoped for the transformation of creation, but its foundation was the Incarnation as the inauguration of God's kingdom and the guarantee for its growth in the world.[117] There was a shift from a pneumatological to a christological orientation.

The emphasis on the Incarnation created an emphasis on the progress of the life of God in Christ throughout history. This progress meant that God was active in helping us in our suffering and distress. There was more of a connection between God and creation in Christoph than Johann, but Christoph also maintained the freedom of God by maintaining that the kingdom developed both within and apart from the world. Christoph likewise rejected the apocalyptic view of history. For him, the parousia and final resurrection were not just a future event, but partially realized in the present, experienced through the incarnate presence of God in Christ, through the ministry of the Spirit and worked out in caring for the sick and suffering. The kingdom was not only realized in waiting on God, but in hurrying to fight against suffering and oppression.[118]

Christoph's theology initially focused on the Incarnation and resurrection of Christ, but later on the cross as a symbol of human participation in the Incarnation of God in history. 'Die that Jesus might live' was Christoph's slogan, '…be poor and miserable, step back, give up your role, and he will appear.'[119] The cross of Christ was equated with denial of the self. ' "Something must die in Christ". The "flesh" must die, not that which God has created, but that which we set up from our own identity that is contrary to the kingdom of God.'[120] Christoph believed that salvation came by the blood of Christ and by human blood in Christ. Blood became the symbol of self-sacrifice. Emulating Jesus' self-sacrifice and waiting passively was better than the miraculous. Yet following the crucified Christ also allowed

Response to World Religions', in Arvind Sharma (ed.), *Religion in a Secular City: Essays in Honor of Harvey Cox* (Festschrift Harvey Cox; Harrisburg, PA: Trinity Press Internation, 2001), pp. 59-77 (73).

117. Macchia, *Spirituality*, p. 116.
118. Macchia, *Spirituality*, pp. 117-18.
119. C. Blumhardt; as quoted by Macchia, *Spirituality*, p. 119.
120. C. Blumhardt; as quoted by Macchia, *Spirituality*, p. 119.

us to participate in the liberation and redemption of the world.[121] Nevertheless, in this period in Christoph's theological development, self-sacrifice became more important than battling for the kingdom in the world.[122]

Consequently, Christoph began stressing the humanity of Christ. In his theology of the cross, Christoph moved away from his father's view that darkness was created by demonic spiritual forces, to stress human responsibility in creating darkness. Christoph also moved away from his father's view that Jesus was a dynamic force in history, to seeing Jesus as a symbol of our human participation in the development of the kingdom. Hereafter, Christoph articulated two parallel Christologies simultaneously: the one focused on the cross of Jesus as the symbol of self-sacrifice and our participation in the progress of the kingdom, and the other focusing on the resurrection as the juncture of God's incarnate presence in creation and the dynamic force of history.[123] He shifted his emphasis from 'waiting on the kingdom' to 'hurrying for the kingdom'.

This particular christological understanding led Christoph to articulate a social critique that would eventually draw him into politics. Picking up on a minor theme in his father's message, Christoph believed that the world needed to be liberated from sickness and suffering. Starvation and war were contextualized examples of suffering in the world. Christoph took his father's 'battle' against spiritual suffering and reinterpreted it in light of the suffering of the poor, the abused and the miserable in the world. Johann's 'groaning' for the suffering of creation and alienation of the creature from the Creator became for Christoph a 'groaning' for oppressed farmers, alienated factory workers and dying trees.[124]

Concern for the oppression and suffering of the workers led Christoph to join the socialist party, the Social Democratic Party (SPD). He was elected to the Landtag in 1900. Christoph believed that the socialist ideals of the SPD were analogues of the kingdom of God, though he never equated the Party with the kingdom. The ideals of socialism could never conquer sin. The cross and resurrection of Christ were needed for this. Nevertheless, Christoph saw wealth and capitalism as social evils and supported the Party's stance against violence, killing and oppression. Capitalism resulted in social bondage. With his turn to politics, however, Christoph shifted in

---

121. Macchia, 'Secular and the Religious', p. 67.
122. Macchia, *Spirituality*, p. 119.
123. Macchia, *Spirituality*, pp. 119-20.
124. Macchia, *Spirituality*, p. 122.

nuance away from the cross as the symbol of judgment on humanity, to the presence of God through the Incarnation and work of the Spirit in historical development.[125] Party members were seen as 'vessels of God'. He believed that Jesus was at the centre of the SPD, because it was open to all peoples and fought for a better humanity. For Christoph, joining the SPD was nourished by ethical, humanitarian and theological ideals.

> He praised the SPD for viewing religion as a private matter, thereby providing an implicit protest against coercion of people into a particular religious confession...this did not mean that Jesus and the kingdom of God did not have universal implications; only religion was private. He saw universalism and pluralism as the heart of the SPD and the kingdom of God.[126]

Through his association with the SPD, Christoph radically relativized ecclesial traditions and doctrines, elevating kingdom ideals above the church.

Christoph did not, however, accept the policies of the SPD uncritically. In 1903, he stated, 'The Social Democrats hope that the proper order will come through the education of people; and I hope that the order will come through the Spirit of God. This is a difference between us.'[127] Contrary to the view of the SPD, Christoph opposed the idea that an ideal society could be attained through education alone. He was also aware that the SPD fell short of the ideals of the kingdom of God, but since the church had abdicated its responsibility in realizing the kingdom, the church was in no position to judge the SPD. However, Christoph's ultimate loyalty was to the kingdom and its liberation of the poor and oppressed.[128] By 1904, Christoph criticized the SPD for not loving its enemies and lacking a vision for worldwide change. In 1907, he retired from politics. Although one reason for his retirement was failing health, he also felt disillusioned by the Party's political infighting, thereby betraying its common vision for liberation. Although Christoph believed that the SPD represented a secular analogue to the kingdom, it ultimately lacked a christological focus in the example of Jesus who helped the poor and oppressed, without succumbing to hatred of his enemies.[129] Christoph remained a socialist until his death, but distanced himself from the Party after his retirement.

---

125. Macchia, *Spirituality*, p. 125.
126. C. Blumhardt; as quoted by Macchia, *Spirituality*, p. 127.
127. Macchia, *Spirituality*, p. 127.
128. Macchia, *Spirituality*, p. 128.
129. Macchia, *Spirituality*, pp. 140-41.

For Christoph, one of the signs of the inbreaking of the kingdom was the betterment of humankind, which ultimately came from God through the Incarnation. The realization of the kingdom was 'supernatural' and 'above nature', but also the experience of God's grace 'wholly through nature'. He continued his father's stress between waiting and hurrying for the kingdom. However, Johann stressed the waiting, while Christoph placed emphasis upon the hurrying. Christoph developed a more prophetic/ethical critique of social oppression. Yet he did emphasize waiting for the kingdom. 'The kingdom develops from within itself. We walk alongside it and are happy to recognize this great movement as the reign of God.'[130] At the same time, 'a movement of the Spirit of Christ proceeds through the times', pushing history ahead to what is new.[131]

Christoph's post-political theology represents his mature thinking, argues Macchia. Overcoming spiritual darkness through God's grace can be seen throughout Christoph's life, but he was dominated by a strong optimism for the betterment of humanity and the progress of the kingdom in the political years. Although Christoph distanced himself from his earlier critique of society, he secularized ecclesial traditions by articulating an ecumenism in which Christians and non-Christians alike must work towards the kingdom. However, he also maintained that piety and Christian virtues are a precondition for the kingdom.[132]

Critique of Pentecostalism

For Macchia, the importance of the kingdom spirituality of the Blumhardts is that it critiques Pentecostal/Evangelical theology by offering a more balanced approach to human participation and responsibility as part of the inbreaking kingdom and the providence of God to bring about the kingdom. Its cosmic and social implications critique the Pentecostal tendency to define healing as otherworldly/supernatural and insists that healing must include liberation from social bondage. Healing is a present foretaste of the future eschatological transformation of creation.

Sickness and suffering are rightly seen by both the Blumhardts and Pentecostals as contrary to God's glory. If there is 'a glorification of suffering and sickness as a source of blessing', then they are sanctioned under divine

---

130. C. Blumhardt; as quoted by Macchia, *Spirituality*, p. 142.
131. C. Blumhardt; as cited by Macchia, *Spirituality*, p. 142; cf. Macchia, 'Secular and the Religious', pp. 67-68.
132. Macchia, *Spirituality*, p. 142.

providence, making God a 'supreme sadist' and Christians masochists.[133] On the other hand, the 'name it and claim it' prosperity gospel, prevalent in the Independent Charismatic movement, wrongly emphasizes physical healing to the neglect of 'social justice, cosmic redemption, the eschatological reservation implied in Christian hope, and the consequent possibility of innocent and even unavoidable suffering'.[134] The prosperity gospel is an influential but distorted view of the Pentecostal doctrine of healing, because it implies a 'realized eschatology available only to elite individuals', while the non-elite (i.e. unhealed) are blamed for their own suffering and sickness. 'By connecting healing to the Blumhardt's message of the coming Kingdom of God in cosmic transformation', argues Macchia, 'healing can then be viewed as an eschatological goal that is never realized fully on this side of eternity. It is simply impossible to assume perfect health on a cosmic scale until the *eschaton*.'[135] Christoph's christological emphasis also offers a way for Pentecostals to connect the pneumatological doctrine of eschatological healing with a pneumatological view of creation, in which healing is a process of the cosmos.[136]

Likewise, the social dimensions of the Blumhardts' theology critiques the Pentecostal tendency to interpret spirituality individualistically, or as limited to the work of the Spirit in the *koinonia* fellowship of the church. The redemptive elements of God's grace must move beyond the individual and the church to include liberating the whole world. This includes a realization that there are social, systemic causes of evil that must be dealt with at the social level. The gifts of the Spirit, then, cannot be limited to individual piety, but must be outward moving into the world and the rest of creation.[137] Liberation from oppressive social conditions and ecological responsibility are vital aspects of this message. This was expressed by Johann as the 'groaning' for all of creation to be freed from bondage in which the kingdom will liberate concrete persons from sickness and

---

133. Frank D. Macchia (in dialogue with Dorothee Soelle and Victor Frankl), 'Waiting and Hurrying for the Healing of Creation: Implications in the Message of the Blumhardts for a Pentecostal Theology of Divine Healing' (SPS and EPTA, Mattersley, Doncaster, England, 10–14 July, 1995), pp. 1-30 (18-19).

134. Macchia, 'Waiting and Hurrying', p. 1.

135. Macchia, 'Waiting and Hurrying', p. 23.

136. Macchia, 'Waiting and Hurrying', p. 23.

137. Frank D. Macchia, 'The Spirit and the Kingdom: Implications in the Message of the Blumhardts for a Pentecostal Social Spirituality', *Transformation* 33 (1994), pp. 1-5 (5).

poverty. For Christoph, the groaning for creation was contextualized in the liberation of the oppressive conditions of both society (especially capitalism) and creation (from pollution) through social-critical and political action. The implication is that Pentecostals must articulate a spirituality that understands signs and wonders as a foretaste of the kingdom in the liberation of society.[138] The kingdom supports human freedom by pointing to the ultimate revelation of human dignity and freedom in the eschaton, as foreshadowed in the christological event of the Incarnation, cross and resurrection of Jesus Christ. The attainment of human dignity, however, does not come simply by waiting in passive resignation for the kingdom, while evil persists in the world, but also through our participation in the growth of the kingdom.[139]

As well, the combined focus on the Pentecostal/christological events by the Blumhardts presents a model for ecumenical dialogue, in which the outbreaking of tongues on the day of Pentecost emphasizes both the unity and diversity of peoples and languages. The Blumhardts stressed the corporateness of prayer. They even insisted that groaning for the redemption of creation and the coming kingdom (Johann) relativized all cultural and religious distinctions (Christoph). The Pentecost/christological nexus means that Jesus Christ is the bearer of the kingdom, and unites all groaners (Christian and non-Christian alike) to participate in the kingdom, a theology with ecumenical significance. 'This ecumenism was not created by unity of doctrine', argues Macchia, '…but through a shared prayer, a shared worship, a shared yearning of the heart for liberation of suffering. What the Blumhardts said about groaning and ecumenism is in the spirit of what Acts 2 depicts concerning glossolalia and prayer as praise.'[140] Although the Blumhardts never connected groaning to glossolalia, Pentecostals and a number of non-Pentecostal theologians have.[141] An implicit diversity is inherent in glossolalic utterances, but Acts also reveals that there was a movement towards unity among tongues speakers. Macchia's latest work has been the development of a theology of tongues that has the Blumhardts' theology of the kingdom and its ecumenical/social implications at its root.

Macchia has revisioned the Pentecostal doctrine of initial evidence in terms of a sacramental theology of tongues. He observes that a number of

---

138. Macchia, 'The Spirit and Kingdom', pp. 3-4.
139. Macchia, 'The Spirit and Kingdom', p. 5.
140. Macchia, *Spirituality*, p. 168.
141. Macchia, *Spirituality*, p. 168 n. 20.

Pentecostal and Charismatic theologians have noted the sacramental character of speaking in tongues.[142] Yet Pentecostals are uncomfortable with sacramental language, preferring instead a belief in the unmediated grace of God and freedom of the Spirit to act directly on the believer. Pentecostals are generally uncomfortable with the mediated liturgical and rational structures of faith, fearing that there is a restriction of the Spirit. Macchia sees this as a false dichotomy, because tongues, as an audible sign of God's presence, takes on sacramental significance.[143]

Macchia's understanding of 'sacrament' is developed in dialogue with Roman Catholic Karl Rahner and Protestant Paul Tillich. Rahner, for instance, locates sacramental efficacy in the 'sign value' of the sacrament, which means that the reality signified in the sacrament is present and experienced through the 'visible sign' (i.e. elements) in the process of signification. The eschatological presence of God is thereby realized through the process of sacramental signification. Rahner questions neo-scholastic theology, which locates 'sacramental efficacy in some kind of material causation necessitated by the elements as elements'.[144] As such, Rahner sees a danger in the neo-scholastic tendency to institutionalize and restrict the free movement of the Spirit. Signs and wonders of the Spirit ' "shock" the liturgical system, making the institutional church seem for a moment "provisional and questionable, incommensurable with the meaning it is supposed to signify". We are suddenly "thrown back" upon an encounter with God that is ultimately beyond our capacities to understand, express or manipulate.'[145] With enthusiasm (tongues included), the church itself is seen as a sign of the kingdom that will disappear with the full self-disclosure of God in the parousia. The eschatological focus of enthusiasm creates a prophetic critique of the status quo. Macchia agrees with Rahner

---

142. For instance, Catholic Charismatic theologian Simon Tugwell believes that glossolalia signifies God's immanent presence in a physically audible way. William Samarin believes that tongues is a 'linguistic symbol of the sacred' that heightens one's awareness of the presence of God similar to the eucharist. Pentecostal theologian Walter Hollenweger insists that tongues represents God presence to the poor, in a way similar to the experience of worship in the Gothic cathedrals for the privileged. See Macchia, 'Tongues as Sign', p. 61.

143. Macchia, 'Tongues as Sign', pp. 61-62.

144. Karl Rahner; as cited by Macchia, 'Tongues as Sign', p. 62.

145. Macchia, 'Tongues as Sign', p. 74; Frank D. Macchia, 'The Church as an End-Time Missionary Fellowship of the Spirit: A Pentecostal Perspective on the Significance of Pneumatology for Ecclesiology' (Pentecostal/National Council of Churches in Dialogue, Oakland, California, 12 March 1997), pp. 1-32 (16-17).

in viewing tongues as a sacrament anticipating the eschatological presence of God, inwardly as an experience of God's presence and outwardly as empowerment of the Spirit for service.[146]

Tillich offers a similar argument when he insists that there is an 'integral connection between the free self-disclosure of God and the physical/audible reality that becomes the occasion in which this self-disclosure is encountered…[and it] is realized from the divine initiative, as God takes the sign up into God's own self-disclosure'.[147] Tillich describes this process as the *kairos* event. For him, the *kairos* event steers a path between one extreme that sees divine self-disclosure as detached from a physical/visible form and the other that sees an objectification of divine action in the physical/visible form itself. An authentic *kairos* event occurs 'when God freely takes that visible human response up into itself to be used as a vehicle of the divine self-disclosure. Though God is never to be identified with the human or creaturely phenomenon used in the *kairos* event, this phenomenon is allowed genuinely to participate in the divine action.'[148] For Macchia, tongues becomes a *kairos* event. God's presence is disclosed in the physical/audible phenomenon of glossolalia, but it also becomes a sign of the presence of the Spirit of God to empower the tongue's speaker. The emphasis is not on tongues, but on the presence of God, identified by Pentecostals as Spirit baptism. Tongues is a sign of divine presence.[149]

A distinction may be drawn, however, between the liturgical view of sacrament and the Pentecostal view inherent in tongues. 'Glossolalia accents the free, dramatic, and unpredictable move of the Spirit of God, while the liturgical traditions stress an ordered and predictable encounter with the Spirit.'[150] Pentecostals value that free and spontaneous movement of the Spirit, a seemingly chaotic and inchoate order of worship that protests formalization and objectification of the Spirit. This explains Pentecostalism's apparent non-sacramental view of water baptism and the eucharist. Yet Macchia believes that a sacramental element is evident in the free and spontaneous manifestation of tongues.[151] In fact, Pentecostal worship has a loose liturgical structure. There are mechanisms used in worship to encour-

---

146. Macchia, 'Tongues as Sign', p. 63.
147. Paul Tillich; as cited by Macchia, 'Tongues as Sign', p. 63.
148. Macchia, 'Tongues as Sign', p. 69.
149. Macchia, 'Tongues as Sign', p. 69.
150. Macchia, 'Tongues as Sign', p. 63.
151. Macchia, 'Tongues as Sign', pp. 63-64.

age the use of tongues.[152] The difference between charismatic and liturgical sacrament, however, is one of emphasis; charismatic signs point to an
eschatological free movement of the redeemer Spirit from above, while
liturgical sacraments point to a continuity with nature and everyday life in
the creator Spirit from below.[153] A sacramental understanding of tongues
explains the integral connections Pentecostals make between tongues
(sign), Spirit baptism (divine presence) and initial evidence (the connection
between the two).

Macchia revisions the Pentecostal 'initial evidence' doctrine, which
asserts that tongues is the initial indicator that one has been baptized in the
Holy Spirit. Pentecostals have so far failed to reflect theologically and con-
structively on their experience of tongues, making the initial evidence concept prone to rigidification, detached from one's in-depth response to the
divine encounter.[154] There is a misunderstanding in Pentecostal circles,
however, that sometimes makes tongues the goal of the Christian life,
rather than the presence of the Spirit, of which tongues are a sign. Tongues
alone are no guarantee of the Spirit's presence. Tongues must also work in
conjunction with other works of the Spirit (i.e. fruit of the Spirit and other
charismata) to confirm the life of the Spirit in the believer.[155] Nevertheless,
there is an important connection between tongues and Spirit baptism. Consequently, Macchia argues that tongues is a sacramental sign of an encounter with the Spirit of God.

The terminology of initial 'evidence' suggests a scientific connotation
inappropriate for describing the divine encounter, though possibly stemming from an early Pentecostal naïveté that saw tongues as 'proof' of God's
presence and existence in the world. Connecting the Pentecostal experience
of the Spirit with the visible/audible phenomenon of tongues in initial
evidence seems 'too scientific, simplistic, and one-dimensional to capture
all of the theological nuances implied by the connection Pentecostals make

---

152. Macchia, 'Tongues as Sign', p. 72; also see Richard Baer, 'Quaker Silence,
Catholic Liturgy, and Pentecostal Glossolalia: Some Functional Similarities', in Russell
Spittler (ed.), *Perspectives on the New Pentecostalism* (Grand Rapids: Baker Book
House, 1976), pp. 150-64.

153. Macchia, 'Tongues as Sign', p. 75.

154. Frank D. Macchia, 'Groans Too Deep for Words: Towards a Theology of
Tongues as Initial Evidence', *AJPS* 1.2 (1998), pp. 149-73 (149); cf. *idem*, 'The Ques-
tion of Tongues as Initial Evidence: A Review of *Initial Evidence*, Edited by Gary
B. McGee', *JPT* 2 (1993), pp. 117-27 (127).

155. Macchia, 'Groans', p. 155.

between tongues and Spirit baptism'.[156] 'Evidence' is a word used for scientific investigation, when data are collected to support an intellectual hypothesis. Tongues are not data for a hypothesis. Tongues express an overwhelming experience of God that become a sign to others to seek similar encounters. Tongues as sacramental sign is a better way of describing the connection between glossolalia and Spirit baptism, because it avoids the 'modernistic (positivistic) preoccupation with empirical proof'.[157]

According to Macchia, the Pentecostal sacramental view of tongues is 'theophanic'. The divine self-disclosure at Pentecost was a dramatic theophany, accompanied by the sound of wind and tongues of fire. Pentecost was an event that not only harkened back to the dramatic events of the giving of the law at Sinai and the presence of God for the prophets, but also centred in God's self-disclosure in the Incarnation, death and resurrection of Jesus Christ. The Pentecost theophany not only inaugurates the kingdom, but also looks forward to the final theophany of God in the *parousia*, when the Lord comes in judgment with signs of blood, fire and smoke (Acts 2.19-20). Tongues, like the *kairos* event of the Pentecost theophany, is a vehicle of divine self-disclosure that transforms language and hints at the future transformation of the world.[158]

A theology of tongues defined as a theophanic encounter with God must be carefully nuanced. The experience of tongues might degenerate into a sensationalistic quest for the miraculous at the expense of the cross and other elements of the Christian life. The initial evidence doctrine might rigidify into criteria for inducing religious experience that betrays the true impulse of Pentecostal worship for the spontaneous and free working of the Spirit. Tongues might also degenerate into an experience of emotional subjectivism that lacks an outward movement into the church and the world. Nevertheless, constructing a theophanic theology of tongues offers the possibility of maintaining the spontaneous, free and wondrous reign of God, who encounters human beings, transforming them and by extension the world through their participation in the kingdom. Tongues are the sign of this transformation.[159]

> Tongues is a sign of the renewed language and renewed human relationships called forth by the dawning kingdom of God in our midst. The fact that language is transcendent points to the unfulfilled mystery of God's

156. Macchia, 'Tongues as Sign', pp. 68-69.
157. Macchia, 'Groans', p. 153.
158. Macchia, 'Sighs', p. 57; *idem*, 'Groans', p. 164.
159. Macchia, 'Sighs', p. 47.

kingdom. The fact that we participate together in glossolalic utterances signifies that the Spirit invites, even requires our participation in the breaking
in of the kingdom in our world.[160]

For Pentecostals, the emphasis on tongues is not so much on Christ as
the incarnate Word, but on the pneumatic Christ who still acts with signs
and wonders to conquer suffering and evil in the world, and to establish
the kingdom. A pneumatic Christology does not see the church as the permanent embodiment of the incarnate Word, but as an 'event' that is continually renewed through obedience and participation in God's redemptive
activity.[161] Elsewhere Macchia argues that the gestalt of Jesus' piety in
Pentecostalism is not concerned with Nicean *homousia* or the hypostatic
union of Chalcedon, but the

> charismatic Christ who now leads the faithful through conversion, holiness,
> Spirit baptism, healing and eschatological hope toward dimensions of the
> messianic experience of the Spirit... This emphasis on the free Spirit of
> God that is connected to the Christ event, particularly the event of the cross,
> exercises a critical function toward our disobedience and self-serving
> ecclesiastical policies.[162]

A theophanic approach stresses the eschatological inbreaking of the Spirit
in extraordinary and unpredictable ways, while the Incarnational approach
stresses the abiding presence of Christ through the Spirit in the sacraments
of the church.[163] A pneumatic Christology that emphasizes the theophanic
and spontaneous opens up history to that which is new to broaden the
future horizon.[164] Worship must break cognitive frameworks to reorder life
into new perspectives. Worship must symbolically reorder experience to
redefine the self. Tongues are a sign of the freedom and spontaneity of the
Spirit and an indicator of the process of personal, historical and cosmic
transformation.[165]

---

160. Macchia, 'Review of *Initial Evidence*', p. 125.
161. Macchia, 'Tongues as Sign', p. 73.
162. Macchia, 'End-Time Missionary Fellowship', p. 13.
163. Macchia, 'Tongues of Pentecost', pp. 11-12.
164. In contradistinction to the Charismatic view which sees Spirit baptism as an
actualization of the Spirit in initiation, Macchia sees the Spirit as eschatological, moving us forward to the final self-disclosure of God. Frank D. Macchia, 'Tradition and the
Novum of the Spirit: A Review of Clark Pinnock's *Flame of Love*', *JPT* 13 (1998),
pp. 31-48 (47-48).
165. Macchia approvingly cites sociologist Robert Bellah here. Macchia, 'Sighs',
pp. 58-59.

Groans 'too deep for words' (Rom. 8.26), understood by Pentecostals and non-Pentecostals as a reference to glossolalia, reveal our human weakness and an eschatological yearning for personal and cosmic redemption. Tongues are not an escape from this world into ecstatic piety, but express strength in weakness and an experience of 'the first-fruits of the kingdom-to-come in the midst of our groaning with the suffering creation. They bring to ultimate expression the struggle that is essential to all prayer, namely, trying to put into words what is deeper than words. They express the pain and the joy of this struggle.'[166] Macchia comments:

> Here we have an eschatology that incorporates transcendent experience with the realities of our creaturely and historical existence, transforming this existence with the promise of redemption, a promise that includes all of creation. We also have a way of developing the theophanic element in the Pentecostal attraction to tongues that avoids a self-centred emotional euphoria or a sensationalist quest for signs and wonders… In glossolalia is a hidden protest against any attempt to define, manipulate or oppress humanity. Glossolalia is an unclassifiable, free speech in response to an unclassified, free God. It is the language of the *imago Dei*.[167]

Tongues are a sign of the future kingdom and draw us in to participate in its unfolding.

Tongues are an aspect of prayer that reveals a disparity between the desire for expression and the means of expression. The abandonment of rational language in our encounter with God reveals that the struggle to express the inexpressible is at the root of all creativity.[168] 'The closer one draws to the divine mystery, the more urgent it becomes to express oneself and, concomitantly, the less able one is to find adequate expression. This is the crisis out of which tongues breaks forth.'[169] Once rational communication of the divine encounter is attempted, one has become distant from God. Tongues express the divine encounter without ending it.

The neo-Pentecostal attempt to define tongues in terms of the depths of the human psyche, as the outflow of human experience or the activation of an inherent human potential has not been the Pentecostal contention. Tongues, for Pentecostals, depict the breakdown of language when God freely and spontaneously acts in self-disclosure.[170] 'Tongues dramatize an

---

166. Macchia, 'Groans', p. 163.
167. Macchia, 'Sighs', pp. 60-61.
168. Abraham Heschel; as cited by Macchia, 'Sighs', p. 62.
169. Macchia, 'Sighs', p. 62.
170. Macchia, 'Sighs', pp. 57, 60.

encounter with God that is filled with awe and wonder.'[171] Tongues are personal, but community-orientated, flowing outward in solidarity with others in *koinonia*. Tongues and other charismata disperse throughout the community, revealing that human existence before God cannot be in isolation. The charismata relativize all social norms, so that there is neither male nor female, Jew nor Greek, free nor slave. All people are valued and respected before God. Tongues therefore point to the hidden mystery of freedom before God, a mystery that cuts through differences of race, class, gender and culture to reveal a solidarity that is essential to our very being and that is revealed to us in God's self-disclosure.[172]

However, glossolalia is more than individual piety and church *koinonia*: it is world transforming. A theology of tongues includes faith in Christ Jesus as the 'universal Lord' and '*Cosmocrator*' and is faithful to the in-breaking kingdom of God through Christ and the work of the Spirit. A theology of tongues must also find its strength in the 'shadow of the cross'. A theology of tongues with the cross at its centre cannot be hidden, but must move into the concrete realities of the world. Glossolalia is praise and prayer that yearns for the deliverance of the suffering in the world and the transformation of creation.

> [G]lossolalia is not simply a celebration of a dynamic encounter with God... The freedom of God has been a freedom *pro nobis* (for us), to deliver us from bondage and death through the cross and resurrection of Jesus Christ. Hence, our freedom *coram Deo* [before God] must also be a freedom committed to the liberation of suffering creation, as we seek to imitate Christ as 'crucified brothers and sisters'. Glossolalia cannot bypass the cross as a direct glorious experience of God.[173]

Tongues are a sign that the gospel of Jesus Christ is transforming social relationships in history and a sign that God incorporates our participation in the transformation of all things, not only in preaching, but in medicine, social action and ecological responsibility.[174]

> The kingdom announced in prophetic utterance is apocalyptic in the sense that it is not directed from this world but from God. Yet, contrary to apocalypticism, the prophetic word of the kingdom opens humanity to free and

---

171. Frank D. Macchia, 'Tongues and Prophecy: A Pentecostal Perspective', in Jürgen Moltmann and Karl-Josef Kuschel (eds.), *Pentecostal Movements as an Ecumenical Challenge* (Concilium, 3; London: SCM Press, 1996), pp. 63-83 (64).
172. Macchia, 'Sighs', pp. 65-66.
173. Macchia, 'Sighs', p. 69.
174. Macchia, 'Signs', pp. 71-72.

responsible participation in redemptive history. Pentecostals…[must incorporate] a broader view of prophecy that would include more reasoned proclamation and social critique.[175]

The kingdom is established sovereignly by God, but God invites us to participate in its history, which includes a prophetic voice to act with social and ecological responsibility.

Macchia asserts that a theophanic understanding of the tongues of Pentecost is a model for ecumenical dialogue. 'The tongues of Pentecost may provide a pregnant metaphor for a distinctly Pentecostal reflection', argues Macchia, on the 'theological promise and challenge of unity in diversity among the churches', that 'exposes that scandal of both a complacent sectarianism that offers no need to strive for unity and a complacent catholicism that is convinced such unity already exists'.[176] The greatest scandal of Pentecostalism is its failure to realize its ecumenical and intracultural potential,[177] a potential reflective of the Azusa Street revival's inclusion of different races, ethnic diversity and religious backgrounds.

The event of Pentecost is a 'metaphor' of the rich theological interplay between unity and diversity which resists domestication and transcends ecclesiastical boundaries.[178] In the theophanic theology of Acts, there is an eschatological movement which includes diversity in a unified witness of the gospel. 'The great *prodigium* of Pentecost, tongues of fire, symbolizes this unity in diversity that is gradually revealed in the story of Acts and prevents Pentecostalism and all Christians from ignoring the scandal of divisions among the people of God.'[179] Tongues are a sign of this expanding diversity of the church—the breakout of tongues occurring at significant junctures of the expanding diversity—but a 'unity in diversity' that is achieved with 'great difficulty and less-than-perfect results'.[180] Although Luke identifies participants of Pentecost as representative of 'every nation under heaven' (Acts 2.5), only diaspora Jews were in attendance. Only at a later time were the Samaritans and Gentiles included in the expanding church. Significantly, their inclusion was symbolized by the manifestation of tongues. Thus the tongues of Pentecost are symbolic of a future unity, as yet unseen but depicted in the unfolding of Luke's narrative. 'Tongues

175. Macchia, 'Tongues and Prophecy', p. 66.
176. Macchia, 'Tongues of Pentecost', p. 1.
177. Macchia, 'Tongues of Pentecost', p. 3.
178. Macchia, 'Tongues of Pentecost', p. 4.
179. Macchia, 'Tongues of Pentecost', p. 5.
180. Macchia, 'Groans', p. 162.

are a sign of our fragmentation and a promise of reconciliation', insists Macchia; 'tongues reflect the struggle and the hope, the tears and the joy. Implied is a catholicity to realize the unity and life of God that is never possessed this side of eternity.'[181]

There is a mystery in the presence of God that surpasses our language and rational concepts. The mystery of tongues at Pentecost is a basis for understanding unity in diversity. All language, culture and theology is relativized under the mystery of the Spirit of God that affirms

> diversity as vehicles for expressing the communion of a free humanity with a free and self-giving God. Such diverse communions can fellowship and work together as equal partners as they dialogue across ecclesiastical lines. Tongues…functions on one level as a kind of 'anti-language' that reveals the utter futility of any effort to articulate absolute status to any one language of faith.[182]

All languages of faith are recognized as worthy and are 'democratized' by placing their ultimate significance in the 'unspeakable' grace of God. The journey of the people of God towards unity in diversity is eschatologically directed.[183]

Macchia notes that the term 'catholic' has numerous definitions and represents one of the challenges of ecumenical dialogue. Qualitatively, however, 'catholic' denotes the fullness of grace, truth and spiritual gifts, located fundamentally though not exclusively in the eucharist. For Pentecostals, catholicity in this sense is located in the baptism/infilling of the Holy Spirit with the outward sign of tongues, indicating the presence of Christ through the Spirit. Quantitatively, 'catholic' denotes, according to the patristic fathers, 'the whole church throughout the world'. Macchia prefers a post-Vatican II definition, which recognizes 'elements of catholicity outside the visible boundaries of the Catholic Church…that as long as the church has not realized the fullness of its God-willed catholicity there are authentic elements of Catholicism existing outside its visible community'.[184] Catholicity is at present imperfect, fragmented and divided. It cannot exist in one church isolated from all others. Although catholicity is in some sense possessed in the present, it is not yet a full reality. The question, for Macchia, is 'how to express theologically the living presence of God and of Christ through the Spirit in the midst of the people of God in a

181. Macchia, 'Tongues of Pentecost', pp. 6-7.
182. Macchia, 'Tongues of Pentecost', p. 14.
183. Macchia, 'Tongues of Pentecost', p. 14.
184. Macchia, 'Tongues of Pentecost', p. 8.

way that does not avoid the full implications of the eschatological and ecumenical nature of catholicity'.[185] In this, Macchia is in agreement with Miroslav Volf, who resists a realized eschatological view of catholicity as a possession this side of eternity. For Volf, catholicity is

> the eschatological gathering of the people of God and their full participation at that time in the intratrinitarian fellowship of God. Individuals and local churches can have experiences through the Spirit that are analogous to the final catholic reality, but this reality is not yet realized until the eschaton.[186]

The danger of envisioning a full possession of catholicity in terms of a realized eschatology is felt by both Pentecostals and Roman Catholics. For Roman Catholics, possession is assumed in the apostolic succession of the Roman pontiff. For Pentecostals, possession is assumed in 'hyper-spiritual experiences',[187] of having the 'fullness' of the Spirit in contrast to other Christian churches who have only a rudimentary experience. Instead of tongues pointing to the fragmentation of the church, they serve as 'evidence' that fullness has been realized.[188] Ironically, such a position betrays the thrust of early Pentecostalism, which saw 'fullness' of the Spirit to be initiated into further Christian service. There is also a danger of seeing tongues as the only sign of catholicity, when the Acts narrative also made apostolic teaching (tradition) and the breaking of bread (eucharist) signs of catholicity. 'In other words', argues Macchia, 'our self-definition as Pentecostals is challenged when we realize that a Catholic presentation on ecumenism could have been just as compelling as a witness to scripture from a eucharistic center as this discussion from the vantage point of glossolalic prayer'.[189]

Macchia is in the process of developing a Pentecostal theology that places tongues within the broader theological context. He takes the Pentecostal distinctive, that tongues is the initial evidence of Spirit baptism, and revisions it to include eschatological, sacramental and catholic dimensions. He also distances himself from Pentecostal apocalyptic eschatology to insist on the inclusion of creation in the eschaton, an inclusion hinted in the sighs/groans of glossolalic prayer 'too deep for words'. Macchia's revision of the Pentecostal distinctive of tongues is interestingly rooted in his earlier analysis of the Blumhardt's kingdom of God theology.

185. Macchia, 'Tongues of Pentecost', p. 9.
186. Macchia, 'Tongues of Pentecost', p. 9; cf. Volf, *After our Likeness*.
187. Macchia, 'Tongues of Pentecost', p. 8.
188. Macchia, 'Tongues of Pentecost', pp. 9-10.
189. Macchia, 'Tongues of Pentecost', p. 10.

What will become evident in the next chapter is that Macchia, Volf, Villafañe and Land are all influenced by the pneumatological eschatology of Jürgen Moltmann. Before placing the Pentecostal theologians in dialogue with Moltmann, his pneumatological eschatology will be addressed.

Chapter 3

The Transformationist Eschatology of Jürgen Moltmann

The prophetic elements of early Pentecostalism's pneumatological eschatology had embryonic implications for a social engagement with the world, encapsulated in the theology of the latter rain. Early Pentecostals believed that the Spirit was being poured out upon all flesh to prepare the people of God for the coming of the Lord. The Spirit's charismatic gifts were not intended simply for personal edification, but intended to bring racial reconciliation, gender equality and unity to the church and the world in preparation for the eschatological kingdom. Although fundamentalist eschatology with its emphasis on passive withdrawal from a doomed world later supplanted the early Pentecostal vision, contemporary Pentecostal theologians are revisioning their eschatology to reflect its original prophetic message. This revisioning process includes a dialogue with non-Pentecostal theologians such as Jürgen Moltmann. Pentecostals find that the emphasis Moltmann places on eschatological hope resonates with their own heritage. This chapter, then, examines elements of Moltmann's pneumatological eschatology that show similarity with, or divergence from, the contemporary Pentecostal theologians of the previous chapter. The concluding chapter places the pneumatological eschatology of early Pentecostalism, the contemporary Pentecostal theologians and Moltmann into dialogue.

University of Tübingen theologian Jürgen Moltmann has made eschatological hope central to his theological vision. For Moltmann, Christian faith is essentially and primarily Christian hope that looks to the eschatological future to transform the present. Yet for him it is deceptive to define eschatology simply as 'the end of all things', because, while hope anticipates the end-time annihilation of suffering and death in the consummation of creation into the future new creation, it announces this future in the present through the proclamation of the risen Christ.[1] The present world will not

1.   Moltmann, *Theology of Hope*, pp. 16-17.

be annihilated, but transformed into the kingdom of God and the new creation. Hope is anticipatory, not because of latent possibilities in the present that can be extrapolated and predictive of the future,[2] but because the triune God stands in that future and draws the present world into himself. The future kingdom cannot be defined as the goal (*telos*) of history, nor in terms of the world as 'becoming', because the kingdom finds its basis in the 'coming of God'. The coming of God from the future draws the whole world into the kingdom and therefore has transformative influence on the present 'godforsaken' world. The eschaton, then, will be the moment when God will fully indwell creation, and fully reveal the divine glory.

This chapter examines Moltmann's theological vision as it pertains to his eschatology. By considering the centrality of eschatology in Moltmann's theology, the importance of Jesus Christ and the Spirit in the coming eschatological kingdom, the political significance of his eschatology, and finally his cosmic eschatology, the general contours of Moltmann's eschatology and its relevance to Pentecostalism will become clear.

The Centrality and Scope of Moltmann's Eschatology

For Moltmann, from his earliest to his most recent work, eschatology is not simply one of the many elements of theology, but central to all of Christian faith. The scope of eschatology is not simply the doctrine of the last things, but includes the 'time between the times' from the resurrection of Jesus Christ and the outpouring of the Spirit in the event of Pentecost to the return of Jesus Christ in universal glory, the final judgment, the consummation of the kingdom, the general resurrection of the dead and the manifestation of the new creation. For Moltmann, however, Christian faith is fundamentally anticipatory hope for the future eschatological kingdom, when all things will be transformed into the new creation. God's coming kingdom has the power to transform the present godforsaken world. Moltmann argues:

> Christianity is eschatology, is hope, forward looking and forward moving, and therefore also revolutionizing and transforming the present. The eschatological is not one element *of* Christianity, but it is the medium of Christian faith as such, the key in which everything in it is set, the glow that suffuses everything here in the dawn of an expected new day. For Christian faith lives from the raising of the crucified Christ, and strains after the

2. See Jürgen Moltmann, 'Methods in Eschatology', in *idem*, *The Future of Creation* (trans. Margaret Kohl; San Franscisco: SCM Press, 1979), pp. 41-48.

promises of the universal future of Christ. Eschatology is the passionate
suffering and passionate longing kindled by the Messiah. Hence eschatology cannot really be only a part of Christian doctrine. Rather, the eschatological outlook is characteristic of all Christian proclamation, of every
Christian experience and the whole church.[3]

Describing the eschaton as 'the end' is misleading. The eschaton will
not be the cataclysmic end of creation, according to Moltmann, but the
fulfilment of Christ's reign. The parousia is not the end of all things, but a
new beginning, when the kingdom of God will appear in its fullness and
the world will be transformed into the new creation. 'In God's creative
future the end will become the beginning', claims Moltmann, 'and the true
creation is still to come and is ahead of us'.[4] Moltmann revisions eschatology to make hope in the future the heart of Christian faith, rather than
dread for the future destruction of the world.

Transformationist Eschatology
Both the eschatological 'kingdom' and the 'new creation' are symbols of
the future reign of God and Moltmann notes that the two are complemen-
tary biblical concepts. The eschatological kingdom is the final transformation of human history, when God will give dignity and joy to those who
have suffered and perished. It is the *telos* and goal of history, restoring to
the poor and suffering of history their rightful place as fellow heirs with
God. The new creation, on the other hand, is the cosmic transformation of
all things into the eschatological creation, when God will 'derestrict' his
glory and fully indwell all of creation.[5] Although the symbol of the kingdom of God is a concept appropriate for describing the eschatological future
in relation to the judgment of God and the suffering of human beings, and a
symbol Moltmann uses extensively in his earlier writings, it is in itself an
inadequate symbol for expressing the eschatological future of the whole
world. Human beings and human history are embedded in nature. This is
why the new creation has become a more appropriate eschatological symbol than the kingdom of God. Moreover, the new creation connotes a cosmic eschatology, including the restoration of all things. The kingdom of

---

3.   Moltmann, *Theology of Hope*, p. 16; also *idem*, *Experiences of God* (trans.
Margaret Kohl; London: SCM Press, 1980), pp. 11-12.
4.   Jürgen Moltmann, *The Coming of God: Christian Eschatology* (trans. Margaret
Kohl; Minneapolis: Fortress Press, 1996), p. xi.
5.   Moltmann, *Coming of God*, pp. 294-95.

God has implications for a political eschatology.[6] Moltmann continues to use 'kingdom' language in a major way even in his most recent work, and considers it a 'more integral symbol of the eschatological hope than eternal life'.[7] He has recently suggested that there will be a transitional period between the eschatological kingdom and the new creation that will be the 'millennial' reign of God. He sees this transitional period as both the hope for Israel's future and the kingdom of peace in history that vindicates their experience of suffering.[8] Nonetheless, Moltmann has a tendency to use 'kingdom' and 'new creation' interchangeably when speaking of the eschaton.

Moltmann's eschatology is best described as an eschatology of transformation. In this theology, the coming kingdom creates possibilities for the present which have transformative and revolutionary power. What can be derived from present-day experience and knowledge is not the basis of the future kingdom, but hope that God will do what has been promised. Faith in the eschaton, which is hope for the beginning of God's new creation, bears upon the present, with the result that it changes the present, awakening in the people of God a passion to participate in that change. Moltmann comments:

> Hope's statements of promise, however, must stand in contradiction to the reality which can at present be experienced. They do not result from experiences, but are the condition for the possibility of new experiences. They do

6.   Moltmann, *Coming of God*, p. 132.
7.   Moltmann, *Coming of God*, p. 131.
8.   Jürgen Moltmann, 'The Hope for Israel and the Anabaptist Alternative', in Richard J. Bauckham (ed.), *God Will Be All in All: The Eschatology of Jürgen Moltmann* (Edinburgh: T. & T. Clark, 1999), pp. 149-54 (151-53). Bauckham questions 'whether the idea of the millennium fulfills a theological need which Moltmann's understanding of the new creation of all things cannot fulfil'. R.J. Bauckham, 'The Millennium', in *idem* (ed.), *God Will Be All in All*, pp. 123-47 (135-36). Volf concurs: 'It can be argued that the millennium (conceived of as transition) is unnecessary in Moltmann's thought. It is unnecessary since he believes that the entrance into "eternity" does not entail flight from time but a restoration of all times and that the "new creation" comes about through the transformation rather than the annihilation of the old'. In fact, Volf sees the millennium transitional period as detrimental to Moltmann's theology, because it risks creating an eschatological millennium in history that shifts into a historical millennium in time (as opposed to eternity) that may become oppressive. Volf's concern is that 'the one future declared as divine, will suppress many human histories whose utopian imaginations diverge from it'. Volf, 'After Moltmann: Relections on the Future of Eschatology', in Bauckham (ed.), *God Will Be All in All*, pp. 233-57 (242-43). It makes more sense to interpret the millennium symbolically as the time of the new creation in eternity.

not seek to illuminate the reality which exists, but the reality which is
coming... Present and future, experience and hope, stand in contradiction to
each other in Christian eschatology, with the result that man is not brought
into harmony and agreement with a given situation, but is drawn into the
conflict between hope and experience.[9]

Hope is therefore not based in the experience of this present world of
suffering and death, but in the world which is to come, a world in which
all evil and death will be annihilated.

Moltmann dialectically juxtaposes the future kingdom with present reality. The eschatological kingdom dialectically transforms present reality,
exposing the godlessness and suffering that exists in the present in the
form of injustice and death, and infusing the present with possibilities for
the new creation. The unlimited possibilities of the future kingdom stimu-
late the human imagination to think and work creatively: 'the hope of faith
must become a source of creative and inventive imagination in the service
of love', insists Moltmann, 'and must release anticipatory thought that
asks about the present possibility of [one's] life here becoming better,
more just, freer, and more humane'.[10] The future possibilities are not self-
evident in history, but reflect the transcendent manifestation of God's
coming kingdom.

For Moltmann, this dialectic is more a paradoxical tension than the resolution of opposites. It exposes the tension between present and future,
between the cross of Jesus Christ and his resurrection, which will be
resolved only in the future eschaton. The resolution of this dialectic will be
a 'negation of the negative', where the elements of suffering, destruction
and death will be transformed by the fullness of life of the new creation.
The resurrection of the crucified Christ corresponds to the negation of the
negative, whereas the cross stands as a symbol of God's ultimate solidarity
with suffering and death in the world. The resurrection is the first-fruits of
the raising of the dead into the fullness of life of the future kingdom. This
dialectic is not a vertical inbreaking, but a horizontal transcendence from
the future. 'In other words, the wholly other God...becomes in Moltmann
the God of a qualitatively other *future*, who in his Word of promise negates
the human present.'[11] Moltmann's dialectical eschatology is thus one of

    9.   Moltmann, *Theology of Hope*, p. 18.
    10.   Jürgen Moltmann, *Religion, Revolution and the Future* (trans. M. Douglas
Meeks; New York: Charles Scribner's Sons, 1969), p. 121.
    11.   Richard J. Bauckham, *Moltmann: Messianic Theology in the Making* (London:
Marshall Pickering, 1987), p. 41.

tension between future and present, between resurrection hope and the cross of suffering and death.[12]

Thus in Moltmann's eschatology God is moving towards humanity from the transcendent future. At the same time, history is being drawn towards the eschaton through the activity of the Spirit.[13] Yet Moltmann rejects the idea that humanity is progressively improving and that this progression will ultimately bring about the kingdom of God. Humanity requires the activity of the Spirit to bring about the kingdom. For Moltmann, the transcendent future which transforms the present provides a better understanding of the dialectic between God's transcendence and immanence than the conception of an 'eternal now', which sees God's transcendence in the present. Such a position, insists Moltmann, lacks the ability to critique the present experience of godforsakenness and often ends up justifying the status quo. He declares that the Word, coming to us from the transcendent future, transforms the godforsakenness of every historical status quo.

Faith and hope in the eschatological horizon is based in the scriptural message of promise. In the Old Testament, appearances of Yahweh are linked to divine promise, in which the unrealized future is announced. Moltmann rejects the idea of the transcendent eternal moment in epiphanic religions, because they confuse epiphanic appearances that announce the promised future with the 'image of an "epiphanic God" who breaks into human experience from a transcendent realm that stands apart from history'.[14] 'The sense and purpose of [God's] "appearances" lies not in themselves', asserts Moltmann, 'but in the promise and its future'.[15] The 'not yet' of the eschatological hope is contained in the promise of God.[16] While the Israelites sometimes restricted the promise of God to the nation of Israel, the New Testament expands the promise to include all nations and people, making the hope of redemption inclusive and universal.[17] The promise of God is revealed decisively in the revelation of the crucified and resurrected Christ.

---

12. Moltmann, *Theology of Hope*, p. 201.
13. Jürgen Moltmann, *The Church in the Power of the Spirit: A Contribution to Messianic Ecclesiology* (trans. Margaret Kohl; London: SCM Press, 1977), pp. 295-96.
14. A.J. Conyers, *God, Hope and History: Jürgen Moltmann and the Christian Concept of History* (Macon, GA: Mercer University Press, 1988), pp. 5-6.
15. Moltmann, *Theology of Hope*, p. 100.
16. Moltmann, *Theology of Hope*, p. 102.
17. Moltmann, *Theology of Hope*, p. 147.

Present experience in history is not the basis for faith and hope in the eschatological kingdom. Rather, the force of the future kingdom acts on present history to transform it. Moltmann uses the concepts of 'tendency' and 'latency' to describe this process. History anticipates the future and reveals tendencies for that future. As such, history is full of possibilities of what the world could potentially be. Yet history is also full of dangers, while at the same time possible salvation. The danger of nuclear holocaust is just as real a possibility as the salvation of creation.[18] Consequently, human beings are required to participate in the future kingdom proleptically through political action.[19] Moltmann states:

> God lets us participate in the reconciliation of the world. Not that we must also make our contribution to this reconciliation, for then reconciliation would be in bad hands; however, he lets us participate in the service of reconciliation to this unsaved world. He does not make us accusers of other men, of the bad, godless society, but agents of reconciliation in this society.[20]

Possibilities and actualized realities are determined, then, not by causal necessity, but by 'tendency, impulse, inclination, trend, specific leanings towards something which can become real in certain historic constellations'.[21] The latency of present history opens possibilities for future realities. The tendency of history has its goal in future reality as it moves towards that reality. Yet each new reality entails a latency for greater fulfilment.[22] In other words, whenever a certain reality is realized in history, there are latencies in that reality which point to a more just reality. Thus latency and tendency stand in dialectic relationship, one disclosing possibilities hidden within present reality, the other disclosing future possibilities. Together they constitute the movement of history. The latency and

---

18. Moltmann, *Theology of Hope*, p. 263.

19. Jürgen Moltmann, 'Theology as Eschatology', in Frederick Herzog (ed.), *The Future of Hope: Theology as Eschatology* (New York: Herder & Herder, 1970), pp. 1-50 (47-48).

20. Jürgen Moltmann, *The Gospel of Liberation* (Waco, TX: Word Books, 1973), pp. 39-40.

21. Moltmann, *Theology of Hope*, p. 243.

22. Randall E. Otto, 'God and History in Jürgen Moltmann', *JETS* 35.3 (1992), pp. 375-88 (377); also see Moltmann, *Future of Creation*, pp. 41-42; also see Douglas J. Schuurman, *Creation, Eschaton and Ethics: The Ethical Significance of the Creation-Eschaton Relation in the Thought of Emil Brunner and Jürgen Moltmann* (TR, 86; New York: Peter Lang, 1991), pp. 90-91.

tendency of history constitute the process of history which is always reinventing itself with new visions of the future.

Although latency and tendencies constitute the process of history in its movement towards the kingdom, Moltmann is clear that the kingdom will not be established through the world of present history, but through the work of the crucified and risen Christ. The kingdom of God is not the *telos* or end of history.[23] The kingdom can only be established through the work of God, breaking into the world from the future. Human beings are called to participate proleptically in the kingdom, but cannot establish the kingdom through their own efforts. Put another way, the vision of the kingdom as revealed by God creates potentialities in the present for the future, which when actualized in history reveal further potentialities. This is a process that will have its ultimate realization in the moment of the eschaton. However, for Moltmann these potentialities are not contained in history *per se*, but are promised by God, who will bring those promises into reality.

Apocalyptic Eschatology

Moltmann makes a distinction between millenarian and apocalyptic eschatology, both having support in Scripture. His view of apocalyptic eschatology, however, has become more nuanced in latter years. Initially, Moltmann noted the difficulties in placing the apocalyptic literature within a theological framework. Are they a continuation of the prophetic message, sometimes radically different, or an imposition of the dualistic cosmology of Iranianism? It appears that the apocalypticists had a religious, deterministic view of history, as divinely predetermined from the beginning: The world under the power of evil will be replaced by the coming world of righteousness; there will be no consummation of creation through a process of overcoming evil with good (as is the case with the prophets), but a complete separation of good from evil; God's judgment is not something that God will recall, even if the world repents, but is a *fait accompli*. Apocalyptic thinking is ultimately non-historical thinking, though apocalypticism is an attempt to interpret the limits of cosmology.[24] Apocalyptic thought comes about in the struggle between historic eschatology and cosmology. Moltmann's own position is clear when he claims:

23.   Jürgen Moltmann, *The Way of Jesus Christ* (trans. Margaret Kohl; London: SCM Press, 1990), p. 303.

24.   Moltmann, *Theology of Hope*, pp. 133-34.

It might well be that the existing cosmic bounds of reality, which the moving historic horizon of the promise reaches in eschatology, are not regarded as fixed and predetermined things, but are themselves found to be in motion. It might well be that once the promise becomes eschatological it breaks the bounds even of that which aetiology hitherto considered to be creation and cosmos, with the result that the *eschaton* would not be a repetition of the beginning, nor a return from the condition of estrangement and the world of sin to a state of original purity, but is ultimately wider than the beginning ever was. Then…cosmology would become eschatological and the cosmos would be taken up in terms of history into the process of the eschaton.[25]

In this perspective, the universe is not to be interpreted as predetermined, but splits into aeons of the apocalyptic process, in which one world is coming and one is passing away.[26] In apocalyptic, it is not simply that world of human beings (i.e. history) that is transformed in the eschaton, but the whole creation (i.e. nature).

Apocalyptic is emphatically not the cataclysmic destruction of the world. Cataclysmic destruction is a secular version of apocalyptic eschatology and has no place in theology. Moltmann's cosmic eschatology insists that the world must be transformed into the new creation as the consummation of God's original creation. This cannot happen if God has predetermined to destroy the world. Yet apocalyptic is an important element in biblical eschatology. In *The Coming of God*, he develops a more nuanced view of apocalyptic in order to incorporate a more fully biblical view of hope. Timothy Gorringe is correct to assert that 'Moltmann develops a far more positive appreciation of apocalyptics…[and] that it is now much clearer that "kingdom eschatology" makes no sense without cosmic eschatol-

---

25. Moltmann, *Theology of Hope*, p. 136.

26. Moltmann rejects the modern notion of time as linear (*chronos*) moving towards its ultimate *telos* and the existential notion of time as *kairos*, when eternity arrives at any moment (*Way of Jesus Christ*, p. 158). Instead, he adopts a patristic view which splits time into different aeons. Translated as eternity, aeonic time is not the absolute eternity of God, but the relative eternity communicated by God. Aeonic time is the time of angels, of the invisible world, called heaven, that stands over the visible world of creation and will be the time of the new creation. The transformation of the temporal time of this creation to the aeonic eternity of the new creation is considered apocalyptic, not because the created world will end in nothingness or even in the eternity of God, but because chronological time will end and be transformed into aeonic time. The death-throws of the last days will be the apocalyptic end of time, but it will also be the eschatological birth pangs of the aeonic eternity of the new creation. Moltmann, *Way of Jesus Christ*, pp. 330-31.

ogy'.[27] He distinguishes between a secular apocalyptic interpretation of end-time annihilation and the eschatological exposure of the historical powers to divine judgment.[28]

For Moltmann, the association of apocalyptic eschatology with some sort of 'nuclear Armageddon' or ecological catastrophe is not only theologically incorrect, but truly frightening. Such an association creates an attitude that human beings can initiate a cataclysmic destruction and bring about the kingdom of God. Moltmann rightly insists:

> The 'nuclear Armageddon' about which Ronald Reagan talked so darkly means annihilation of the world without the kingdom of God. The ecological end of the world which many people are afraid of, and not without cause, means the destruction of nature without a new creation.[29]

Human destruction of the world may bring about the end of life, but it will be without the kingdom of God or new creation.

Thus the apocalyptic is not equated with cataclysmic destruction. Apocalyptic, rightly understood, is the destruction of sin and the powers of evil. Those elements of Christianity that interpret eschatology apocalyptically tend to do so because they are dominated and powerless in the face of oppression. People who are powerless do not want to see the prolongation of history; instead, the powerless want to see the end of history. The powerless want an alternative future, one that will liberate them from the misery of the present and deliver them from their helplessness.[30] According to Moltmann, 'Anyone who talks here about "the apocalypse" or the battle of Armageddon, is providing a religious interpretation for mass human crime, and is trying to make God responsible for what human beings are doing'.[31] The true interpretation and theological intention of apocalyptic is to 'awaken the *resistance of faith* and the *patience of*

27. Timothy Gorringe, 'Eschatology and Political Radicalism: The Example of Karl Barth and Jürgen Moltmann', in Richard Bauckham (ed.), *God Will Be All in All: The Eschatology of Jürgen Moltmann* (Edinburgh: T. & T. Clark, 1999), pp. 87-114 (109).

28. Moltmann, *Coming of God*, p. 146.

29. Moltmann, 'What Has Happened to our Utopias: 1968-1989?', in Bauckham (ed.), *All in All*, pp. 115-21 (119); *idem*, 'God and the Nuclear Catastrophe', *Pacifica* (1988), pp. 157-70 (166-67); *idem*, 'The Possible Nuclear Catastrophe and Where Is God?', *ScotJRS* 9 (1988), pp. 71-88 (71-73).

30. Moltmann, *Coming of God*, p. 135.

31. Moltmann, *Coming of God*, p. 203.

hope.[32] An apocalyptic reading of eschatology spreads hope when there is danger, because God's new beginning is expected. Moltmann comments:

> The earlier apocalypticists expected that the end of the world and judgment would come from God, who judges and saves; our apocalypticists today expect the annihilation that is caused by and made by human beings themselves... The biblical apocalypses associate the expected end of this perverted world with the hope for the beginning of God's new, just world. But 'our' apocalypses are godless, knowing no judgment and no grace, but only the self-inflicted self-annihilation of humanity. The 'nuclear apocalypse' is 'a naked apocalypse, that is to say the apocalypse without a kingdom'.[33]

For Moltmann, apocalypse means the disclosure of sin and evil in the world by God's judgment. Apocalyptic eschatology reveals the forms of oppression. The perpetrators of oppression will finally and truly see themselves through the eyes of their victims.[34] He states:

> The apocalyptic interpretation of the catastrophes of world history, or cosmic catastrophes is something different from the eschatological apocalypse of the powers of the world in the judgment of God, whose purpose is the birth of a new world. The modern apocalyptic interpretations of human endtimes are secularizations of biblical apocalyptic, and now have in common with it only the catastrophe, no longer the hope. They talk about an end without a beginning, and about judgment without a kingdom... Apocalypticism belongs to eschatology, not history. And yet eschatology begins with apocalyptics: there is no beginning of a new world without the end of this one, there is no kingdom of God without judgment on godlessness, there is no rebirth of the cosmos without 'the birth pangs of the End-time'.[35]

Thus for Moltmann, apocalyptic eschatology rightly belongs to a theology of hope, according to which the godless and corrupt powers of this world will stand under divine judgment to make way for the new creation, but wrongly when it predicts the utter destruction of the world by human beings without hope for the new creation.

Millenarian Eschatology

More recently, Moltmann has examined the eschatological symbol of millenarianism. According to Moltmann, millenarian theology was transformed from a pre-Constantinian belief in the expectation of a literal

32. Moltmann, *Coming of God*, p. 203.
33. Moltmann, *Coming of God*, p. 217.
34. Moltmann, *Coming of God*, p. 218.
35. Moltmann, *Coming of God*, p. 227.

thousand-year reign of Christ in the future, to a post-Constantinian eccle-siastical self-confidence that the triumph of the expansion of the patristic church was itself the millennial reign on earth.[36] A distinction is made, however, between millenarianism and eschatology:

> Eschatology is more than millenarianism, but millenarianism is its historical relevance... Millenarianism is the special, this-worldly side of eschatology, the side turned towards experienced history; eschatology is the general side of history, the side turned towards what is beyond history. Millenarianism looks towards future history, the history of the end; eschatology looks towards the future of history, the end of history. Consequently, the two sides of eschatology belong together as goal and end, history's consummation and its importance.[37]

The importance of millenarianism, for Moltmann, is that it incorporates world history, and the future earthly fulfilment of God's promises for the church *and* Israel. It represents a transitional stage between this world and the new creation, which is identified as the kingdom of God.[38]

Moltmann makes a further distinction between *eschatological millenari-anism* (also called messianism, millennialism and chiliasm)[39] and *historical millenarianism* (also called presentative, amillennialism and amillenarian-ism). Eschatological millenarianism is the 'expectation of the universal kingdom of Christ and the saints on earth in the final future of the world, as a kind of this-worldly, historical transition to the new creation at the end of history'.[40] *Historical millenarianism* interprets the thousand-year reign of the future as a period in history and conceives of the present as the earthly reign of Christ and the last stage of history. It represents a type of realized millenarianism, in which the millennial stage is already present.[41]

Eschatological millenarianism and historical millenarianism stand in contradiction to each other. Eschatological millenarianism offers an alter-native to present existence in a vision of the future, while historical

---

36. Moltmann, *Coming of God*, p. 181.
37. Moltmann, *Coming of God*, p. 197.
38. See Moltmann, *Coming of God*, pp. 199-202. See n. 8 above.
39. Moltmann argues that the Jewish concept 'messianism', the Latin concept 'millennialism' and the Greek concept 'chiliasm' are similar in that they depict a thou-sand-year reign in which Christ and his church will 'reign on earth before the end of history'. Moltmann, *Coming of God*, p. 147. Millenarian tends to be a term used in America, while chiliasm tends to be used in Europe.
40. Moltmann, *Coming of God*, p. 146; Bauckham, 'The Millennium', p. 124.
41. Bauckham, 'The Millennium', pp. 125-26.

millenarianism sees the present as the unfolding realization of Christ's kingdom on earth. For instance, the early church represented a form of eschatological millenarianism with a martyr eschatology that critiqued the evils of the Roman empire. Historical millenarianism dominated in the Constantinian church when the Roman empire became the *imperium Christianum*. After the Roman empire fell, a different form of historical eschatology developed, in that the church saw itself as the medium through which Christ exercised his sovereign reign of the millennial kingdom, starting with Christ's ascension and spanning to his coming again. After 1000 years had passed, eschatological millenarianism once again dominated in the form of post-millennialism. Apocalyptic interpretations abounded and there was a widespread belief that the world was in the end-time tribulations, because Satan had been loosed to precipitate the final battle between Christ and the Antichrist. Even the Reformers believed that the millennium was a past era and Luther, especially, saw his struggles with the Pope as representative of the end-time battle with the Antichrist.[42] Thus Moltmann claims that eschatological millenarianism is an authentic vision of Christian hope, because it identifies the sin and oppression of the present world and seeks to overcome them, but it has often been condemned by the historical millenarian tradition. Eschatological millenarianism offers a counter vision to the ruling powers. Because historical millenarianism allies itself with the political powers of the status quo, it cannot tolerate the revolutionary potential of any alternative vision of reality that threatens its power base.

Making a distinction between pre-millenarianism (the belief that the thousand-year reign will occur in the future after Christ's second coming), post-millenarianism (the belief that the thousand-year reign is unfolding in present history as preparation for Christ's second coming) and amillenarianism (the denial of any millenarian reign),[43] Moltmann argues that the importance of millenarianism is that it expresses the this-worldly character of Christian hope.[44] Nevertheless, he is critical of eschatological millenarianism when its emphasis is not on the delayed *parousia*, but on a premature fulfilment of the eschatological reign. Millenarianism can be ambivalent:

> It can fill the present with new power, but it can also draw power away from the present. It can lead to resistance—and also to spiritual escape… If the call is no longer to resistance against the powers and their idols, but if

42. Moltmann, *Coming of God*, pp. 153-55.
43. Moltmann, *Coming of God*, p. 147.
44. Moltmann, *Coming of God*, p. 153.

instead escapades into religious dream worlds are offered in the face of a
world destined for downfall—a downfall that is even desired—the meaning
of this millenarian hope is turned upside down. This is always the case
when it is no longer resistance that is at the centre, but 'the great rapture' of
believers before the annihilation of the world in the fire storm of nuclear
bombs.[45]

The difficulty with American fundamentalism in particular, argues
Moltmann, is that it seeks spiritual escape and world annihilation. Although the American fundamentalist apocalypticism of John Darby, D.L.
Moody and C.I. Scofield was also millenarian, it was the exact opposite of
the pre-millenarianism of the early church. While early church apocalyptics were defined by resistance to the powers of sin and oppression in the
world, fundamentalist apocalypticism emphasizes a spiritual flight from
the world. The doctrine of the 'Rapture' embodies this flight.[46]

Of particular importance in Moltmann's analysis is his examination of
the distinctions and development of eschatological millenarianism and
historical millenarianism throughout the history of Christianity. The pre-
Constantine church had a pre-millenarian view focused in a martyr eschatology of suffering with Christ. The Constantinian church after 313 CE
shifted to a presentative eschatology that saw the millennial rule of Christ
as already being present in history under the rule of the Roman empire.[47]
With Augustine, presentative eschatology shifted once again from the
collapsing rule of the Roman empire to the rule of the church. The ramification of this shift was that the church insisted that society must conform
to the principles of the church, and the focus of the church shifted from the
gathering of the community to the hierarchy of the church. Eschatology
was then reduced to the expectation of judgment and the spiritualization of
Christian hope, because the church saw itself as the millennial reign. Hope
was spiritualized as hope for the soul only. Moltmann suggests that this
did not represent a waning of chiliasm, but was the 'ecclesiastical occupation' of chiliasm. The church saw itself in the middle of the millennium.[48]
Yet in both the Constantinian and post-Constantinian churches, the millenarian rule was believed to be present in history as Christ's rule in the
empire and later in the church.

45. Moltmann, *Coming of God*, p. 153.
46. Moltmann, *Coming of God*, p. 159.
47. Moltmann, *Coming of God*, p. 153.
48. Moltmann, *Coming of God*, p. 182.

After the first millennium passed into history (i.e. 1000 CE), various post-millenarian eschatologies surfaced. These eschatologies were apocalyptic, believing that the end of the millennium meant that Satan had been loosed and the end-time tribulations were unfolding. They saw a cosmic struggle between Christ and the Antichrist that would end in divine judgment. Apocalyptic eschatologies of this type dominated the Middle Ages. Even the Reformers believed that the millennium was a time of the past. Luther, for instance, believed that the tribulation was evident in his struggles with the Roman church. The Reformers condemned therefore all forms of pre-millenarianism, believing that the millennium had already ended.[49]

In general, the post-Reformation period witnessed a rebirth of millenarianism. In Germany, this rebirth was found in the Pietist movement. For instance, Moltmann comments that Friedrich Christoph Oetinger added a 'theology of hope' to the mediaeval theology of love and the Reformation theology of faith. The seventeenth century saw a new optimistic theology of the kingdom of God orientated towards the world in missionary action, in a new *diakonia*, new forms of education, and for the first time a dialogue with the Jews. German Pietism remained optimistic towards the future and open to the world.[50]

Yet American millenarian hope represents a political form of historical millenarianism. The United States sees itself as a nation whose destiny is to redeem the world, a political philosophy which is fuelled by a messianic vision.[51] Along with this messianic Spirit is an

> end-of-the-world apocalypticism, the expectation of the final battle of good against evil, and a total destruction of the world on the day of Armageddon... Nowhere else in the world is this doomsday apocalyptic so widespread, and apparently so firmly held as in the United States. 'The doom boom' is evidently the inescapable reverse side of the political messianism in the USA's political mythology.[52]

The messianic spirit of the USA was depicted in Israel's liberation from Egyptian slavery. Emigrants to the States saw themselves as slaves to European feudalism and the state church. America was pictured as the promised land. The messianic dream was then interpreted in terms of 'the Manifest Destiny'. Expansion into the West in the 1800s was interpreted

49. Moltmann, *Coming of God*, pp. 153-55.
50. Moltmann, *Coming of God*, pp. 157-58.
51. Moltmann, *Coming of God*, p. 169.
52. Moltmann, *Coming of God*, pp. 169-70.

as equivalent to Israel's occupation of the promised land. Native Americans were driven out, just like the Canaanites and Amalekites. As the land was subjugated, America began to feel its dominance in the world. 'The old nation of the chosen people and its religious mission was transmuted into the concept of the "favoured people" and its God given successes.'[53] America's manifest destiny was justified in terms of divine providence, though its successful expansion was unfortunately also realized through conquest and domination of indigenous peoples.[54]

The political experiment of liberty and self-government was justified through special providence. Yet there was a corresponding loss of the biblical place of a 'chosen people' that gave way to a destiny in world history through 'success'.

> From being a refuge for the persecuted saints and an experiment in freedom and democratic self-government, America turned into a world power with a world mission... If America had been chosen for the salvation of all nations and humanity in general, then its policies not only can but *must* be measured against their promotion of the liberty of other peoples, the self-government of those peoples, and their human rights.[55]

Yet American 'Manifest Destiny' contains both the seeds of hope and danger. On the one hand, its millenarian-conceived world mission is able to critique and resist narrow-minded nationalism and uphold human dignity and rights. On the other hand, there exists the danger of falling victim to its own form of nationalism, which has in fact been used to expel and conquer other peoples, to support dictatorships that bolster America's own self-interests and to quash the human rights it tries to defend.[56]

Early Pentecostal eschatology is clearly situated within American millenarianism, making Moltmann's discussion of special interest to us here. As an oppressed people, early Pentecostals rejected the triumphalism of America's 'manifest destiny' and 'success' orientation and saw themselves as a 'chosen people' or 'remnant' empowered by the charismatic gifting of Spirit to proclaim the coming of the Lord. This empowerment of the Spirit did not result in passive resignation to the sinful powers of this world, but called the Pentecostal to engage the world through resistance. The charismatic Spirit not only restored personal relationships, but encouraged social and racial reconciliation in anticipation of the imminent kingdom.

53. Moltmann, *Coming of God*, p. 173.
54. Moltmann, *Coming of God*, p. 173.
55. Moltmann, *Coming of God*, p. 174.
56. Moltmann, *Coming of God*, p. 174.

Jesus Christ, the Holy Spirit and the Kingdom

Since my concern in this chapter is Moltmann's eschatology, I will not be able to expound his Christology or pneumatology thoroughly, but only as they are integrally related to his eschatology. Nevertheless, for Moltmann, 'Every eschatology that claims to be Christian, and not merely utopian or apocalyptic, or a stage in salvation history must have a christological foundation…[It is founded in] Christian hope based on Christ's coming, his surrender to death on the cross and his resurrection from the dead.'[57] Moltmann's Christology is strongly influenced by Luther's theology of the cross, both the suffering of the cross as Christ's solidarity with the suffering of all life, and the resurrection of Christ as the foretaste or first-fruits of the general resurrection of the dead and transformation of creation. However, where Luther's theology of the cross and its delineation through the pietistic tradition tended to emphasize passive resignation, Moltmann's theology of the cross emphasizes solidarity in suffering and social protest against oppression. His Christology is also influenced by a messianism forged in Jewish–Christian dialogue that takes seriously the Jewish rejection of Jesus Christ as Messiah.[58] He articulates a messianic Christology of Christ in movement, as being-on-his-way, or Christ as becoming.[59] Moltmann articulates a cosmic Christology in which Christ is the *pantocrator* of creation and will restore all things in the new creation. This cosmic Christology is ecological because 'there can be no redemption of human beings without a redemption of the whole of perishable nature'.[60] He develops a Spirit-Christology that refuses to restrict the movement of the Spirit to Christ's sending, insisting that Christ's coming, life and ministry are also made possible through the indwelling of the Spirit. One can therefore see that Moltmann's Christology, pneumatology and eschatology are intricately connected.

Eschatological Significance of the Crucified Christ

The dialectical relation of the cross and resurrection of Jesus Christ is eschatological. The resurrection gives humanity hope for both the future

57. Moltmann, *Coming of God*, p. 194.
58. Moltmann, *Way of Jesus Christ*, pp. 28-37.
59. Moltmann, *Way of Jesus Christ*, p. xiii.
60. Jürgen Moltmann, *Jesus Christ for Today's World* (London: SCM Press, 1994), p. 83.

resurrection of the dead and the redemptive transformation of this godforsaken world. The cross reveals an incarnate God who identifies with the suffering and death of the present godforsaken world. Through the cross God stands in solidarity with creation, and seeks to overthrow every form of oppression. The dialectic of cross and resurrection is a total contradiction, however, parallel to the total contradiction of the present godforsaken world and the future hope of God's kingdom. Yet the two are inseparable as part of the revelation of the resurrected Christ, the crucified. Thus the resurrection of Jesus Christ gives human beings hope for the future. 'The resurrection has set in motion', declares Moltmann, 'an eschatologically determined process of history, whose goal is the annihilation of death in the victory of the life of the resurrection, and which ends in the righteousness in which God receives in all things his due and the creature thereby finds its salvation'.[61] Yet the hope of the resurrection is not simply hope for the resurrection of the dead, but hope that all of creation will be transformed by God in the new creation. Resurrection hope will not see the destruction of this world but its transformation.

The cross of Christ stands in total opposition to the resurrection. The cross is identified with the present godforsaken world. Yet the cross is more than God's identification and solidarity with a suffering world. In the cross, Jesus is utterly abandoned by God. Moltmann argues:

> The abandonment on the cross which separates the Son from the Father is something which takes place within God himself; it is *stasis* within God— 'God against God'—particularly if we are to maintain that Jesus bore witness to and lived out the truth of God. We must not allow ourselves to overlook this 'enmity' between God and God by failing to take seriously either the rejection of Jesus by God, the gospel of God which he lived out, or his last cry to God upon the cross.[62]

Jesus Christ is totally abandoned by God in order for God to be revealed *sub contraria* (Luther) and in order to redeem all of creation.[63] The suffering of the cross of Christ finds its correspondence in the suffering of God. Suffering, then, must be understood as an ontological structure in the being of God. Love is open to suffering and pain, because God suffers in love.

61. Moltmann, *Theology of Hope*, p. 163.

62. Jürgen Moltmann, *The Crucified God: The Cross of Christ as the Foundation and Criticism of Christian Theology* (trans. R.A. Wilson and John Bowden; London: SCM Press, 1974), pp. 151-52.

63. Moltmann, *Crucified God*, pp. 27-28.

In *The Way of Jesus Christ*, Moltmann develops a thoroughly eschatological ('messianic') Christology, which sees Jesus as '...Christ-in-his-
becoming, the Christ on the way, the Christ in the movement of God's
eschatological history'.[64] This Christology combines the concepts of eschatological 'process' and 'relationality' in which God will redeem all
reality in the new creation. Also, Jesus is who he 'becomes' in trinitarian
relationship with the Father and the Holy Spirit, and in his social relationship with humanity and nature. 'In each stage of his way Jesus is who
he is not merely as divine person or as private human person, but in solidarity with or representation of others.'[65] Jesus Christ is therefore moving
towards his future transcendence in the eschaton and is consequently
bringing creation along with him.

The implication of the cross and resurrection is that Christian participation in the coming kingdom must include human identification with the
apocalyptic sufferings of the crucified Christ. Just as Christ's resurrection
anticipates the future resurrection of the dead and the coming of the new
creation, his death anticipates the universal and absolute death of this world
under God's judgment and the beginning of the new one. Moltmann links
the cross with the new creation:

> But if he [Christ] has suffered vicariously what threatens everyone, then
> through his representation he liberates everyone from this threat, and throws
> open to them the future of the new creation... 'The suffering in this cosmos
> is universal because it is a suffering with the suffering of Christ, who has
> entered this cosmos and yet burst the cosmos apart when he rose from the
> dead'.[66]

In identity with the crucified Christ, Christians are called to live in solidarity with the suffering of the poor, the oppressed and the oppressors,
who through their godless oppression of others become oppressed themselves.[67] In identity with the resurrected Christ, Christians have hope for
the future, when all creation will be transformed by God's indwelling
presence. Through this solidarity, Christians have a social responsibility to
effect change, not only in the church but in the world as well. This responsibility is the basis for political action.

Moltmann also articulates a cosmic Christology that moves beyond the
limitations of seeing redemption solely for human beings and their history.

---

64. Moltmann, *Way of Jesus Christ*, p. 33.
65. Bauckham, *Theology of Jürgen Moltmann*, p. 206.
66. Moltmann, *Way of Jesus Christ*, p. 155.
67. Moltmann, *Crucified God*, p. 25.

It includes nature in salvation. 'Unless nature is healed and saved', declares Moltmann, 'human beings cannot ultimately be healed and saved either, for human beings are natural beings'.[68] Cosmic Christology does not replace personal faith in Christ, but places personal faith under the universal lordship of Christ who will restore all things in himself.[69] The personal side of salvation is the resurrection of the dead. The cosmic side is the annihilation of death through the apocalyptic suffering of the cross.[70]

This cosmic Christology harkens back to an earlier patristic Christology, especially within the Eastern church, which sees Christ as the first-born of all creation and the head of a reconciled cosmos.[71] Christ's *parousia* cannot be restricted to the end or goal of history (*telos*), but must be 'conceived of and awaited as the final coming forth of the Pantocrator hidden in the cosmos, and as the finally accomplished manifestation of the hidden subject of nature in the reconciled, redeemed and hence newly created cosmos'.[72] For the apostle Paul, Christ's cosmic dimension is seen in his mediation of creation. All things are 'from God' the creator and 'through' Christ the Lord. Christ is identified as God's Wisdom, who was with God before creation, for it is through Christ that all things are made (Prov. 8; 1 Cor. 8.6). Paul envisions the universal lordship of the exalted Christ (Phil. 2.9-11). In Acts, Christ is presented to the Gentiles as the universal creator who will raise the dead, a shift from the Jewish notion of Christ as Israel's Messiah.[73]

68. Moltmann, *Jesus Christ for Today's World*, p. 88.
69. Moltmann, *Way of Jesus Christ*, p. 306.
70. Moltmann, *Jesus Christ for Today's World*, p. 109.
71. Moltmann, *Way of Jesus Christ*, p. 275.
72. Moltmann, *Way of Jesus Christ*, p. 280.
73. Moltmann, *Way of Jesus Christ*, pp. 280-81. The implication of Moltmann's theology is that it may lead to universalism in its vision of 'universal reconciliation' and 'restoration of all things' when God is 'all in all'. Moltmann addresses the issue himself when he writes: 'If we think humanistically and universally—God could perhaps be a particularist. But if we think pietistically and particularistically—God might be a universalist. I find that I have to say: I myself am not a universalist, but God may be one' (*Jesus Christ for Today's World*, p. 143). Moltmann relies on Christoph Blumhardt's statement: 'There can be no question of God's giving up anything or anyone in the whole world, either today or in eternity...' Moltmann states his own position: 'I am not preaching universal reconciliation. I am preaching the reconciliation of all men and women in the cross of Christ. I am not proclaiming that everyone will be redeemed, but it is my trust that the proclamation will go forward until everyone has been redeemed. Universalism is not the substance of the Christian proclamation; it is its presupposition and its goal' (*Jesus Christ for Today's World*, p. 143). In other

The theology of the cross is once again an important aspect of Moltmann's cosmic, eschatological Christology. The epistemological foundation for faith in the cosmic Christ is the Easter experience of the resurrection. It moves beyond the limits of human history and experience to await the resurrection of the dead and the perfecting of creation by the God who created the world *ex nihilo*. Christ is the first to be resurrected and the first-born of all creation.[74] The ontological foundation is Christ's death, as the suffering of God. The cosmic dimension of his resurrection connotes that the cross has universal significance. Christ did not die simply for the reconciliation of human beings, but for the whole cosmos. Bodily resurrection, then, presupposes the restoration of nature which includes the body. 'The reconciliation "of all things" through his blood on the cross is not the goal', insists Moltmann, 'but the beginning of the gathering together of "all things" under Christ who is "the head"; and hence the beginning of the new creation of all things through the annihilation of death itself'.[75]

Eschatological Goal of the Triune God

Moltmann's theology of the Trinity is also integrally connected to his eschatology as indicated by the title: *The Trinity and the Kingdom*. The root concept in his theology of the Trinity is the experience of God's suffering. As we have seen, he rejects the notion of the impassability of God and instead argues that God suffers with us. The 'pathos' of God is the root concept of the Trinity, not merely as the outward expression of God's redemptive acts, but also as inward experience of intra-trinitarian suffering. This suffering is the consequence of the vulnerability of love. To say that God is love is to say that God suffers. 'If God were incapable of suffering in every aspect', insists Moltmann, 'then he would also be incapable of love'.[76] 'For the divine suffering of love outwards is grounded on the pain of love within.'[77] The suffering of God is not a result of some deficiency in God, but from the outpouring of love. The pain of God is reflected in the human experience of love and joy, sorrow and pain. 'God suffers with us—God

words, there is the possibility for universal redemption, but it is not a surety.

74. Moltmann, *Way of Jesus Christ*, p. 281; *idem, Jesus Christ for Today's World*, pp. 83-86.

75. Moltmann, *Way of Jesus Christ*, p. 284.

76. Jürgen Moltmann, *The Trinity and the Kingdom* (trans. Margaret Kohl; Minneapolis: Fortress Press, 1991), p. 23.

77. Moltmann, *Trinity and the Kingdom*, pp. 24-25.

suffers from us—God suffers for us: it is the experience of God that reveals the triune God.'[78]

Moltmann's trinitarian understanding of God overcomes 'monotheistic monarchicalism' through an emphasis on the perichoretic interdependence of the three Persons of the triune God. This 'social doctrine of the Trinity' emphasizes the 'community' of the divine Persons of the triune God in perichoresis as correspondent to human community.[79] He is critical, therefore, of the tendency of Western theology to define the divine Persons by their 'relations', while minimizing the concept of Person as 'being' or 'existent'. He is likewise critical of the tendency in Eastern theology to define Person as 'being' or 'existent', while minimizing their 'relations'. For Moltmann, 'It is impossible to say: person *is* relation; the relation constitutes the person'.[80] The fact that the Father and Son are related and defined by fatherhood and sonship does not in itself constitute the existence of Father and Son. Their existence is presupposed. If trinitarian 'Person' is defined by its relation without its constitution of existence, then there is a tendency in trinitarian theology to slip into modalism. Thus he claims: 'But the fact that God *is* the Father says more than merely that: it adds to the mode of being, being itself. Person and relation therefore have to be understood in a reciprocal relationship. Hence there are no persons without relations; but there are no relations without persons either'.[81] So Moltmann insists that the trinitarian Persons have both 'personality' or 'beingness' and 'relations'.

Moltmann believes he has protected the unity of God in the doctrine of perichoresis. In perichoresis, the Persons are not defined as separate individuals, nor as merely three modes of being that are repetitions of the One God. The perichoresis does not reduce the three into the One, nor dissolve the One into the three. 'In the perichoresis, the very thing that divides them, becomes that which brings them together. The "circulation" of the eternal divine life becomes perfect through the fellowship and unity of the three divine Persons in eternal love.'[82] In perichoresis, the human community is the divine image, not only in terms of the single person or

78. Moltmann, *Trinity and the Kingdom*, p. 4.
79. Elisabeth Moltmann-Wendel and Jürgen Moltmann, 'Social Understanding of the Trinity', in their *Humanity in God* (Cleveland, OH: Pilgrim Press, 1983), pp. 90-106 (96-100).
80. Moltmann, *Trinity and the Kingdom*, p. 172.
81. Moltmann, *Trinity and the Kingdom*, pp. 172-73.
82. Moltmann, *Trinity and the Kingdom*, p. 175.

the social relationship of Persons to each other, but the whole human community corresponds to the triunity of God.[83] Unity with the triune God is the eschatological goal of all creation.

He also discusses the various orderings of the Trinity, and the ultimate eschatological purpose of the triune God. In Jesus' baptism, the trinitarian activity is as follows: the Father sends the Son through the Spirit, the Son comes from the Father in the power of the Spirit, and the Spirit comes to bring people into communion with the Father and fill them with liberating power.[84]

This ordering changes in Jesus' passion. Here the Father delivers up the Son for us, the Son willingly gives himself, and the Spirit is the medium through which the common sacrifice of the Son and the Father occurs; the Spirit unites the abandoned Son to the Father.[85]

In Jesus' resurrection, the order changes once again and can be seen in three different ways: (1) The Father resurrects the Son through the Spirit, the Father reveals the Son in the Spirit and the Son is established as Lord of the kingdom through the Spirit of resurrection. (2) It can also be seen as the Father raises up the dead Son through the life giving Spirit, the Father establishes the Son as Lord of the kingdom, the resurrected Son sends the creative Spirit from the Father to renew creation and the Spirit comes from the Father and the Son. (3) In Christian baptism, the triune God is unfolded as the open and eschatological history of God, the unity of the Father, Son and Spirit is an open and inviting community, and the unity of the triune God is open for unification with the people of God, with humanity and with all creation.[86]

Yet the goal of the work of the triune God is eschatological. In relation to the *parousia*, the trinitarian ordering can be seen in two ways: (1) The Father surrenders all things to the Son, the Son surrenders the consummated kingdom to the Father, and the Son surrenders himself to the Father. (2) The sending, delivering up and resurrection of Christ is seen as the movement of Father—Spirit—Son. In the lordship of Christ and the sending of the Spirit it is Father—Son—Spirit. In the eschatological fulfilment

---

83. Moltmann-Wendel and Moltmann, 'Social Understanding of the Trinity', pp. 99-100.

84. Moltmann, 'The Trinitarian Story of Jesus', in Moltmann-Wendel and Moltmann, *Humanity in God*, pp. 70-89 (75).

85. Moltmann, 'The Trinitarian Story of Jesus', p. 78.

86. Moltmann, 'The Trinitarian Story of Jesus', pp. 81-82.

and glorification the ordering is Spirit—Son—Father.[87] In all trinitarian orderings, the Spirit plays an important role in the action of God. These orderings allow Moltmann to emphasize a pneumatology that does not subordinate the Spirit to the Father and Son, but reveals their mutual participation in the work of God. The eschatological goal is to take up all creation into the eternal life of the open Trinity.

Messianic Significance of Christ and the Spirit
Moltmann also articulates a Spirit-Christology in which the efficacy of the Spirit is considered the first facet of the mystery of Jesus Christ. He moves beyond his earlier work in *Theology of Hope*, where he viewed the resurrection as the eschatological horizon of the future, to a Spirit-Christology that sees Jesus as the messianic prophet to the poor.[88] The 'poor' is a collective term that includes the hungry, unemployed, sick, discouraged, the sad and suffering, the crippled and homeless, those who are subjugated, oppressed and humiliated, those who are 'non-persons', 'sub-human' and 'human fodder'.[89] He still depicts the eschatological history of Christ in messianic categories, but expands this to develop 'the Spirit-history of Jesus Christ: the coming, the presence and the efficacy of the Spirit in, through and with Jesus is the hidden beginning of the new creation of the world'.[90] The appearance of the risen Christ and the outpouring of the Spirit are a single whole, undifferentiated in time.[91] Spirit-Christology takes up the messianic history and promise to Israel as the presupposition of Christology. Israel's eschatological expectation was for an anointed King, or suffering servant on whom the Spirit would rest (Isa. 11.42)[92] and Jesus' earthly messianic mission fulfils this expectation in a fully Incarnational Christology. Spirit-Christology, then, is not a rejection of Incarnational Christology or a rejection of the two natures doctrine, but absorbs these doctrines into a greater wealth of relationships. The premise of this Spirit-Christology is not a christocentrism, but an affirmation of the

---

87. Moltmann, 'The Trinitarian Story of Jesus', p. 84.
88. Moltmann, *Way of Jesus Christ*, p. 3.
89. Moltmann, *Way of Jesus Christ*, p. 99.
90. Moltmann, *Way of Jesus Christ*, p. 73.
91. Jürgen Moltmann, *The Source of Life: The Holy Spirit and the Theology of Life* (trans. Margaret Kohl; Minnesota: Fortress Press, 1997), p. 16. Moltmann believes that the times between Christ's crucifixion and resurrection and then the tarrying for the outpouring of the Spirit must be interpreted symbolically.
92. Moltmann, *Way of Jesus Christ*, pp. 9-10.

trinitarian presence of God in Jesus. To talk about Jesus is also to talk about the work of the Spirit in and through him. In Spirit-Christology, the 'Being of Jesus Christ is from the very outset a Being-in-relationship and where his actions are from the very beginning interactions and his efficacious co-efficacious'.[93]

Before there can be a theological discussion of Christ's act of sending the Spirit as the Spirit of Christ, one must remember that the Spirit precedes Christ's Incarnation in the annunciation and birth of Christ and later descends on Jesus in his baptism. The historical Jesus must also be seen in theological terms as 'God's messianic child, the Spirit-imbued human being who comes from the Spirit, acts and ministers in the Spirit, and through the Spirit surrenders himself to death on the cross'.[94] The Spirit is active with Christ in creation, is the giver of life and not only raises Christ from the dead, but also is the celebrating vitality of the Christian community in its hope-filled movement towards the kingdom. Moltmann claims:

> The 'Spirit of Christ' effects in us the raising of new energies through the word of the gospel. The 'Spirit of God' opens new possibilities round about us through the circumstances of history. If the workings of the Holy Spirit are seen only as the subjective operation of the objective word of God in the hearts of believers, they are being too narrowly defined. In the experienced reality of our lives the two work together and show themselves to be one— the Spirit of Christ and the Spirit of God, the word and the *kairos*, inward powers and outward possibilities.[95]

For Moltmann, pneumatology does not stand under Christology, but stands beside it, for both Christ and the Spirit lead us towards the kingdom. Christ's history is predetermined by the Spirit from the beginning.[96] Thus Moltmann states:

> We can see at a glance that the history of Christ and the history of the Holy Spirit are dovetailed and indissolubly intertwined: according to the Synoptic Gospels Christ comes from the Holy Spirit—'conceived by the Holy Spirit', baptized by the Holy Spirit—performs miracles and proclaims the kingdom of God in the power of the Spirit, surrenders himself to his redeeming death on the cross through the Spirit, and in the Spirit is present among us now. *Christ's history in the Spirit* begins with his baptism and ends in his resurrection. Then things are reversed. Christ sends the Spirit upon the

---

93.   Moltmann, *Way of Jesus Christ*, p. 74.
94.   Jürgen Moltmann, *The Spirit of Life*, p. 58.
95.   Moltmann, *Spirit of Life*, p. 103.
96.   Moltmann, *Way of Jesus Christ*, p. 77.

> community of his people and is present in the Spirit. That is *the history of
> the Spirit of Christ*. The Spirit of God becomes the Spirit of Christ. The
> Christ sent in the Spirit becomes Christ the sender of the Spirit.[97]

The experience of the presence of the Spirit as an experience of the risen
Christ reveals the whole messianic history of Christ 'on his way' to his
consummated reign, and the workings of the Spirit in and through him.[98]

The story of the virgin birth is in fact the story of how the life of the
Spirit is linked to the life of Christ. Two theological points can be derived
from the story of the virgin birth. One is that God enacts the miracle of
Mary's pregnancy through the Spirit. The second is that behind Mary's
human motherhood stands the motherhood of the Holy Spirit.[99] In fact, the
Holy Spirit is depicted in feminine and motherly imagery, with concepts
such as birth, 'born again' and comforter.[100] Both points indicate that Jesus
Christ is the Son of God, not from the moment of the Spirit's descent on
him in his baptism, but from the very beginning with his birth in the
Spirit.[101] Christ owes his existence to the Spirit, who descends and indwells Jesus from his conception, even before his messianic mission as the
Son of God. Yet the Spirit does not create Jesus Christ, but engenders or
brings him forth as the messianic Son of God. Through Christ's coming,
the Spirit not only indwells the Son of God, but indwells the world. This
indwelling comes initially through the rebirth and fellowship of the children of God and eventually through the rebirth and renewal of the entire
cosmos. As such, the Spirit is the source of all life.[102]

Jesus' baptism coincides with the 'descent of the Spirit' on him 'like a
dove' to indwell him. Jesus is indwelt by the Spirit from the moment of his
begetting, but the descent of the Spirit in Jesus' baptism connotes 'condescension' and 'kenosis'. It also marks him as the hoped-for messianic
bearer of the Spirit, the one who will bring the eschatological realm of
justice and peace.[103] The Spirit emptied herself and descends from eternity
to dwell in the vulnerable and mortal human Jesus. The Spirit fills Jesus
with authority and healing power, signs of the coming kingdom, not to

---

97. Moltmann, *Source*, p. 15.
98. Moltmann, *Way of Jesus Christ*, p. 78.
99. Moltmann, *Way of Jesus Christ*, pp. 82-83.
100. Moltmann, *Way of Jesus Christ*, p. 86; *idem*, *Source*, pp. 35-37; *idem*, *Spirit of
Life*, p. 158.
101. Moltmann, *Way of Jesus Christ*, p. 84.
102. Moltmann, *Way of Jesus Christ*, p. 86.
103. Moltmann, *Way of Jesus Christ*, pp. 9-10.

make him into a superman, but to participate in the weakness and suffering of Jesus on the cross. When the Spirit indwells the human Jesus, the Spirit binds itself to Jesus' destiny. This binding is evident when the Spirit leads Jesus into the desert to be tempted. Jesus is tempted to become the messianic Son of God through the seizure of economic, political and religious power. Instead, the Spirit enables Jesus to accept the messianic mission of surrendering himself to helplessness and suffering of death on the cross.[104]

Eschatological Mission of the Charismatic Spirit

Moltmann argues that the Spirit is the Spirit of Christ in the sense that the Spirit proceeds from the Father and rests on Jesus and through Jesus goes forth to communicate the presence of God to human beings.[105] The Spirit makes the mission of Christ universal. The sending of the Spirit is in fact the eschatological history of Christ.[106] Moltmann states:

> In so far as the life, death and resurrection are formed by the Spirit, the Holy Spirit reveals, glorifies and completes the lordship of Christ in believers, in the church and in the world. It is not that the gift of the Holy Spirit is merely the subjective side of the objective divine acts of salvation in Christ, nor is it as if its dispensation and intercession for us could be added to the salvation really gained on the cross. The history of Christ and the history of the Holy Spirit are so interwoven that a *pneumatological christology* leads with inner cogency to a *christological pneumatology*.[107]

So the history of Jesus is also the history of the Spirit. The special feature of Spirit-Christology, however, is that the activity of the Spirit moves beyond the history of Jesus. The Old Testament prophets spoke in the power of the Spirit as did John the Baptist. The Spirit is the creative energy of God that vitalizes all life, moving creation towards the eschatological kingdom of the new creation.[108] Yet it is through Jesus that the saving power of the Spirit is sent to the community of believers. Thus it is the Spirit who 'constitutes the social person of Jesus as the Christ of God'.[109]

For Moltmann, pneumatic Christology leads easily to charismatic ecclesiology.[110] Elsewhere he states that it is pneumatology that brings Christology

---

104. Moltmann, *Way of Jesus Christ*, p. 93; idem, *Spirit of Life*, pp. 61-62.
105. Moltmann, *Way of Jesus Christ*, p. 94.
106. Moltmann, *Church in the Power of the Spirit*, p. 34.
107. Moltmann, *Church in the Power of the Spirit*, p. 23.
108. Moltmann, *Way of Jesus Christ*, pp. 91-92.
109. Moltmann, *Way of Jesus Christ*, p. 94.
110. Moltmann, *Church in the Power of the Spirit*, p. 36.

and eschatology together. 'There is no mediation between Christ and the kingdom of God except the present experience of the Spirit, for the Spirit is that Spirit of Christ and the living energy of the new creation of all things.'[111] However, the charismatic rule of Christ is first of all and essentially liberation from violence and the worldly powers of oppression. Christ's resurrection, through the energies of the Spirit, anticipates the new creation, when death will be no more. The Spirit is the energy that draws the world into the new creation. The community of Christ (i.e. church) is the sign and instrument of the inbreaking lordship of Christ[112] and the 'new order of all things'. 'The community which is filled with the different energies of Christ's liberating power is therefore not an exclusive community of the saved', claims Moltmann, 'but the initial and inclusive materialization of the world freed by the risen Christ'.[113] The gifts and powers of Christ's Spirit in the church are directed towards freeing the world from the power of death. The work of the Spirit in the church is therefore eschatologically orientated towards the new creation. For Moltmann:

> The Spirit of the last days and the eschatological community of the saved belong together. The new people of God see themselves in their existence and form as being 'the creation of the Spirit', and therefore the initial fulfilment of the new creation of all things and the glorification of God. The Spirit calls them into life; the Spirit gives the community the authority for its mission; the Spirit makes its living powers and the ministries that spring from them effective; the Spirit unites, orders and preserves it. It therefore sees itself and its powers and tasks as deriving from and existing in the eschatological history of the Spirit.[114]

According to Moltmann, the charismata are the energies of new life and the power of the Spirit that spring from God's creative grace. Moltmann understands 'charismatic' to mean the 'crystallization and individuation of the one charis given in Christ. Through the powers of the Spirit, the one Spirit gives every individual his specific share and calling, which is exactly cut out for him, in the process of the new creation.'[115] Every Christian is called and gifted by Christ through the Holy Spirit and therefore every Christian is charismatic.

111. Moltmann, *Spirit of Life*, p. 69.
112. See Moltmann, *Church in the Power of the Spirit*, p. 293.
113. Moltmann, *Church in the Power of the Spirit*, pp. 293-94.
114. Moltmann, *Church in the Power of the Spirit*, pp. 294-95.
115. Moltmann, *Church in the Power of the Spirit*, p. 295.

> Calling and giftedness, *klēsis* and *charisma*, belong together and are
> interchangeable. From this it follows that 'Every Christian is a charismatic'
> even when many do not realize their gifts. Gifts which one brings or
> receives stand in the service of his or her calling because by the call God
> reaches people and accepts them just as they are.[116]

Moltmann also makes a distinction between kerygmatic gifts (apostles,
prophets, teachers, evangelists, exhorters, as well as inspiration, ecstasy
and speaking in tongues), diaconical gifts (deacons and deaconesses, care
for the sick, charity, care for widows, as well as healing, exorcising demons
and other forms of help) and cybernetic gifts (shepherds, bishops, peacemakers and the formation of the community). He argues that one cannot
make a distinction between supernatural and natural gifts, because the gifts
are placed into the service of the community. Talents in service of the
Christian community and talents in service of the family, work and society
are inseparable.[117] Speaking in tongues is a 'strong inner grasp of the
Spirit that its expression leaves the realm of understandable speech', an
intense expression of an experience of God's presence.[118] Tongues is 'an
inward possession by the Spirit which is so strong that it can no longer
find expression in comprehensible speech—just as intense pain expresses
itself in unrestrained weeping, or overwhelming joy in laughing, "jumping
for joy" and dancing'.[119]

Thus the charismatic, for Moltmann, is one who is called by Christ and
endowed by the Spirit to serve the church and the world in preparation for
the new creation. The charismatic's service is both in the church and in the
world, breaking down the distinction between the sacred and the secular.
He writes:

> The charismata are by no means to be seen merely in the 'special minis-
> tries' of the gathered community. Every member of the messianic commu-
> nity is a charismatic... For the call puts the person's particular situation at
> the service of the new creation. The Spirit makes the whole biological,
> cultural and religious life history of a person charismatically alive... In

116. Moltmann, 'Spirit Gives Life', p. 23.

117. Moltmann, 'Spirit Gives Life', p. 25; *idem, Source,* pp. 57-59; *idem, Spirit of Life,* p. 183.

118. Moltmann, 'Spirit Gives Life', pp. 26-27; see *idem, Church in the Power of the Spirit,* p. 296.

119. Moltmann, *Source,* pp. 61, 68-69; *idem, Spirit of Life,* p. 185. This definition of tongues and the gifts of the Spirit places Moltmann in the Charismatic tradition, rather than the Pentecostal one.

principle every human potentiality and capacity can become charismatic through a person's call, if only they are used in Christ.[120]

In other words, the natural potentialities that every individual has become vitally and actively charismatic in the Spirit through Christ's calling. The Spirit is poured out on all flesh, not simply for the church, but for cultural and historical movements in the world.[121] Moreover, Moltmann adopts a functionalist understanding of the charismata. The Spirit's gifting does not become charismatic by its fact, but by its modality. 'It is not the gift itself that is important, but its use.'[122]

Nevertheless, the charismata stand in service to the new creation as revealed in Acts when the Spirit is poured out upon 'all flesh'. For Moltmann, this outpouring has universal intent. 'All flesh' is usually thought of as human life, but according to Gen. 9.10 it includes all life (plants, trees and animals). 'If the Holy Spirit is God's Spirit and the special presence of God', argues Moltmann, 'then when God's Spirit is poured out, "all flesh" will be deified. All mortal flesh will be filled with the eternal life of God for what comes from God is divine and eternal like God himself.'[123] The Pentecost event is a prolepsis of the *parousia* of God. Therefore, confessing faith in Jesus Christ and invoking the Holy Spirit is not only a reference to the event of Pentecost, but involves the 'wider cosmic dimensions of the coming of the Holy Spirit for the redemption and transfiguration of the world'.[124] Consequently, the charismatic enlivening in us becomes 'the coming springtime of the new creation, and we ourselves become a "living hope" '.[125]

Like the cosmic dimension of the resurrection of Christ, the cosmic dimension of the Spirit who indwells creation is that the Spirit draws creation into the new creation. Moltmann articulates a cosmic pneumatology that insists that life itself is possible only through the vitalizing energies of the Spirit. It starts from the Hebrew concept of *ruach* and sees the redeeming Spirit of Christ and the creative life-giving Spirit as one. The cosmic Spirit guides us to respect all created things, for God is present in all living things through the Spirit.[126] He states:

---

120. Moltmann, *Church in the Power of the Spirit*, pp. 296-97.
121. Moltmann, *Spirit of Life*, p. 240.
122. Moltmnn, *Church in the Power of the Spirit*, p. 297.
123. Moltmann, *Source*, pp. 12, 23.
124. Moltmann, *Source*, p. 93.
125. Moltmann, *Source*, pp. 94-95; *idem*, *Spirit of Life*, p. 194.
126. Moltmann, *Spirit of Life*, pp. 9-10, 274.

> The dynamic of the life process is always greater than the diversity of the
> forms of life and the living relationships which the process creates. Life is
> fathomless, and is more than any individual expression of life. It is these
> creative living energies which we call *divine Spirit* because it transcends all
> the beings it creates, and even its own created energies. We call it the
> *cosmic Spirit*, because it is the life in everything that lives…*because* God is
> the Creator, his creative Spirit is the dynamic of the universe and the power
> that creates community in the widening, differentiating network of the
> living.[127]

The energy of the Spirit is present, then, in all of life. If God were to withdraw the Spirit from creation, all life would cease to exist and become
nothingness.

Cosmic pneumatology is an attempt to rediscover the immanence of the
transcendent Creator in creation.[128] Moltmann claims that there is a mutual
indwelling of God in creation and creation in God. He articulates his theology through the concept of 'shekinah'. God's 'shekinah' is the indwelling
of the glory of God in creation, so that the Spirit not only draws creation to
its eschatological glory, but also suffers with the suffering of creation:

> The Spirit indwells. The Spirit suffers with the suffering. The Spirit is
> grieved and quenched. The Spirit rejoices when we rejoice. When it
> descends and takes up its habitation and indwelling in wandering and suf-
> fering created beings, the Spirit thrusts forward with intense longing for
> union with God, and sighs to be at rest in the new, perfected creation.[129]

The cosmic Spirit indwells creation and creation indwells God, so that
God's immanence is felt throughout the cosmos.

The cosmic Spirit therefore is understood as '*the divine wellspring of
life*—the source of life created, life preserved and life daily renewed, and
finally the source of the eternal life of all created being'.[130] However,
when life is called by God,[131] it enjoys a more intimate communion with
God. Moltmann states:

> In the charismatic experiences, God's Spirit is felt as a *vitalizing energy*. In
> the nearness of God we are happy, and life begins to vibrate. We experience

127. Moltmann, *Spirit of Life*, p. 227.
128. Moltmann, *Source*, p. 115.
129. Moltmann, *Spirit of Life*, p. 51.
130. Moltmann, *Spirit of Life*, p. 82.
131. Moltmann is unclear whether this calling is a specific call to the Christian
community, or a universal call to participate proleptically in the new creation when all
life will be reborn. However, the universalistic implications of his theology suggest
that this calling is universal to all created life. See n. 73 above.

> ourselves in the divine field of force. That is why charisma is also described
> as *dynamis* and *energeia*... In the charismatic experience of the Spirit, we
> experience the reciprocal perichoresis of God and ourselves. That is a much
> more intimate communion than the community between Creator and
> creature. It is the communion of reciprocal indwelling. In the Holy Spirit
> the eternal God participates in our transitory life; and we participate in the
> eternal life of God.[132]

The charismatic vibrancy of the Spirit creates a closer, more intimate communion with God.

In Moltmann's cosmic theology, then, the Spirit is not restricted to the
church, but is at work in creation to bring the cosmos to its new creation.
Emphatically, the Holy Spirit is not the monopoly of the church. Rather,
the Spirit uses the church to bring about the eschatological rebirth of life
and the new creation of all things.

Political Significance of Eschatology

Moltmann's theology, from beginning to end, is intentionally political in
orientation. The combination of eschatological hope with the theology
of the cross has specific sociopolitical ramifications, already evident in
Theology of Hope (1964), where he spoke of the 'Exodus of the Church',
and in *The Crucified God* (1972), where he wrote about the 'way to the
political liberation of humanity'. His latest work on method, *Experiences in
Theology* (2000), continues to be thoroughly political in orientation. 'Political theology', in Moltmann's terms, seeks the liberation of the weak, the
poor, the suffering, the hungry, the disabled, any who have been victimized,
or marginalized, and the victimizers as well, who need to be liberated. He
sides with the feminist critique of theology which seeks to breakdown the
patriarchal structures of church and society. His political theology is akin
to Latin American liberation theology in that it emphasizes a 'preferential
option for the poor',[133] but differs in that it has developed within the

---

132. Moltmann, *Spirit of Life*, pp. 195-96.

133. Along with J.B. Metz and D. Sölle, Moltmann's political theology may have
been influential on the beginnings of Latin American liberation theology. Moltmann
saw a similarity between the two: 'I found there [in Gustavo Gutiérrez's liberation
theology] the perspectives of my own *Theology of Hope* and the praxis of political
theology...the first books on the theology of liberation that was just developing in Latin
America still reflected an entirely European influence'. Jürgen Moltmann, *Experiences
in Theology: Ways and Forms of Christian Theology* (trans. Margaret Kohl; London:
SCM Press, 2000), p. 217. However, Latin American liberation theologians later

Spirit of the Last Days

context of post-war and cold war Europe, and the threat of global nuclear holocaust.[134] His political theology seeks world peace, ecological responsibility and the affirmation of human rights and dignity.[135] It seeks a way for human beings of differing national, racial and ideological contexts to live together humanely.[136] The following will sketch the contours of Moltmann's political theology.

Political theology in Germany, in which Moltmann was associated with J.B. Metz and D. Sölle, developed after the Second World War following the shock of the Jewish holocaust. Moltmann himself was a captured German soldier during the war and experienced the despair of imprisonment and the shock of learning about the Jewish atrocities perpetuated by his own people. It was during his imprisonment that Moltmann became a Christian. Nevertheless, awareness of Auschwitz was the crisis that characterized the theological context in Moltmann's early years as a theologian. How could Christians have allowed the atrocities of Nazism to occur? Both the Catholic and Protestant traditions had failed to speak out effectively against Nazism. Moltmann believes that it was the emphasis on the privatization of faith as personal piety that separated Christians from politics. Instead of speaking out against Hitler, Christians who abhorred what was occurring 'interiorized' their faith in order to preserve their innocence. Luther's two kingdom doctrine contributed to the privatization of faith and the 'pietistic' withdrawal of Christians and the church from the political sphere. Religious conscience was then confined to the church, while society was left to the 'unscrupulous politics of power'.[137]

An older political theology, articulated by National Socialist theorist Carl Schmitt, argued as early as 1922 that a correspondence existed

distanced themselves from First World theology in an effort to find their own identity in the 'liberation of the suffering and dying of the poor'. Moltmann, *Experiences in Theology*, pp. 218-20; cf. Miroslav Volf, 'A Queen and a Beggar: Challenges and Prospects of Theology', in *idem* (ed.), *The Future of Theology* (Grand Rapids: Eerdmans, 1996), pp. ix-xviii (ix).

134. Jürgen Moltmann, 'Political Theology and Theology of Liberation', in Joerg Rieger (ed.), *Liberating the Future: God, Mammon and Theology* (Minneapolis: Fortress Press, 1998), pp. 60-80 (61-62).

135. Jürgen Moltmann, 'Christian Theology and Political Religion', in Leroy S. Rouner (ed.), *Civil Religion and Political Theology* (BUSPR, 8; Notre Dame: University of Notre Dame Press, 1986), pp. 41-58 (44).

136. Jürgen Moltmann, 'Politics and the Practice of Hope', *CC* (March 1970), pp. 288-91 (290).

137. Moltmann, 'Political Theology and Theology of Liberation', pp. 62-63.

between political concepts and theological concepts. Political concepts, according to Schmitt, were nothing more than secularized theological concepts. He defended the political policies of the National Socialist dictatorship through the existential categories of being and non-being and the dualistic friend/foe thinking of political Manichaeism. Schmitt's theology was really a political theory designed to support the status quo of the state and effectively reduced theology to political ideology.[138]

Moltmann's political theology, however, started to take shape in the Christian-Marxist dialogue of 1965–67. It may be seen as the first truly post-Marxist theology, in that following Barth it took seriously the Feuerbach/Marx critique of religion and took up concrete political/theological stands. In response to the Marxist critique, political theology revisioned Christian theology in view of 'the passion of Jesus for the poor'. For Moltmann, this found roots in the criticism of religion by the Old Testament prophets. The Jewish-Marxist philosophy of Ernst Bloch, which traced the 'principle of hope' to biblical sources, had a profound influence on Moltmann's eschatological vision, linked to *theologia crucis*. This was articulated in *Theology of Hope* and *The Crucified God*. Unfortunately, the Marxist–Christian dialogue was effectively curtailed in 1968, when the Soviet Union invaded Czechoslovakia.[139]

Political theology seeks to free the church from its captivity to the ruling power structures of society. It is critical of the notion that there is such a thing as 'apolitical theology'. Those who insist that theology must be apolitical are covertly allied with conservative politics and are in reality politically involved. Although an alliance of private 'apolitical' religion with conservative politics protects its privilege in society, this happens at the cost of the church's critical force. 'The real question is not whether the churches should be allowed to become political, as the critics keep on fearing, but whether the Church [*sic*] can extricate itself from the unconscious, hidden compromising practice of political theology. The Church must develop a critical and self-conscious political theology.'[140]

---

138. Moltmann, 'Christian Theology and Political Religion', p. 43.

139. Moltmann, 'Political Theology and Theology of Liberation', pp. 63-64; Elisabeth Moltmann-Wendel and Jürgen Moltmann, *God—His and Hers* (trans. John Bowden; New York: Crossroad, 1991), pp. 34-35.

140. Jürgen Moltmann, 'The Cross and Civil Religion', in Institute of Christian Thought (ed.), *Religion and Political Society* (trans. Institute of Christian Thought; New York: Harper & Row, 1970), pp. 14-47 (19).

Political theology for Moltmann, then, is the public, critical and liberative analysis of the church's role and responsibilities in society.[141] It is not simply the analysis of the relationship between theology and politics, church and state, but is an attempt to become aware of the political dimensions inherent in faith and theology. As the attempt to awaken the political consciousness of all aspects of theology,[142] political theology is not simply political ethics, but asks about the political consciousness of theology itself.[143]

> The new political theology presupposes the public witness of faith and the political discipleship of Christ. It does not aim at 'politicizing' the churches, a frequently made accusation, but asks rather to 'christianize' the political existence of churches and Christians according to the standard of Christian discipleship given in the Sermon on the Mount.[144]

The teachings of Jesus are seen as critical for the transformation of society.

Political theology is 'not a "progressive", liberal theology of the established middle class, but rather a politically and socially critical theology of those who are victimized by the First World'.[145] Moreover, it is not simply an academic theology, but is rooted in the experience and expectations of different praxis groups and protest movements throughout Europe. It is not the 'progressive theology' of liberal Protestantism or modern Catholicism (an accusation made by liberation theologians against European political theology), but has its roots in the anti-establishment theology of Karl Barth and the resistance of the Confessing Church. This political theology adopts a critical position towards the self-justification of power establishments. It takes a critical stance against 'political religion', 'civil religion', 'patriotism', the 'Christian West' and 'anti-Communism' in order to demythologize the political and economic powers. Political theology speaks on behalf of the victims of violence to give them voice. It is embedded in various praxis groups and highlights the revolutionary traditions of Scripture and church history, particularly Jesus' message of the reign of God coming to

---

141. Moltmann, 'Christian Theology and Political Religion', p. 43.

142. Moltmann, 'Cross and Civil Religion', p. 19.

143. Jürgen Moltmann, 'Political Theology', in *idem, The Experiment Hope* (ed. M. Douglas Meeks; trans. M. Douglas Meeks; Philadelphia: Fortress Press, 1975), pp. 101-118 (102-103).

144. Moltmann, 'Political Theology and Theology of Liberation', p. 63.

145. Moltmann, 'Political Theology and Theology of Liberation', p. 60.

the poor. Political theology is contextual, but also has universal dimensions because theology itself has universal implications.[146]

Political theology, for Moltmann, is not one-sided in the sense that its sole purpose is social improvement, but insists that the suffering of humanity is also related to human anxiety and alienation from God. While sociopolitical transformation is essential, liberation must also come through faith. Thus liberation through faith, and through social improvements, go hand-in-hand.[147] In fact, Moltmann criticizes liberation theology, not for its vision of socio-economic liberation of the poor, but because it sometimes neglects the cultural and religious dimensions of liberation. He thinks that the rise of Pentecostalism in Latin America is related to the deficit of the cultural and religious dimensions in liberation theology. 'The poor want to be addressed not only in terms of what they do not have, but also be respected for who they are.'[148]

Moltmann's political theology takes its bearing from an eschatological understanding of the theology of the cross. As already discussed, the dialectic of cross and resurrection is important in Moltmann's Christology as the anticipation of the eschatological kingdom. The passion of the crucified Christ takes on the universal dimensions of apocalyptic suffering, in that the 'apocalyptic sufferings of "this present time" are gathered up in "the sufferings of Christ" on Golgotha. Jesus suffers them in solidarity with others, and vicariously for many, and proleptically for the whole suffering creation.'[149] The theology of the cross is not to be understood as passive resignation in human suffering. If the cross is seen as the 'opiate of the people' (Marx) that forces people to be subservient to dominant masters, then it becomes a blasphemy. However, Christians find in the cross 'the expression of human dignity and self-respect in the experience that God counts them worthy and the belief that Christ loves them'.[150] This *theologia crucis* moves beyond the mysticism of the cross as passive suffering to recognize the active suffering of Christ, and calls for our imitation of the crucified Christ as the basis of solidarity and resistance to suffering and all forms of oppression.[151]

146. Moltmann, 'Political Theology and Theology of Liberation', pp. 69-71.
147. Moltmann, 'Political Theology' (*Experiment Hope*), p. 115.
148. Moltmann, 'Political Theology and Theology of Liberation', p. 74.
149. Moltmann, *Way of Jesus Christ*, p. 152.
150. Moltmann, *Crucified God*, p. 50.
151. Moltmann, *Crucified God*, p. 53.

Moltmann is greatly influenced by Luther's theology of the cross and the 'functional' analyses of Feuerbach, Marx and Freud. The latter three give rise to the question of how the cross should function politically within a community. The cross is not indifferent to history or resigned to circumstances, but functions as critique and divine rejection of all political and civil religions that support oppression. The symbol of the crucified Christ opposes all forms of political oppression and domination.

> Functionally, Christ was seditious. Functionally, his crucifixion was a regnant government's repression of an alternative ultimate value that would relativize its own claims to be absolute. Functionally, the cross was the initial rejection by the Church of all political structures seeking to become religious.[152]

By applying a functional methodology to the theology of the cross, Moltmann is able to address the Marxist critique of religion through the symbol of the suffering Christ who stands against all forms of oppression.

Moltmann also relies on Luther's theology of the cross, which contrasts the knowledge of God through Christ's suffering to knowledge of God derived through creation and history (natural theology). Although Luther was willing to admit that there could be 'indirect' knowledge of God through creation, this knowledge was distorted through human sinfulness. Human beings use this knowledge for self-deification. However, knowledge of the cross and the suffering of Christ caused by inhumane human beings destroys the human attempt at self-deification by restoring to humanity an abandoned and despised humanity. The cross is the picture of true humanity.[153] Moltmann's critique, however, is that while Luther employed the cross in theoretical and practical terms, he failed to use it politically. Instead of applying the theology of the cross critically to the Peasant Wars

---

152. Thomas Hughson, 'Introduction', in Institute of Christian Thought (ed.), *Religion and Political Society*, pp. 11-13.

153. Moltmann, *Crucified God*, pp. 70-73. In his 1518 'Thesis for the Heidelberg Disption', Luther clearly identifies the sufferings of the cross, rather than natural theology, as the basis for theological discourse. He states: '19. The one who beholds what is invisible of God, through the perception of what is made [cf. Rom. 1.20], is not rightly called a theologian./ 20. But rather the one who perceives what is visible of God, God's "backside" [Exod. 33.23], by beholding the sufferings of the cross./ 21. The "theologian of glory" calls the bad good and the good bad. The "theologian of the cross" says what a thing is./… But without a theology of the cross, man misuses the best things in the worst way'. John Dillenberger (ed.), *Martin Luther: Selections from his Writings* (New York: Anchor Books, 1961), pp. 502-503.

of 1524–25 and standing in solidarity with the oppressed against the oppressors, Luther reverted back to a 'non-Protestant mysticism of suffering and humble submission'. According to Moltmann,

> The task therefore remained of developing the theology of the cross in the direction of an understanding of the world and history. The theology of the cross had to be worked out not merely for the reform of the church but a social criticism in association with practical actions to set free both the wretched and their rulers.[154]

The suffering of Christ is the point of solidarity and resistance to the suffering humanity and through human solidarity with the crucified Christ, the dawning of the eschatological kingdom approaches. The visionary eschatological contours of what Moltmann sees as the political implications of his theology include a theology of human rights and dignity, the feminist critique of patriarchy, a theology of peace and an ecological theology.

Moltmann is clear that 'The *political and social directions of the churches gain* their *universal significance* only in relationship to human rights. With regard to human rights, the church necessarily becomes the "church for others" or the "church for the world".'[155] The inviolability of human rights was first spelled out in the United Nations' 'General Declaration of Human Rights' of 1948 and includes but is not limited to the Human Rights Treaty of 1966. Although the concept of human rights emerged in the context of post-war Europe, it is universally axiomatic irrespective of its European origins. Human rights now have an overriding authority over any and all national, religious and cultural interests.[156]

Yet human rights must be distinguished from human dignity. Moltmann writes:

> Human rights exist in the plural, but there is only a single human dignity. Human dignity is one and indivisible. It does not exist to a greater or lesser degree, but only wholly or not at all. Human dignity means the quality of being human, however the various religious and philosophies may define this. At all events, human dignity makes it illegitimate to subject human beings to acts which fundamentally call in question their quality as what Kant called 'determining subjects'. Because human dignity is one and

---

154. Moltmann, *Crucified God*, pp. 72-73.

155. Jürgen Moltmann, 'The Theological Basis of Human Rights and the Liberation of Human Beings', in *idem*, *Experiment Hope*, pp. 147-57 (147-48).

156. Jürgen Moltmann, 'Human Rights, the Rights of Humanity and the Rights of Nature', in Hans Küng and Jürgen Moltmann (eds.), *The Ethics of World Religions and Human Rights* (Concilium, 2; London: SCM Press, 1990), pp. 120-35 (121).

indivisible, human rights are a single whole too, and cannot be added to, or subtracted from, at will.[157]

Human dignity, then, is fundamental to what it means to be human, but human rights exist in plurality and can generally be grouped in the following categories as: '1. protective rights—the rights to life, liberty and security; 2. freedom rights—the rights to freedom of religion, opinion and assembly; 3. social rights—the right to work, to sufficient food, to a home and so forth; and 4. rights of participation—the right to co-determination in political and economic life'.[158]

The Christian theological basis of human rights and dignity is rooted in the image of God in humankind and the future, eschatological orientation of the gospel. The human being has been fashioned in the image of God, so that the inner dignity, freedom and responsibility of the human being is not located in the state, as was the case in the divine rule of kings, but in the human being.

> If man is God's image, he is a responsible person and bears the rights and duties of freedom... The state is therefore no longer 'God on earth', but has to respect and guard the dignity of man. [*sic*]... Basic rights are the standards by which civil rights and state power must be criticized and judged.[159]

At the same time, the future orientation of humanity in the coming kingdom of God means that the goal of God's liberative acts is to create a new and just humanity. The image of God in the human being and the future orientation of this image in the kingdom binds human beings together so that historical and cultural differences are overcome.[160]

Moltmann insists, however, that human rights and dignity are effective only when human beings stand up for the oppressed. Human rights are still at risk because there are too few sociopolitical powers that support them and ensure their continued existence.[161] Nevertheless, human rights and dignity can be upheld through resistance, whether resistance to racism,[162]

---

157. Moltmann, 'Human Rights, the Rights of Humanity and Rights of Nature', p. 122.

158. Moltmann, 'Human Rights, the Rights of Humanity and Rights of Nature', p. 122.

159. Moltmann, 'Human Rights and the Liberation of Human Beings', p. 150.

160. Moltmann, 'Human Rights and the Liberation of Human Beings', pp. 149-50.

161. Moltmann, 'Human Rights and the Liberation of Human Beings', p. 149.

162. Jürgen Moltmann, 'Racism and the Right to Resist', in *idem, Experiment Hope*, pp. 131-46.

socio-economic oppression,[163] mistreatment of the disabled, or any other instance where human beings stand in need of liberation.

Moltmann also argues that rights must extend to nature. First, the protection of the environment is a minimal condition of human dignity, for if the natural environment were to collapse, the human race itself would be threatened. Yet nature must be protected for its own sake and therefore has its own dignity. As such, creation is seen as the source of natural rights for all living creatures on the earth. Animals are living creatures with rights of their own and may not be mistreated or manipulated for economic gain. They must be protected. Otherwise, the moral cost will result in indifference towards the life of animals, embryos and other people.[164]

Moltmann's political theology is also evident in his use of the feminist critique of patriarchy. He argues for a revision of Christian anthropology to eliminate patriarchy and male-domination within the church and throughout society at large. He argues, though, that with the 'Constantinian captivity' of the church, Christianity was soon dominated by men and made to serve patriarchy. 'This had a crippling effect on its liberating potential', claims Moltmann, '…the liberation of women and then of men from patriarchy goes hand in hand, therefore, with the rediscovery of the freedom of Jesus and of the energies of the Spirit'.[165]

Moltmann's starting point for the critique of patriarchy is different than the feminists who want to revision the image of 'God as mother'. Moltmann's attitude is ambivalent to this approach. Feuerbach's critique of 'God as Father' is just as relevant to 'God as Mother'. However, it is through the social doctrine of the Trinity and the rediscovery of the femininity of the *ruach* of God that Moltmann believes the 'feminine side' of God can be discussed.[166] As already mentioned, Moltmann believes that there needs to be a rediscovery of the 'feminine' imagery of God through the 'maternal' understanding of the work of the Spirit.

163. Moltmann, 'Political Theology and Theology of Liberation', pp. 64-65.

164. Moltmann, 'Human Rights, the Rights of Humanity and Rights of Nature', pp. 128-33.

165. Elisabeth Moltmann-Wendel and Jürgen Moltmann, 'Becoming Human in New Community', in their *Humanity in God*, pp. 109-125 (112); also in Constance F. Parvey (ed.), *Community of Men and Women in the Church* (Philadelphia: Fortress Press, 1983), pp. 29-42 (31-32). Moltmann argues that this patriarchy was essentially foreign to Christianity until the time of Constantine, but he avoids the issue of patriarchy in the Old Testament in the genealogy of Abraham, Isaac and Jacob and in the New Testament.

166. Moltmann-Wendel and Moltmann, *God—His and Hers*, p. 36.

The patriarchalization of human relations, along with other forms of oppression, dehumanize both the oppressed and oppressor, women and men. 'On the one side, there is the tyrant, on the other side the slave; here the dominating man and there the serving woman. Oppression destroys humanity on both sides. The oppressed person is robbed of humanity, and the oppressor becomes an inhuman monster.'[167] For the man, oppression takes the form of suppressing so-called feminine feelings to control certain instincts. The man is forced to be a subject of reason and will, while denying his heart, feelings and physical needs, which is a subjugation of his so-called 'frail', 'emotional' and 'physical' feminine side. Patriarchy forces women into the role of mother and wife, corresponding to feminine stereotypes. The man then vacillates between unresolved 'mother-fixation' and 'machismo'. These wrongly enforced roles must end, argues Moltmann, if humanity is to become free and mature.[168]

Patriarchy also has an unhealthy influence on how we view God. God is seen as an isolated male, depicted in concepts such as Almighty, Absolute Ruler, who determines everything but is influenced by nothing. God is therefore incapable of suffering. Authority ascends from the patriarchal family, to the national patriarchy, to the patriarch of the church, and finally to the patriarch of heaven. Authority is legitimized through the descent of the heavenly patriarch downwards. God is defined by the function of ruler of the world. God is seen as head of Christ, Christ as head of the church and the man as head of the woman. However, this model of God has no relevance to the mystery of Jesus and his 'Abba Father'.[169] Creation is in a state of senseless suffering, making the patriarchal model of God problematic. For the Christian, God is 'solely and exclusively the "Father of Jesus Christ" ', because only Christ who endures all suffering makes this address to God 'possible and meaningful'.[170] Jesus' reference to God as Abba Father is linked to their mutual suffering, not to God's description as male.

---

167. Moltmann-Wendel and Moltmann, *Humanity in God*, p. 113.

168. Moltmann-Wendel and Moltmann, 'Becoming Human in New Community', in their *Humanity in God*, p. 113. Moltmann identifies specifically how patriarchical stereotypes hurt men, but leaves the discussion of how patriarchical stereotypes hurt women to others.

169. Moltmann-Wendel and Moltmann, 'Becoming Human in New Community', in their *Humanity in God*, p. 114; Moltmann-Wendel and Moltmann, *God—His and Hers*, pp. 5, 18, 35.

170. Moltmann-Wendel and Jürgen Moltmann, *God—His and Hers*, p. 35.

Moltmann's theology of peace is another point of political criticism and initially a response to the cold war and the proliferation of nuclear armaments. A focal point for Moltmann was the Vietnam War (one of the many conflicts related to the cold war). Although this war ended in 1973 after worldwide protests, there remained the deadly arms race between the Soviet Union and the Western world. Political-theological criticism took shape against the proliferation of arms through theologically legitimized protest movements and civil disobedience.[171] According to Moltmann, the non-violent peace movement was one of the factors that led to the collapse of 'forced socialism' in East Germany. Yet with the subsequent collapse of the Soviet Union the threat of nuclear disaster is no less dangerous.

Since the nuclear bombing of Hiroshima in 1945 we have lived in 'the last epoch of humankind; for we live in the time in which the end of humankind can be brought to pass at any moment'.[172] This means that politics has moved (and needs to move further) away from national interests to a 'common age of all nations and all people'.[173] We live in an epoch that needs to shift away from a military system of nuclear deterrence as a means of ensuring peace, to developing a political system for securing peace, and this will require radically different theological thinking.[174]

The way to peace, then, is twofold: The first is, as has already been discussed, through the cross of Christ which is the 'justifying, reconciling and peacemaking action of God'.[175] The second is through the church as the 'instrument' of God's justice and sign of the coming new creation. Yet peace cannot come until there is justice in the world. Justice creates peace. The justice of God creates rights for human beings and thereby creates the 'kind of peace that endures: "shalom". It follows from this that there is no peace where injustice and violence rule… Peace does not bring justice, but justice brings peace.'[176] Christians as peacemakers therefore have a political

---

171. Jürgen Moltmann, 'Political Theology and Theology of Liberation', p. 66.

172. Jürgen Moltmann, 'Political Theology and the Ethics of Peace', in Theodore Runyon (ed.), *Theology, Politics and Peace* (Maryknoll, NY: Orbis Books, 1989), pp. 31-42 (32); also in Leroy S. Rouner (ed.), *Celebrating Peace* (BUSPR, 11; Notre Dame: University of Notre Dame Press, 1990), pp. 102-117; *idem*, 'God and the Nuclear Catastrophe', pp. 160-64.

173. Moltmann, 'Political Theology and the Ethics of Peace', p. 32.

174. Moltmann, 'Political Theology and the Ethics of Peace', p. 33.

175. Moltmann, 'Political Theology and the Ethics of Peace', p. 36.

176. Moltmann, 'Political Theology and the Ethics of Peace', pp. 37-38.

calling, because they are participants in the coming kingdom. Moltmann writes:

> From every *gift* (*Gabe*), however, arises a corresponding task (*Aufgabe*). If the Christians are the *handiwork* (*Werk*) of this justice creating and peace-making action of God, then they are also and with equal seriousness the *instrument* (*Werkzeug*) to express this divine action in this world... If the peace of God is experienced in the church, then the *hope* for 'peace on earth' also originates here. If *faith* responds to the experienced justice of God with thoughts, words and works, *hope* anticipates a new just world. If *faith* embraces the peace of God, *hope* anticipates a new world of peace. If *faith* finds the comfort of God in all suffering, hope *looks* toward a new creation in which there will be no suffering, pain or crying.[177]

The 'shalom' of the new creation is the basis for peace and political action in the present world. Yet peace must ultimately come from God.

> Because God creates justice, Christ is. Because God establishes peace there is a Church. Therefore Jesus Christ's Church has to be the Church of peace. Accordingly all divine service in the Church of Christ begins with a salute of peace, and the Church's blessing is pronounced with the peace of God, which passes all understanding.[178]

'Shalom', then, is an inclusive term that first of all means 'blessed joy of a successful life', and the sanctification of life and all its relationships. 'Shalom' does not distinguish salvation from well-being or the peace of God from secular peace, but is universal. It is a prophetic term connoting the promised future salvation for all creation, in which violence, suffering and death will be abolished. 'Shalom' is recognized in the messianic Christ as the experience of salvation through the Spirit as the sign of universal peace in God for the entire cosmos.[179] It is also the basis for ecological responsibility in the world as anticipation of the peace of the new creation, a subject I will now address in more detail.

Cosmic Eschatology and the Transformation of Creation

In *God in Creation*, Moltmann affirms that the whole world that God has created will be included in the eschaton as part of the new creation. He

---

177. Moltmann, 'Political Theology and the Ethics of Peace', pp. 36-37.

178. Jürgen Moltmann, 'Peace the Fruit of Justice', in Hans Küng and Jürgen Moltmann (eds.), *A Council for Peace* (Concilium, 1; Edinburgh: T. & T. Clark, 1988), pp. 109-119 (110).

179. Moltmann, 'Peace the Fruit of Justice', pp. 111-13.

also argues that a modified concept of evolution must be understood as the self-movement of the cosmic Spirit as the Spirit of creation,[180] and divides creation into three parts: creation in the beginning; continuous creation; and the consummation of creation in the kingdom of glory. Creation in the beginning is understood pantheistically as 'God "withdrawing himself from himself to himself" in order to make creation possible'.[181] By withdrawing himself, God creates an open-ended system of space and time. Moreover, creation in the beginning is not the goal which was ruined by original sin, but the goal is the future kingdom of glory which is the new creation.[182] Continuous creation does not contradict creation in the beginning, but takes its being from it. Continuous creation includes the evolutionary process which creates new life and it includes the process of history. Continuous creation is not simply the re-creation of what God has already created, but is directed towards the final consummation of creation. Thus continuous creation must be viewed as 'the *preservation* of the world he has created, and the *preparation* of its completion and perfecting'.[183] Finally, the future of creation is the eschatological consummation of creation as the new creation. The consummation of creation, however, is not the end of creation, but a new beginning. It is the time when God will indwell creation and manifest divine glory.[184] All creation is an open system in that the eschaton is open to the fullness of life through the eternal indwelling of God.

Yet Moltmann does not wholeheartedly adopt the concept of evolution as the epitome of the process of continuous creation. He discusses both the promise and problems of the evolutionary process in dialogue with Teilhard de Chardin, who was optimistic that the evolutionary process would lead to a new 'ultrahuman' state. Teilhard questions the one-sidedness of the doctrine of redemption and original sin, arguing that it fails to envision 'the completion of creation through the gathering together of all things under the head, who is Christ, and through their entry into that fullness of God which will one day be "all in all"'.[185] Teilhard shifts the focus from 'Christ the redeemer' to 'Christ the evolutor'. This ultrahuman perfection

180. Jürgen Moltmann, *God in Creation: An Ecological Doctrine of Creation* (trans. Margaret Kohl; London: SCM Press, 1985), p. 19.

181. Moltmann, *God in Creation*, p. 88.

182. Moltmann, *Crucified God*, p. 207.

183. Moltmann, *God in Creation*, p. 209.

184. Moltmann, *God in Creation*, pp. 212-13.

185. Moltmann, *Way of Jesus Christ*, p. 292.

will take place through the process of evolution and will coincide with the crowning of the Incarnation in the future. The completion of evolution corresponds to 'the completion of God', making the divinization of creation the reverse side of God's Incarnation. Thus the Incarnation is not exhausted in the historical person of Jesus of Nazareth, but includes the evolutionary process of 'Christificating' the cosmos through the cosmic Christ. God comes to us from in front of us and draws the cosmos to God's self.[186] This future is defined by Teilhard as the 'Omega point'.

One can see an influence of Teilhard's cosmic theology on Moltmann, particularly as it relates to the consummation of creation by the cosmic Christ, who stands in the future and beckons creation to its glorification in him. However, Moltmann is critical of Teilhard's callousness towards the suffering of life. Teilhard continually tries to find the meaning of natural and human catastrophes for the evolutionary process, so much so that when the atomic bomb was dropped on Hiroshima,

> Teilhard was filled with enthusiastic admiration for the scientific and technological advance which the achievement of a scientific super-brain acting in teamwork had brought to humanity. He believed that the control of atomic power would promote the evolution of humanity and the human consciousness in a hitherto unheard-of-way. Here Teilhard gave no thought to Hiroshima's hundred thousand dead and the people who are still dying today from radiation damage.[187]

Teilhard was incapable of believing that there could be a nuclear holocaust or ecological disaster that would annihilate humanity, trusting instead in 'life's planetary instinct for survival'. Yet, for Teilhard, whether it be in the victims of the evolutionary competition for survival or the extinction of different species, the suffering and death of evolution must also be embraced and transformed by God in the consummation of creation. Moltmann is critical of this lack of concern for 'evolution's victims'. 'Evolution is not merely a constructive affair on nature's part. It is a cruel one too. It is a kind of biological execution of the Last Judgment on the weak, the sick and "the unfit".'[188] Defining Christ as the cosmic evolutor without redemption makes God cruel:

> A *Christus evolutor* without *Christus redemptor* is nothing other than a cruel, unfeeling *Christus selector*, a historical world-judge without compassion for the weak, and a breeder of life uninterested in the victims... The

186. Moltmann, *Way of Jesus Christ*, pp. 292-93.
187. Moltmann, *Way of Jesus Christ*, p. 295.
188. Moltmann, *Way of Jesus Christ*, pp. 294-95.

history of every form of progress has its other side in the history of its victims. The history of the victors, the survivors and the well-adapted 'fittest' has its price in the suppression of those who are called 'the unfit'.[189]

Because evolution is ambivalent, Moltmann argues that it has no salvific significance in itself. Evolution must be redeemed by Christ in its eschatological transformation as the reversal of evolutionary suffering.

Moltmann's doctrine of creation also calls into question the body/soul dichotomy as it relates to redemption. The doctrine of the immortality of the soul is rooted in Platonic thought, which asserts that only the soul attains immortality while the body remains mortal and corruptible. The body is seen as no more than the husk for the soul, and through death is the soul liberated. It is only the soul that possesses the imprint of the divine image.[190] The body/soul dichotomy is likewise preserved in modern philosophy in the subject/object dichotomy. In the Cartesian model, for instance, the human subject becomes aware of itself through self-reflection. The body is relegated to the objective sphere of bodily, sensory perception and is seen as the corporeal extension of the cognitive subject. The body is the instrument of the mind.[191]

Moltmann is sharply critical of this body/soul dichotomy, arguing that it does not represent the biblical data or patristic doctrine. The Old Testament defines the human being as a constituent whole; body and soul are not component parts of the person, but dimensions of the whole. The inclusion of body and soul in God's eschatological redemption is rooted in 'covenant, community, reciprocity, a mutual enriching, regard, agreement, harmony and friendship'.[192] The relationship between body and soul corresponds to the relationship between individual and community. Moltmann finds trinitarian correspondence to the body/soul distinction in the doctrine of perichoresis. The unity of body and soul corresponds to the 'unique, perfect, perichoretic fellowship of the Father, the Son and the Holy Spirit', not in the sense that there is a hierarchical relationship of the superiority of the Father over the inferior Son, but one of 'mutual interpenetration and

189. Moltmann, *Way of Jesus Christ*, p. 296.

190. Moltmann, *God in Creation*, p. 249; *idem, Coming of God*, pp. 58-59; *idem,* 'Love, Death, Eternal Life: Theology of Hope—The Personal Side', in Frederic B. Burham, Charles S. McCoy and M. Douglas Meeks (eds.), *Love: The Foundation of Hope. The Theology of Jürgen Moltmann and Elisabeth Moltmann-Wendel* (San Francisco: Harper & Row, 1988), pp. 3-21 (6-9).

191. Moltmann, *God in Creation*, pp. 251-52.

192. Moltmann, *God in Creation*, pp. 256-58.

differentiated unity'. 'This presupposes theologically that the presence of God in the Spirit is not located solely in the soul, or in the subjectivity of reason and will; but its place is the whole human organism—that historical Gestalt which people, body and soul, develop in their environment.'[193]

Moltmann rightly points out that the belief of the patristic church was that the whole person would be resurrected. 'I believe in the resurrection of the body and the life everlasting', states the Apostles' Creed. The body itself will be resurrected.[194] The body and soul are inseparable and destined to resurrection. Conversely, both body and soul are affected by death.

The resurrection of the person is contingent, however, on the resurrection of the crucified Christ. 'If Christ has been risen *from* the dead', argues Moltmann, 'then he takes on proleptic and representative significance *for* the dead. He is "the leader of life" (Acts 3.15), "the first to rise from the dead" (Acts 26.23), "the first-born from the dead" (Col. 1.18). He is therefore "the resurrection and the life" in person (John 11.25).'[195] The resurrection has begun in Christ, continues in the life-giving Spirit and will be completed in the general resurrection of the dead. The implication of the resurrection is that the human being can embrace the whole continuum of life, the joys and sorrows, love and suffering, pleasures and pains, because the person need not withdraw from the material conditions of life, but live life to the fullest according to God's intent.[196] Moreover, the resurrection of the body implies that all of creation is to be included in God's salvific transformation. The person cannot be extracted from the natural conditions that produces that person. Both body and soul are the product of nature. If the body is to be resurrected and transformed, then the material conditions that produce and sustain the body must also be transformed. Moltmann thus argues for the cosmic transformation of creation.

The cosmic transformation of creation into the new creation is embodied in two doctrines: the sabbath rest as the feast of creation and God's 'shekinah' indwelling of creation. Moltmann shifts the focus of creation away from the anthropological belief that humankind is the crowning glory of creation, to the more biblical and messianic view that the sabbath day of rest is the crowning of creation. It shifts from the work of creation that culminates in the creation of the human being who is given dominance over the earth, to the seventh-day rest that brings peace ('shalom') to

193. Moltmann, *God in Creation*, p. 259.
194. Moltmann, *God in Creation*, p. 246.
195. Moltmann, *Coming of God*, p. 69.
196. Moltmann, *Coming of God*, pp. 68-69; *idem, Way of Jesus Christ*, p. 235.

creation. The sabbath represents peace with God, peace between body and soul, individual and family, human beings and animals, heaven and earth. The sabbath rest is the beginning of peace with nature.[197] It is the feast of creation that hints at the consummation of creation as creation's redemption. Moltmann writes:

> If we combine the two—the sabbath as the completion of creation and the sabbath as the revelation of God's reposing existence in his creation—then these two elements point beyond the sabbath itself to a future in which God's creation and his revelation will be one. That is redemption. We therefore have to understand redemption as both 'the eternal sabbath' and 'the new creation'. When 'the whole earth is full of his glory' (Isa. 6.3), when God is 'all in all' (I Cor. 15.28 AV) and when God 'dwells' in his whole creation (Rev. 21.3), then creation and revelation are truly one.[198]

The sabbath rest contains the promise of the future, by opening creation up to the coming kingdom. The sabbath is both futurized and universalized as the 'eternal sabbath', when the whole cosmos will be full of God's presence.[199]

The sabbath is such an important theological concept in the Old Testament that, when the Israelites failed to observe the weekly sabbath (Exod. 20.8-11), the yearly sabbath (Lev. 25.1-7) and the sabbath Year of Jubilee (Lev. 25.8-55), God punished them. The Israelites were commanded to allow the land a time of fallowing. They disobeyed. The Babylonian exile was viewed as punishment for the abuse of the land (2 Chron. 36.19-21). Moltmann sees this as a basis for ecological responsibility in modern times. The modern world also needs to allow the land a time of peace and rest, so that it can recover from its overproduction.[200]

However, early in the history of the church the sabbath feast was combined with the feast of Christ's resurrection, identified as 'the Lord's Day'. Where the sabbath hinted at the completion of the present creation, the Lord's Day hinted at the beginning of the new creation, which brings with it Christ's resurrection from the dead and looks to the new creation, when all will be raised from the dead. 'Just as Israel's sabbath turns our gaze back to God's work in creation and to our human week-day work', claims Moltmann, 'the Christian feast of the resurrection looks forward into the

197. Moltmann, *God in Creation*, p. 277.
198. Moltmann, *God in Creation*, pp. 287-88.
199. Moltmann, *God in Creation*, p. 288.
200. Jürgen Moltmann, *Creating a Just Future: The Politics of Peace and the Ethics of Creation in a Threatened World* (London: SCM Press, 1989), pp. 61-66.

future of the new creation'.[201] In this way, the sabbath and 'the Lord's Day' are combined.

God's 'shekinah', on the other hand, is the indwelling of God's presence in the new creation. Present creation will not be annihilated in the new creation, though in Moltmann's articulation of apocalyptic eschatology sin and death will be destroyed, but God's presence will be fully manifested. Where 'creation-in-the-beginning' is the beginning of time, brought about through God's panentheistic self-restriction, the new creation will be the de-restriction of God's glory to enfold the whole cosmos. Moltmann writes:

> The sabbath as the time of the first creation links this world and the world to come. It is *the presence of God* in the *time* of those he has created or, to put it more precisely, the dynamic presence of eternity in time, which links beginning and end, thus awakening remembrance and hope. The eschatological indwelling of God in 'the new heaven and the new earth' is *the presence of God* in the *space* of his created beings... We can continue to relate the two ideas to one another: the weekly sabbath, with the sabbath year, is God's homeless Shekinah in the time of exile from Jerusalem, and in the far country of this world, estranged from God. The eschatological Shekinah is the perfected sabbath in the spaces of the world. Sabbath and Shekinah are related to each other as promise and fulfilment, beginning and completion. In the sabbath, creation holds within itself from the beginning the true promise of its consummation. In the eschatological Shekinah, the new creation takes the whole of the first creation into itself, as its harbinger and prelude, and completes it. Creation begins with time and is completed in space.[202]

God dwells in part in this world through the crucified Christ, but it is through the risen Christ in the presence of the Spirit that the universal 'shekinah' of the new creation is anticipated.

Human beings become 'vessels' of God's indwelling Spirit in the forgiveness of and liberation from sins. They are filled with hope and anticipate God's universal indwelling presence in the new creation.[203] In the new creation, however, God dwells in creation as the *cosmic 'shekinah'*. 'What in history is experienced only among the people of God and in the temple, in Christ and in the Holy Spirit, and was expected of God's future,

---

201. Moltmann, *God in Creation*, pp. 294-95.

202. Moltmann, *Coming of God*, p. 266. In the English translation, sabbath and shekinah are sometimes capitalized and sometimes not.

203. Moltmann, *Coming of God*, p. 267.

is there fulfilled: God's immediate presence interpenetrates everything.'[204] The 'eternal sabbath' is the new creation, when the whole earth is full of God's glory (Isa. 6.3), when God will be 'all in all' (1 Cor. 15.28) and when God 'dwells' in the whole of creation (Rev. 21.3).[205]

The political implications of Moltmann's cosmic eschatology are obvious. If present creation is to be included in the new creation, then it is incumbent on human beings to look after the world in an ecologically responsible manner. Likewise, the doctrine of the sabbath means that creation must be given a chance to recover from overproduction if it is to remain fruitful. This was the lesson of Israel's Babylonian exile. Human beings must also embrace and experience the fullness of life, both body and soul. Embracing life critiques the escapist mentality of withdrawing from the world (whether through monasticism or pietistic traditions). Christians must politically engage the world as a proleptic participation in the coming kingdom, which is our service to God.

Moltmann's eschatological focus is helpful for the four Pentecostal theologians under discussion. Not only do they engage Moltmann's theology (among others), but they revision Pentecostal eschatology by shifting it from the fundamentalist vision of world destruction to hope for the transformation of creation. This includes a corresponding shift from passive resignation to the evil powers of the world to an active political engagement to transform the world as our service to the kingdom. By engaging Moltmann in various ways and to varying degrees, the four Pentecostal theologians are bringing Pentecostals back to their early heritage that prophetically called into question the status quo of church and society. The following chapter, then, is a dialogue between the theologies of Moltmann and the Pentecostals.

204. Moltmann, *Coming of God*, p. 317.
205. Moltmann, *God in Creation*, p. 288.

Chapter 4

ESCHATOLOGICAL DIALOGUE: CONVERGENCES AND
DIVERGENCES BETWEEN MOLTMANN AND THE PENTECOSTALS

Pneumatological eschatology is central to Moltmann's theology and an important component in the theological proposals of Land, Villafañe, Volf and Macchia. The early Pentecostal movement was as eschatological in its orientation as it was pneumatological. The move of the Spirit in charismatic dimensions, and especially speaking in tongues as the sign of baptism of the Holy Spirit, was seen as the latter rain outpouring of the Spirit in preparation for the Lord's return. Although the latter rain doctrine waned and fundamentalist eschatology influenced the development of Pentecostalism in the middle part of the twentieth century, at least for the Classical Pentecostals stemming from the Azusa Street revival, eschatology is still an important component of the full gospel. The theological revisions offered by the aforementioned Pentecostals are an effort to retain the eschatological and pneumatological fervour of the early movement, while contextualizing Pentecostal theology within the contemporary context. These revisions not only critique the alliance Pentecostals made with fundamentalism, but also re-evaluate the more prophetic vision of early Pentecostalism as a critique of current social-political conditions.

One cannot overstate the influence that Moltmann has had in the latter half of the twentieth century on Pentecostals and non-Pentecostals alike. One may ask what accounts for Moltmann's influence on these Pentecostal theologians. It is obvious that the concerns of Moltmann's theology are similar to those of many Pentecostals. Eschatological hope is central to his theology and his later emphasis on the indwelling of the Spirit in the believer, the church and creation is appealing to many Pentecostal theologians, whose heritage is highly eschatological and pneumatological. His position makes room for 'experience' as an active component of theology, not in the sense of a structure of consciousness, or as a disposition of subjectivity in the human being, but in terms of the indwelling of the Spirit. Once again Pentecostals have an affinity with this position. For the

Pentecostal, too, experience of God is specifically viewed as the experience of the Holy Spirit, rather than as an inward human disposition.

Moltmann's social critique may be less appealing to Pentecostals in general, but the Pentecostal theologians in question see a need to move Pentecostalism in a social-critical direction. Villafañe and Volf show more similarity to Moltmann's political theology than Land and Macchia, though social criticism is evident in the theology of the latter two as well. Interest in Moltmann's liberationist thrust may come through a convergence of liberation theology and Pentecostalism in Latin America and Africa. Moltmann's panentheistic theology, with its rejection of a pristine creation damaged by sin and its implied universalism, may be less appealing to some Pentecostal theologians, yet Volf and Land appear to adopt its basic structure.

The influence of the Pentecostals on Moltmann is more difficult to ascertain, and it may come more through Pentecostalism in general than through the four Pentecostals under discussion. Moltmann notes that his first exposure to Pentecostalism came after a lecture series in Linköping, Sweden, for the Missionary Alliance church. At one point in the final service, which was held in a Pentecostal church, someone spoke in tongues. His translator 'suddenly stopped translating', said Moltmann, 'telling me he could not understand it. This was followed by interpretations of what had been spoken.'[1] Moltmann goes on to suggest that with the vital role of charismata at play, the Pentecostal church is in a better position to express itself than the German state-supported churches. Moreover, Pentecostals can help the ecumenical community define charisma more broadly than the rite of ordination. 'I believe', states Moltmann, 'that we need to move away from the state church and toward the church as a community of faith. We would then discover the charismatic gifts presently in all our churches.'[2]

A number of official dialogues have taken place between Moltmann and Pentecostal/Charismatic scholars. The first occurred at the Brighton Conference on World Evangelization in 1991, for which Moltmann was the keynote speaker. His paper later became a chapter in *The Spirit of Life*.[3] It was Miroslav Volf, one of his former doctoral students, who responded to the

---

1. Miroslav Volf, 'An Interview with Jürgen Moltmann', in G. McLeod Bryan (ed.), *Communities of Faith and Radical Discipleship: Jürgen Moltmann and Others* (Macon, GA: Mercer University Press, 1986), pp. 5-12 (7).
2. Volf, 'Interview', p. 8.
3. Moltmann, 'Spirit Gives Life', pp. 22-37.

paper.[4] Other prominent Pentecostal scholars were also in attendance. A subsequent dialogue took place between Moltmann and various international Pentecostal theologians in the *Journal of Pentecostal Theology* over the publication of *The Spirit of Life*.[5] Frank Macchia was one of the dialogue partners. In fact, Macchia writes a further response to Moltmann[6] and translated Moltmann's 'A Pentecostal Theology of Life',[7] later included as a chapter in *The Source of Life*. Furthermore, Moltmann recommends Land's book *Pentecostal Spirituality* in *The Source of Life*,[8] and Land and Macchia were involved in a Concilium dialogue co-edited by Moltmann and Kuschel.[9]

A broad correlation can be seen between Moltmann's pneumatology and Pentecostalism. The rich development of healing and speaking in tongues in his eschatological pneumatology seems odd within his own Reformed tradition, which provides him with neither the resources nor the background for such a development. Arguably, the worldwide presence of Pentecostalism has provided him with these theological resources. Moreover, a broad correlation may be drawn between Moltmann's liberationist concerns and those of some Third-World Pentecostals.[10]

Although Moltmann's theology appeals to the Pentecostal theologians under scrutiny, it is questionable whether it would find resonance with the general Pentecostal constituency. While contemporary Pentecostal theologians are questioning Pentecostalism's alliance with fundamentalism and its damage to the early Pentecostal vision, the general Pentecostal constitu-

4.   Miroslav Volf, 'A Rhythm of Adoration and Action: A Response to Jürgen Moltmann', in Harold Hunter and Peter Hocken (eds.), *All Together in One Place: Theological Papers from the Brighton Conference on World Evangelization* (JPTSup, 4; Sheffield: Sheffield Academic Press, 1993), pp. 38-45.

5.   The respondents included Mark Stibbe, Peter Kuzmic (Volf's brother-in-law), Frank Macchia, Simon Chan, Juan Sepúlveda and Japie Lapoorta. See *JPT* 4 (1994), pp. 3-70.

6.   Frank D. Macchia, 'The Spirit and Life: A Further Response to Jürgen Moltmann', *JPT* 5 (1994), pp. 121-27.

7.   Moltmann, 'Pentecostal Theology of Life', pp. 3-15. Later published as a chapter in Moltmann, *Source*.

8.   Moltmann, *Source*, p. 146.

9.   Moltmann and Kuschel (eds.), *Pentecostal Movements as an Ecumenical Challenge*.

10.   See Cox, *Fire from Heaven*, pp. 173-84.

ency may in fact be tightening its alliance with fundamentalism.[11] The social-critical elements of Moltmann's eschatology may be more in line with the emerging Pentecostal scholarship than the Pentecostal-in-the-pew. Nonetheless, there appear to be varying degrees of influence among Moltmann, Land, Villafañe, Volf and Macchia. This chapter sets up a present dialogue among them, showing both points of convergence and divergence. It focuses on the centrality of eschatology and the continuity/discontinuity of the kingdom, Christ and the Spirit of the kingdom, and the implications of the kingdom for political theology and cosmic eschatology.

The Centrality of Eschatology

In Chapter 3 we saw that eschatology is undeniably central for Moltmann, from his first to his latest work. We also saw in Chapter 2 that eschatology has a central place for all four Pentecostal theologians. Moltmann goes so far as to claim that eschatological hope is not merely one element of Christianity, but characteristic of all Christianity and transforms the present world.[12] Although he has examined other doctrinal issues over the course of his career, eschatological hope for the new creation undergirds his entire theological enterprise.

Land too makes eschatology central, especially for understanding the charismatic impulse of the early Pentecostal movement. The inbreaking of the Spirit of the last days comes through the outpouring of the Spirit at Pentecost, which constitutes the church as an eschatological community, through the universal mission, power and demonstration of the Holy Spirit.[13] Eschatology is an emphasis for Villafañe as well, though his main concern is the development of a pneumatological social ethic for Hispanic Pentecostals. However, this ethic of the Spirit hinges upon the 'reign of God' that is already present in the world, but not yet fully realized.[14] The role of the Christian is to participate in the historical reign of the Spirit to overthrow all forms of oppression and suffering. Volf also makes eschatology central to his theology, and offers a revision of the theology of work and embrace based on the eschatological vision of the new creation. Even his recent work on ecclesiology makes the eschatological gathering of the

---

11. Edith L. Blumhofer, *Restoring the Faith: The Assemblies of God, Pentecostalism and American Culture* (Chicago: University of Chicago Press, 1993), pp. 250-52.

12. Moltmann, *Theology of Hope*, p. 16.

13. Land, *Pentecostal Spirituality*, pp. 59-61.

14. Villafañe, *Liberating Spirit*, pp. 182-83.

whole people of God in the new creation the basis for defining the catholicity of church.[15] For Macchia, eschatology is central as well, but he views the kingdom of God as not only awaiting its future fulfilment in the new creation, but also breaking into history through the events of the Incarnation, Pentecost and the theophanic experiences of God. He is similar to Moltmann when interpreting the Incarnation and Pentecost as eschatological, but dissimilar when emphasizing the theophanic inbreaking of the Spirit as eschatological. All four contemporary Pentecostal theologians have shifted the emphasis from the soon return of Christ to the delayed *parousia*, and from the fundamentalist cataclysmic destruction of the world to an eschatology that seeks the transformation of creation into the kingdom of God.

Also, as we saw in Chapter 1, early Pentecostalism was defined by its latter rain eschatology, with its emphasis on the charismatic moving of the Spirit in the last days as reflective of the outpouring of the Spirit on the day of Pentecost. This eschatology was millennial and dispensational in structure, but different from fundamentalist dispensationalism which sought a withdrawal from the world as a precondition for the world's destruction. The emphasis of early Pentecostalism was on the soon return of Jesus Christ. The outpouring of the Spirit on all flesh as the pre-event of Christ's kingdom was believed to restore personal and social relationships in the church and the world. Early Pentecostals expected that the social damage of sectarian-mindedness, racism and gender divisions would be transformed by the power of the Spirit. There is no question, then, that eschatology was central for the early Pentecostal movement.

The Continuity/Discontinuity of the Kingdom

Eschatologies differ on the question of the continuity or discontinuity of the kingdom of God in the present with its ultimate consummation. Among our four Pentecostal theologians we find varying degrees of convergence or divergence with Moltmann on this question. Steven Land is clearly influenced by Moltmann's theology of hope[16] and proposes a Pentecostal transformationist eschatology as an apocalyptic passion for the kingdom, in which the charismatic manifestations of the Spirit in the present are a prolepsis of the coming kingdom of God. Although Land tends to discuss

15. Volf, *After our Likeness*, p. 280.
16. Land publicly claimed to be influenced by Moltmann at the annual meeting for the Society for Pentecostal Studies, Tulsa, Oklahoma, 8–10 March 2001.

the future *parousia* in terms of the kingdom of God, he does refer to it as the new creation of the new heaven and new earth as well.[17] This kingdom as an apocalyptic vision includes the transformational inbreaking of the kingdom into creation in the present. The tongues of Pentecost (Acts 2) is the 'eschatological key' for understanding the impulse of the Pentecostal movement. Land argues that the eschatological outpouring of the Spirit in the here and now is a sign of hope. Commenting on early Pentecostalism he claims:

> Hope is not given by and in and for the present world order that is passing away. This does not mean they [Pentecostals] demeaned this world. It was in hope which had continuity—a new body, a new earth, a new heaven. But this hope was at the same time discontinuous because it is new—a new creation. With one foot in creation and the other in the age to come, the Pentecostals hoped for the salvation of the lost and hoped for Jesus to come.[18]

Land's own eschatology involves both discontinuity and continuity between the present and the future, at times described by him as a crisis-development dialectic. For the early Pentecostal, significant points of crises were moments when God did something decisive, which made the impossible possible in personal or corporate development. At the same time, salvation history was ongoing and moving towards its fulfilment in the kingdom.[19] Land also cites Moltmann to argue in agreement with him that apocalyptic theology must view the apocalyptic as the separation of sin and death from creation, rather than creation's destruction.[20] For Land apocalyptic hope is discontinuous with the world, for it involves the cosmic separation of the 'powers and principalities' of this world from Christ's kingdom, but continuous in that creation will not be destroyed but transformed.[21]

The eschatological 'reign of God' is prominent in Villafañe's theological proposal as well. His theology is intentionally contextual, addressing especially Hispanic Pentecostals in North America, and is influenced as well by liberation theologians. It is designed to develop a stronger social ethic among Pentecostals. For Villafañe, the reign of God has broken into

17. Land, *Pentecostal Spirituality*, p. 65.
18. Land, *Pentecostal Spirituality*, p. 65.
19. Land, *Pentecostal Spirituality*, pp. 117-18.
20. See Land, *Pentecostal Spirituality*, p. 70 n. 1, where he cites Moltmann's apocalyptic theology in Moltmann, *Theology of Hope*, pp. 124-38; and a secondary source on Moltmann's eschatology by Conyers, *God, Hope and History*, p. 77.
21. Land, *Pentecostal Spirituality*, p. 66.

present creation in the person of Jesus Christ, but awaits its final consummation in the not yet future.[22] As for Moltmann and Land, so also for Villafañe, God's reign involves both continuity and discontinuity between history and God's rule. The reign of God is experienced in the present as the 'Spirit's total liberation', affecting the whole person (both spiritual and physical) in 'concrete historical reality'.[23] While creation awaits the reign of God, we share even now as participants in Jesus' mission of liberation, through 'proclamation' and 'demonstration' of the kingdom in the power of the Spirit of the charismatic Christ. Participation in God's present reign is participation in the power of the future reign which demands political action as a sign of the reign of God and the Spirit's work to restrain evil and to help create a just and peaceful moral order for all humanity.[24]

Villafañe's eschatology resembles that of Moltmann, though there is a strong influence of liberation theology as well.[25] As discussed earlier, an affinity exists between Moltmann's political theology which protests social-political oppression, and liberation theology which emphasizes Jesus' preferential option for the poor. In fact, Moltmann's political theology was probably a powerful impetus for the development of liberation theology.[26] Villafañe argues that the reign of God is the inbreaking of the future reign in the person of Jesus Christ that is already present, but not yet realized. History is therefore continuous and discontinuous with God's rule. The inbreaking of the reign of God through the Spirit brings liberation to the social-political structures of the concrete historical experiences of marginalized Hispanic people. Liberation demands participation in the political process as a sign and instrument of the kingdom. Participating in social-political struggles to expose the elements of oppression and to create change for human betterment is our service to the kingdom. Although Villafañe's transformationist eschatology is akin to that of Moltmann, the only evidence that actually connects them is Villafañe's reference to Moltmann's theology of the cross.[27] Nevertheless, for both Villafañe and Moltmann, the inbreaking of the reign of God in the power of the Spirit not only

22. Villafañe, *Liberating Spirit*, p. 184.
23. Villafañe, *Liberating Spirit*, p. 186.
24. Villafañe, *Liberating Spirit*, pp. 196, 200.
25. There are scattered references to various Latin American liberation theologians, including Leonardo Boff, Gustavo Gutiérrez and Juan Luis Segundo, as well as African American liberation theologians, such as Martin Luther King and James Cone.
26. See Volf, 'A Queen and a Beggar', p. ix.
27. Villafañe, *Liberating Spirit*, p. 172 n. 22.

transforms the person, but the social-political structures of history as well. However, Villafañe prefers to discuss the kingdom in terms of the 'reign of God', whereas Moltmann prefers the 'kingdom of God' and the new creation.[28]

Generally, Moltmann's eschatology is presupposed by Volf, and eschatology is certainly central for him. Volf critiques the fundamentalist influence on Pentecostalism which insists on the apocalyptic destruction of the world, revealing his agreement with Moltmann that the apocalyptic is not to be defined as the destruction of creation. He argues that there must be continuity between the present and the future new creation and that it is inconsistent to assert an otherworldly existence for the soul and the destruction of the world, while at the same time maintaining the resurrection of the body.[29] If anything, Volf is more radically in favour of the continuity between creation and the new creation than the other Pentecostals. For instance, divine healing is not seen by Volf as an element of the atonement, the typical approach articulated by Classical Pentecostals, but as a partial manifestation of the future kingdom in the present. Healing is a proleptic, material manifestation of the resurrection of the new creation.[30]

Volf's eschatological framework, which hopes for the future transformation of creation, underscores his theology of work as well as his theology of embrace. Volf credits Moltmann's eschatology as the basis for his theology of work, arguing that 'at its very core, Christian faith is eschatological. Christian life is life in the Spirit of the new creation or it is not Christian life at all.'[31] Work, articulated as the outward expression of the charismatic gifting of the Spirit, is rooted in the eschatological new creation which will transform the cumulative efforts of work.[32] This is not an evolutionary view of work which will find its *telos* in the kingdom through moral progress, but a contribution by human beings called by God whose work will be transformed by God in the eschaton. The new creation will be established solely by the power of God.[33] Even though Volf identifies

---

28. Throughout his work, Moltmann prefers the term *Reich Gottes* (translated as 'kingdom of God'). In *Jesus Christ for Today's World*, he states that even though 'rule of God' has recently come into greater use, this term implies the seizure of personal, professional or political power and therefore must be used with caution (pp. 8-9).

29. Volf, 'Loving with Hope', pp. 28-29.

30. Volf, 'Materiality', pp. 457-58.

31. Volf, *Work in the Spirit*, p. 79.

32. Volf, *Work in the Spirit*, pp. ix-x.

33. Volf, *Work in the Spirit*, p. 84.

the new creation as a discontinuous gift from God and human participation as prayerful waiting as opposed to doing,[34] there appears to be a stronger continuity between the present and the future creation. This can be seen, for instance, in his articulation of work as 'cooperation' with God for the kingdom, rather than service to the kingdom. Nevertheless, he does state that the new creation will be established in the gracious sovereignty of God.

Volf's theology of embrace is likewise rooted in the eschatological new creation. It allows one to maintain distance from one's own cultural systems, because ultimate allegiance is to God and the future kingdom rather than to the present. This allows one to critique one's own culture and expose areas of oppression and sin (i.e. exclusion). As embryonic creatures of the eschatological new creation, the Christian and the church are expected to criticize and participate in the transformation of the social-political powers that dehumanize, oppress and exclude. Volf's political theology will be discussed below. For now it is important simply to underscore that Moltmann's transformationist eschatology is presupposed in Volf's work.

Macchia's eschatological proposal is dissimilar in that it stems from a Pentecostalist's reading of Wuerttemberg Pietism, specifically that of Johann and Christoph Blumhardt. As an Assemblies of God theologian, Macchia has a more Reformed Pentecostal view of grace and the baptism of the Spirit and displays the influence of Barth. The coming kingdom is not located solely in the future *parousia*, but has already come in the outpouring of the Spirit at Pentecost (Johann Blumhardt) and is anchored in the Incarnational/christological event of the cross (Christoph Blumhardt). Since the kingdom is already present in some measure, history is an important component in the unfolding of the kingdom. The kingdom is already present but hidden. Yet the kingdom breaks into creation from beyond history as well. Thus the event of Pentecost and the future *parousia* are two poles in the revelation of God's eschatological kingdom.[35] For Johann Blumhardt, healing was a sign of the inbreaking kingdom, offered to the church through the outpouring of the Spirit in Pentecost. For Christoph Blumhardt, social-political action was the Christian's service to the kingdom as the healing of history and creation.

Macchia extrapolates from the Blumhardts' theology to argue that a more balanced approach between human participation in the inbreaking of

34. Miroslav Volf, 'The Church as a Prophetic Community and a Sign of Hope', *EJT* 2.1 (1993), pp. 9-30 (20).

35. Macchia, *Spirituality*, p. 161.

the kingdom, and the providence of God to establish the kingdom, is needed in Pentecostalism. Human beings are not instruments for bringing in the kingdom, nor are they passive recipients of the kingdom, but are called to work for the kingdom. The social/cosmic implication is that healing cannot be viewed solely as supernatural, but must include a social-liberationist dimension. Bodily healing is a prolepsis of the resurrection of the dead and the healing of creation. This is akin to Moltmann's argument that the resurrection of the body necessitates the transformation of all creation. For Macchia, social liberation is thus an important component of the inbreaking kingdom.[36] Also, the Pentecostal doctrine of initial evidence, which fundamentally connects Spirit baptism to speaking in tongues, needs to be seen as a sacramental sign of the outpouring of Pentecost and the kingdom. One can push the issue further and suggest that Pentecost itself is an eschatological event, and that tongues as a sign of Pentecost and the kingdom, is eschatological.

Macchia reveals his Pietist and Barthian influence by interpreting the kingdom as already present in history through the Pentecost event. The kingdom is already present but hidden in the unfolding of history, but the kingdom also breaks into history and cannot be seen simply as history.[37] For Macchia, sacrament must include the eschatological dimension of the new creation as the proleptic sign of the inbreaking of the kingdom of God. Macchia's view of sacrament is not dissimilar to Moltmann's, especially as articulated in *The Church in the Power of the Spirit*. Moltmann argues that the sending of the Holy Spirit must be viewed as the eschatological sacrament of the kingdom.[38] 'In the eschatological gift of the Holy Spirit', argues Moltmann, ' "word and sacrament", "ministries and charismata" become comprehensible as the revelations and powers of Christ and his future'.[39] The difference is that for Moltmann all workings of the Spirit are sacramental revelations of Christ, whereas Macchia is specifically interested in defining evidential tongues as one among many sacraments of the eschatological future.

There are other dissimilarities as well. Moltmann's early theology tends to focus on the 'not yet' of the kingdom and therefore calls for the radical transformation of the present. His more recent theology tends to affirm a stronger continuity between the future and the present through the concept

---

36. Macchia, *Spirituality*, pp. 159-61.
37. Macchia, *Spirituality*, p. 163.
38. Moltmann, *Church in the Power of the Spirit*, p. 202.
39. Moltmann, *Church in the Power of the Spirit*, p. 205.

of the indwelling presence of God in creation. Macchia has consistently emphasized a balanced view between the already/not yet dialectic, seeing the kingdom already present but hidden in the Incarnation, cross and resurrection of Christ. As well, the kingdom is already here in the Pentecost event as the Spirit of Pentecost, yet the kingdom is not yet fully revealed. This full revelation will occur in the eschaton.

As has been argued, Moltmann articulates an apocalyptic and transformative eschatology. The apocalyptic is not seen as the destruction of the world, but envisions the cosmic separation of sin and death from creation. The consummation of creation-in-the-beginning will occur in the eschaton simultaneously with the coming of God and the new creation. The new creation will involve the de-restriction of God's glory, so that God will dwell fully in creation, and creation in God. The new creation will be an eternal creation, relative to the eternal God. The kingdom, for Moltmann, is the transformation of history and the social-political realm under the rule of Christ. It does not represent the *telos* of history, but its new beginning. 'The last days' is a concept that points to the juncture between creation and the new creation, when God will judge sin and death and separate them from creation. The millenarian rule of Christ is the time when Christ will rule 'in history' before the new creation to vindicate the suffering of the oppressed who long for justice within history.

All four Pentecostal theologians stand in agreement with Moltmann in revisioning eschatology to reject the fundamentalist's vision of the apocalyptic destruction of the world in favour of the transformation of history and creation into the kingdom of God and the new creation. Land emphasizes the kingdom of God and Volf the new creation, but both concepts are evident in their theologies. For Land, the charismata of the Spirit are the proleptic inbreaking of the kingdom into the present. For Volf, the cumulative effects of work are viewed as the charismata of the Spirit which will be transformed in the eschatological new creation. He too sees healing as the inbreaking of the new creation. Land does not deal with the millenarian aspect of Moltmann's theology, probably because it was articulated after Land's publication, and Volf thinks it unnecessary and even detrimental to Moltmann's eschatology. The millenarian rule of Christ in history risks becoming a historical eschatology that will suppress all contrary viewpoints. Macchia articulates an eschatology that rejects the apocalyptic destruction of the world as well, but he is influenced more by Pietism than by Moltmann. The interpretation of apocalyptic as world destruction was a strain in Wuerttemberg Pietism, especially in Bengel's theology, but

Macchia prefers the prophetic/ethical eschatological vision of the Blum-hardts. The kingdom is already in history and as such will move history to its fulfilment in God, but is not to be identified with history. We are called to participate in the unfolding of the kingdom. Villafañe does not explic-itly reject eschatological world destruction, but his theology of liberation from social-political evil as a sign and instrument of the kingdom, and belief that the fullness of salvation must include the social sphere of his-tory, contradicts apocalyptic destruction.

Dialogue on Jesus Christ, the Holy Spirit and the Kingdom

The emphasis in early Pentecostalism was on the outpouring of the Spirit as both sign of, and preparation for, Jesus' soon return. Although speaking in tongues as the sign of the baptism of the Holy Spirit and divine healing were the most dominant features, the outpouring of the Spirit was seen in the whole plethora of charismata. The emphasis on the Spirit was not to the exclusion of Christ, for the Spirit is the Spirit of Christ and the Spirit's work glorified Christ. However, early Pentecostals exhibited a Christology that was characterized by a 'Jesus piety', rather than attention to historical, christological issues.[40] Nevertheless, the eschatological dimensions of Jesus Christ and the Spirit were important foci in early Pentecostalism.

The relationship of Jesus Christ and the Spirit to the kingdom are major emphases for Land, Villafañe, Volf, Macchia and Moltmann as well. Land argues that early Pentecostals were christocentric precisely because they were pneumatic. The 'full gospel' focuses on Christ because it starts with the Holy Spirit.

> Indeed, Jesus Christ is the center and the Holy Spirit is the circumference of a distinctive Pentecostal spirituality… But the decisive context and ever-present horizon for most usefully and comprehensibly displaying those beliefs, practices and affections is eschatological: the presence of God, as Spirit, is the agent of the inbreaking, soon-to-be consummated kingdom of God.[41]

Land insists that Pentecostals display a 'functional' Christology which focuses on the work of Jesus Christ in justification, sanctification, Spirit-baptism, healing and soon return. He is critical of the argument that Pente-costalism represents a shift from Christology to pneumatology with a

---

40. See Faupel, *The Everlasting Gospel*, p. 283; also see Land, *Pentecostal Spiri-tuality*, p. 96.
41. Land, *Pentecostal Spirituality*, p. 23.

corresponding emphasis on the Spirit over against Christ. Instead, he argues that Christ and the Spirit, love and power, instantaneous and gradual in the divine encounter, are correlative and integrative.[42]

Although Land's emphasis is upon a pneumatology situated within the fivefold gospel of the Wesleyan Holiness and Pentecostal traditions, there is an intimation of Moltmann's christological pneumatology in the background. Land publicly credits Moltmann as being influential in the development of his theology.[43] Land also articulates a functional Spirit-Christology which resembles that of Moltmann. For Moltmann, a perichoretic unity exists between Christ and the Spirit, in which the Spirit acts in, with and through Christ to communicate God's love. The charismatic energies of the Spirit are operative in the church, the world and creation to communicate the kingdom and bring it to fulfilment. Christ acts in the Spirit to bring creation to its fulfilment in God. The relationship between Christ and the Spirit as the eschatological movement of the kingdom are therefore important for both Land and Moltmann.

Land also shows reliance on Moltmann's trinitarian doctrine, not only in the trinitarian correlatives of orthodoxy, orthopraxy and orthopathy, but also by his insistence that the eschatological trinitarian presence of God must permeate Pentecostal faith.[44] For Land, history is the eschatological trinitarian process, in which God was and is the goal and limit of all things. History moves '*by* God *in* God *to* God'.[45] Thus Land argues that:

> God acts in history and is affected by history. Jesus and the Spirit 'sigh and groan' as do creation and believers who share in the eschatological trinitarian process that is in actuality a processional into the new heaven and new earth. Pentecostal spirituality narrates the journey and acts in God in the light and goal of the consummated kingdom reign begun in Jesus and carried forward in the Spirit.[46]

Land starts with Moltmann's claim that the trinitarian origin, presence and goal of Christian existence is summarized in the monarchical, eucharistic and doxological movements. In the monarchical, salvation progresses

---

42.   Land, *Pentecostal Spirituality*, p. 63.

43.   Land publicly noted Moltmann's influence on him at the Society for Pentecostal Studies, Tulsa, Oklahoma, 11–13 March 2001, and credited Moltmann's influence in Land, 'The Triune Center', p. 84.

44.   Land, *Pentecostal Spirituality*, p. 197. Land cites Jürgen Moltmann, 'The Fellowship of the Holy Spirit: Trinitarian Pneumatology', *SJT* 37 (1984), pp. 287-300.

45.   Land, *Pentecostal Spirituality*, p. 198.

46.   Land, *Pentecostal Spirituality*, p. 199.

from the Father through the Son in the Spirit. In the eucharistic, salvation progresses in the Spirit through the Son to the Father. In the doxological, 'God is all in all' and the Godhead opens up to us as 'we know that we are known'.[47] Land diverges from Moltmann to argue that a dispensational understanding of history best describes God's eschatological trinitarian presence, but insists that a threefold dispensation view of history like that of Joachim of Fiori, the Cappadocian fathers, John Fletcher or even Moltmann, is more compatible with Pentecostal dispensationalism than fundamentalist dispensationalism.[48] Thus the Spirit cannot be limited to scriptural inspiration, illumination and empowerment of the believer as certain fundamentalists and some Reformed theologians argue,[49] but the Spirit was and is involved in all things, in creation, in sustaining and directing people towards God.[50]

Thus Land believes that God's trinitarian presence opens up the eschatological horizon. The Father, the Son and the Holy Spirit actively work towards the transformation of creation, not its destruction.[51] According to Land, the 'Spirit-filled Christian is to become part of the teleological process of suffering, healing, hope and victory which presses toward the kingdom of God'.[52] This process includes the charismatic manifestations of the Spirit as part of the journey, intended to move the church and the world towards the final transformation of the kingdom.

For Villafañe, the person of Jesus Christ is the one who brings the reign of God into history. Jesus proclaims the kingdom and demonstrates its miraculous power through the Holy Spirit. Christ's life and mission is inaugurated and empowered by the Spirit. Jesus must therefore be considered the charismatic Christ.[53] The reign of God is particularized in Jesus Christ and made efficacious through the cross. However, the reign of God is universalized through the Spirit as the mediation of the risen Christ in

47.   Land, *Pentecostal Spirituality*, p. 200; cf. Moltmann, 'Fellowship of the Holy Spirit', pp. 298-300.

48.   Steven J. Land, 'A Passion for the Kingdom: Revisioning Pentecostal Spirituality', *JPT* 1 (1992), pp. 19-46 (29-30). The difficulty with Land's argument here is that Moltmann does not argue for a dispensational understanding of history. He is sympathetic with the dispensationalist's eschatological yearnings, but his interest is a transformative eschatological view of history.

49.   See Ruthven, *On the Cessation of the Charismata*, pp. 23, 33-38.

50.   Land, *Pentecostal Spirituality*, p. 200.

51.   Land, *Pentecostal Spirituality*, p. 200.

52.   Land, *Pentecostal Spirituality*, p. 201.

53.   Villafañe, *Liberating Spirit*, p. 184.

us.[54] History is the realm of the Spirit, seeking its liberation of humanity from the oppressive 'powers-that-be'. Creation is likewise in need of the Spirit's liberation.[55] Thus Villafañe's social ethic demands the liberation of the entire social sphere. This social ethic is the purview of pneumatology. This ethic must come first through the liberating Spirit, which looks back to the crucified and risen Christ and forward to the reign of God.[56]

Villafañe does not explicitly argue for a 'Spirit-Christology', but this is implied when he argues that Jesus Christ brings in the reign of God through the kerygmatic and demonstrative power of the Spirit. Jesus is defined as the charismatic Christ and the reign is proclaimed and demonstrated through the miraculous working of the Spirit of God. Christ's life and mission is inaugurated and empowered by the Spirit. The Spirit universalizes the reign of God through the mediation of the crucified and risen Christ.[57] For Villafañe, the cross and resurrection are the focal point for a liberating ethic of the Spirit. Making reference to Moltmann's theology of the cross, Villafañe argues that the cross and resurrection are the point of solidarity and liberation from the oppressive powers-that-be for marginalized Hispanic people. The resurrection is the inbreaking reign of God through the Spirit, and implies an ethic of the Spirit. One can see, then, the similarities between Villafañe's and Moltmann's theology of the cross as the moment of solidarity in, resistance to and liberation from suffering and oppression, as well as a Spirit-Christology that articulates the power and work of the Spirit to bring forth Christ's kingdom.[58]

Volf's Christology and pneumatology are strongly influenced by Moltmann as well and therefore integrally connected to the kingdom. His Christology is a wholehearted adoption of Moltmann's theology of the cross and trinitarian thrust. According to Volf, Moltmann's mature theology of the cross not only sees solidarity as the identity of the suffering Christ with the victims of oppression, but also develops the theme of atonement for the perpetuators of oppression. The sufferings of Christ are not merely his own sufferings, but the point of God's identification with the sufferings of the poor and the weak. Because God is in Christ in the suffering of the cross, the cross becomes the event through which the eternal fellowship of God, divine justice and righteousness flow outward

54. Villafañe, *Liberating Spirit*, p. 195.
55. Villafañe, *Liberating Spirit*, p. 187.
56. Villafañe, 'Contours', p. 6.
57. Villafañe, *Liberating Spirit*, p. 195.
58. Villafañe, *Liberating Spirit*, p. 172 n. 22.

into the world.⁵⁹ Moltmann's mature Christology, argues Volf, supplements the theme of solidarity with the mutual theme of atonement for the perpetuators of oppression. 'Just as the oppressed must be liberated from the suffering caused by oppression, so the oppressors must be liberated from the injustice committed through oppression.'⁶⁰ Volf's theology of embrace, then, is an effort to flesh out this divine self-giving on the cross, so that the godless are not abandoned to their evil but are called into divine communion through atonement. Atonement through God's embrace then becomes the model for human embrace of the other.⁶¹ Thus Volf takes Moltmann's functional understanding of the cross as solidarity for the victims of oppression and atonement for the perpetuators of oppression and further develops the theme of atonement through the metaphor of embrace.

Although not a primary focus under discussion, Volf's ecclesiology reveals a trinitarian perspective influenced by Moltmann. Volf adopts a social understanding of the Trinity and its authoritative implications for the church. He writes: 'a hierarchical notion of the Trinity ends up underwriting an authoritarian practice in the church. In contrast, I have tried to develop a nonhierarchical but truly communal ecclesiology based on a nonhierarchical doctrine of the Trinity.'⁶² Although the Trinity is a mystery that can only be worshipped, the trinitarian history of God with the world is a history of mutual indwelling. The world's *telos* is ultimately to become the dwelling place of the triune God.⁶³

Volf borrows directly from Moltmann and argues that the trinitarian Persons cannot be defined as pure relationality, lest they become transparent and indistinguishable. The 'one substance' then dominates, dissolving the Persons into their relations, so that the Father is defined as fatherhood, the Son as sonship and the Spirit as procession. However, the trinitarian Persons cannot be defined as pure Person either. The divine Persons are constituted 'as subjects', but Person and relation arise simultaneously and mutually in perichoretic unity.⁶⁴ The triune God is the community of Per-

---

59. Volf, *Exclusion and Embrace*, pp. 22-23; citing Moltmann, *Spirit of Life*, pp. 130-38, and with reference to Moltmann's *Crucified God*, *Trinity and the Kingdom*, and *Way of Jesus Christ*.

60. Volf, *Exclusion and Embrace*, p. 23.

61. Volf, *Exclusion and Embrace*, p. 23.

62. Volf, *After our Likeness*, p. 4.

63. Volf, *After our Likeness*, p. 192.

64. Volf, *After our Likeness*, pp. 204-205, 215-16; cf. Volf's citation of the German editions of Jürgen Moltmann, 'Die einladende Einheit des dreieinigen Gottes', in *In*

sons who fully interpenetrate each other. In this social doctrine of the Trinity, the Spirit is not subordinated to Christ, but stands with Christ to bring about the new creation. In human embrace, the peculiarities of the other are inclusively affirmed, not to force uniformity, but to include the other's diversity into my own distinctiveness. This political theology resembles the social doctrine of the Trinity. Because the Trinity is 'open to creation' for both Moltmann and Volf, eschatological hope for humanity and the world has this trinitarian character.

One can also see the influence of Moltmann's pneumatology in Volf's theology of the Spirit. His theology of work shifts from a soteriological understanding of vocation to a charismatic understanding of the gifting of the Spirit.[65] The pneumatological model of work is the proleptic coopera- tion with God's future new creation. Similar to Moltmann's definition of charism, which makes no distinction between the natural and supernatural, the secular and the sacred,[66] Volf argues that the charisms of the Spirit are the basis for the varieties of human work. Charisms are not defined en- tirely in ethical terms, nor are they restricted to the church or to an elite group of Christians in the church, but are ordinary and extraordinary gifts given by the Spirit to all human beings. Thus work as charism is for both the sacred and the secular spheres. The gift of administration is just as much a gifting of the Spirit as the gift of healing.[67] Because work is seen as pneumatological, the alienating element of work is criticized as contrary to God's new creation. Also, because work is based in the Spirit's charisms, a person is not restricted to a single gift or a single task, but may be gifted with many charisms and therefore able to perform many tasks. As such, one may work in several occupations simultaneously or sequentially.[68] All such gifts and tasks are directed by the Spirit towards service to the king- dom.

Although the basis of individual work is the charismata of the Spirit, cumulative work will be transformed and incorporated by the Spirit in the new creation. Work will be transformed and incorporated in the eschaton.

---

der Geschichte des dreieinigen Gottes: Beitrage zur trinitarischen Theologie (Munich: Kaiser, 1991), pp. 117-28 (123-29) and *Trinity and the Kingdom*, p. 172.

65. Admittedly, charismatic gifting is soteriological in nature. The shift Volf is suggesting is from a specifically Lutheran view of work as calling to the Christian life.

66. Moltmann, 'Spirit Gives Life', pp. 23-27; *idem, Church in the Power of the Spirit*, pp. 293-95.

67. Volf, 'Human Work', p. 185.

68. Volf, *Work in the Spirit*, pp. 16-17.

Volf does not believe that human work is part of an evolutionary progress moving towards the kingdom, but he does believe that the cumulative achievements of humanity change what it means to be human and must therefore be included in God's new, transformed creation. All human beings, then, are gifted by the Spirit to work. Work in the Spirit is a proleptic glimpse of the new creation. Yet Volf and Moltmann adopt a charismatic pneumatology that is more in line with the view of the Charismatic movement than that of the Pentecostals. They have also broadened the definition of 'charismatic' to go beyond ecclesiastical activity; the charismatic activity of the Spirit reaches into all of creation to include all things in God's redemptive purpose.

Macchia too argues for an eschatology similar to that of Moltmann with a strong christological and pneumatological framework, but rooted in Johann Blumhardt's focus on the outpouring of the Spirit of Pentecost hidden in history, and Christoph Blumhardt's christological focus on the Incarnation, cross and resurrection of Jesus Christ as the basis for social criticism. Macchia uses the Blumhardts' theology as a foil to point out Pentecostalism's overemphasis on the supernatural aspects of the Spirit in healing and other charismata, and on the individualistic aspects of piety. The pietistic tradition can be a resource for the incorporation of faith and social responsibility into Pentecostalism. This includes criticism of sinful social structures, but also a positive assertion of the Christian's responsibility to participate in the healing of creation.[69]

Macchia also argues that Pentecostals exhibit a Spirit-Christology in which signs and wonders announce the kingdom. This pneumatic Christology does not see the church as the permanent embodiment of the incarnate Word, but as the place for the continual event of renewal through obedience and participation in the life of God.[70] The charismatic Christ leads us through the journey of salvation into conversion, holiness, Spirit baptism, healing and eschatological hope as the messianic experience of the Spirit. The freedom of the Spirit is inseparable from the event of the cross as the critique of disobedience in ecclesiastical policies.[71]

For Macchia, pneumatic Christology emphasizes a 'theophanic' eschatological inbreaking of the Spirit in interruptive, extraordinary and unpredictable ways. The Spirit opens history up to a broader future horizon.[72]

---

69. Macchia, 'Waiting and Hurrying', p. 23.
70. Macchia, 'Tongues as Sign', p. 73.
71. Macchia, 'End-Time Missionary Fellowship', p. 13.
72. Macchia, 'Tradition and the *Novum* of the Spirit', pp. 47-48.

However, Macchia diverges from Moltmann here, because in *Theology of Hope* Moltmann understands 'epiphanic' pejoratively and thinks it confuses the promise of the future kingdom with a religious sanctioning of the present.[73] For Moltmann, epiphanic and eschatological are contradictory terms; for Macchia they are compatible. Nevertheless, the continuity of history with the kingdom is through the cross and revealed in the event of Pentecost, claims Macchia, but its discontinuity is through God's theophanic inbreaking into history. God thus works within history, but above and beyond history as well. For Macchia, tongues is a sign of the theophanic revelation of God. It points to an encounter with God that is not an expression of an inward disposition of the human being, but a divine interruption into the human sphere and into the church. This encounter is beyond words. Tongues is the breakdown of speech in the meeting with the divine.[74]

Macchia and Moltmann converge when they argue that a Spirit-Christology best articulates the relationship and work of Christ and the Spirit. For Macchia, Pentecostalism exhibits this Spirit-Christology by calling for the continual event of renewal in the church, leading Christians through the journey of salvation. For Moltmann, Spirit-Christology is the outward expression of trinitarian fellowship, in which the Spirit binds herself to Christ in condescension and the kenosis of the cross to communicate the message of liberation and the future kingdom to the poor.[75] Macchia diverges from Moltmann when he insists that this Spirit-Christology is 'theophanic', in that Christ interrupts the present through the power of the Spirit to encounter the person in history in order to broaden the eschatological horizon. Although Moltmann argues that the eschatological future breaks into the present through Christ and the Spirit to revolutionize the present, he also sees a continuity of history as the unfolding of the kingdom through the indwelling of the Spirit. The gifts of the Spirit are differentiated from the one gift of Christ and should be seen as natural potentialities in the individual that are actualized for use in the service of the kingdom. He is rightly opposed to an inappropriate distinction between natural and supernatural gifts.[76] Macchia, on the other hand, argues that the kingdom is unfolding in history, but insists that the gifting of the Spirit is not the

73. Moltmann, *Theology of Hope*, pp. 95-102.
74. Macchia, 'Sighs', pp. 57-60.
75. Moltmann, *Way of Jesus Christ*, p. 93; *idem*, *Spirit of Life*, pp. 61-62.
76. Jürgen Moltmann, 'A Response to my Pentecostal Dialogue Partners', *JPT* 4 (1994), pp. 59-70 (67).

actualization of inward potential, but the penultimate inbreaking of the Spirit of Pentecost.

In a dialogue between Moltmann and a number of Pentecostal theologians over the publication of *Spirit of Life*, Macchia states, in agreement with Moltmann, that Pentecostals value the notion that there can be an upwelling of the Spirit of God from within us to move us towards God. But in distinction from Moltmann, Macchia wants to make room for the divine encounter that interrupts us in 'unanticipated ways', revealing God's majesty and power through charismatic signs and wonders. He draws upon Barth's notion of Wholly Other to insist that our encounter with God is 'ambivalent'. Yet it is God who lays claim to all dimensions of life as an act of grace, anticipating the eschatological new creation. Macchia is critical of Moltmann's assumption that the Wholly Other creates a dichotomy between Spirit and life. Macchia claims:

> Moltmann's rejection of God's 'otherness' is one of the basic problems that I, as a Pentecostal, have with his pneumatology. As Barth noted in his *Humanity of God*, a one-sided notion of God's otherness can create the kind of horrifying distance between God and life that Moltmann rightly rejects. Yet God's otherness can also grant us an adequate appreciation for the ambivalence we often feel in the indepth encounter with God—both embraced and alienated, or both comforted and feared. This is because God's awesome presence that lays claim to us in promise and hope can never be associated with created life, nor can it be demonstrated or manipulated. By way of contrast, the Spirit's presence described by Moltmann is indeed identified with life, despite Moltmann's effort to include an element of divine transcendence that 'comforts' us. With Moltmann's notion of life as 'emanating' from the Spirit, any 'confrontation' Moltmann might inject into the discussion will not grasp us very deeply and will certainly not provoke the *mysterium tremendum* that we Pentecostals have come to value in our experience with God.[77]

Not only does the close correspondence between Spirit and creation in Moltmann's theology make Macchia uncomfortable, but he believes that Moltmann is unsuccessful in constructing a Spirit-Christology that frees the Spirit from subordination to Christology, despite his efforts.[78] Macchia would like to see the development of a pneumatology that sees the Spirit 'as an independent eschatological force, calling radically into question our

---

77. Frank D. Macchia, 'A North American Response', *JPT* 4 (1994), pp. 25-33 (26-27).
78. Macchia, 'A North American Response', pp. 32-33.

ecclesiological *and* secular fellowships and institutions and opening them up to *praxis* in unexpected and truly miraculous ways'.[79]

Moltmann's brusque response to Macchia's use of Wholly Other is that it is simply another emphasis on transcendence over against immanence.[80] However, Macchia is really emphasizing the freedom of the Spirit to call into question the status quo in order to transform it. He questions whether it is even possible to emphasize the immanence of the Spirit in life and still stress the eschatological freedom of God and criticism of the Spirit upon our world. Macchia believes that Moltmann's stress on the immanence of the Spirit in all life is important, lest the church slip into passive resignation. But we need to place a corresponding stress on the freedom of the Spirit to break into life from beyond to bring in the new.[81] Curiously, Macchia seems to be drawing Moltmann back to his earlier theological position which called for the revolutionary transformation of the world from the Wholly Other eschatological future. In *Theology of Hope*, Moltmann claims that revelation must be understood as 'promise' which 'announces the coming of a not as yet existing reality from the future'. The kingdom is not simply the anticipation of a future that unfolds through the latent possibilities already contained in history, but the eschatological history that comes entirely from the promise of God's future.[82] It is God's promise of the coming kingdom that transforms the world.

I suggest that an aspect of Moltmann's theology which could help to deepen the thought of the Pentecostal theologians, with the possible exception of Volf, is his theology of the cross. Moltmann's theology of the cross is developed within the Lutheran heritage, and points to God's solidarity, in Christ, with all the suffering of creation. Christ's resurrection is the foretaste of the kingdom, when the dead will be resurrected and creation will be utterly transformed. The dialectic of cross and resurrection is the moment of the inbreaking of the eschatological future into the present. The cross reveals the incarnate and suffering God, totally identified with the godforsakenness of creation, and is the symbol of resistance to all forms of oppression. The resurrection is the symbol of future hope for God's kingdom and a new creation, which seeks the annihilation of death through the victory of

---

79. Macchia, 'A North American Response', pp. 31-32.

80. Moltmann, 'A Response', p. 64.

81. Frank D. Macchia, 'The Spirit and Life: A Further Response to Jürgen Moltmann', *JPT* 5 (1994), pp. 121-27 (122-23).

82. Moltmann, *Theology of Hope*, p. 85.

life, and finds its meaning in the glorification of God.[83] Moltmann addresses the Pentecostal concern to discern the Spirit, and sees the cross as the point of discernment for the Christian life. What endures in the face of the cross is truly of the Spirit of God.[84] Although the Pentecostal theologians, especially Macchia and Villafañe, do see the cross as an important element of a pneumatological eschatology, they could strengthen their theologies through a stronger integration of the theology of the cross with a pneumatological eschatology.[85]

Dialogue on the Political Significance of Eschatology

The message of the latter rain outpouring of the Spirit in Pentecostalism implied a social-political demand upon the church and the world through its prophetic voice. The outpouring of the Spirit on all peoples called into question the racial and gender prejudices of certain segments of society, especially in the United States. All people were called to worship in the Spirit and commissioned to work together in preparation for the soon expected kingdom. Although the critical force of the message shattered within a few years, the seeds of a pneumatological eschatology that envisioned the end of racism and gender division were sown. A revision of Pentecostal theology can revitalize the social-political dimensions of the Pentecostal message as a prophetic call to church and society.

We have seen that Moltmann's theology of hope was immediately a political theology of social justice and international peace, and later became a political theology of the environment as well. The political implications of eschatological hope can also be seen in all four Pentecostal theologians. Volf is the most similar to Moltmann in his political theology and continues to develop the implications of eschatological hope in his theology of work and theology of embrace. Villafañe's social ethics also show similarity to Moltmann's political theology, but Villafañe is probably as much influenced by Latin American liberation theology. However, as Moltmann himself argues, a similarity between German political theology and libera-

---

83. Moltmann, *Theology of Hope*, p. 163.

84. Macchia, 'A Response', p. 67.

85. Although not within the purview of this book, a theology of the cross could be developed within the Pentecostal heritage through its potent symbol of 'pleading the blood of Christ'. The Pentecostal pleads the blood in prayer for salvation, for healing, for help in the face or suffering and torment. The blood is viewed as an important element in the fullness of salvation.

tion theology exists, in that they seek liberation from oppressive conditions, even though the contexts of the two are so different. Land too shows affinity with Moltmann's political theology, but he has not yet fully developed the political implications of eschatological hope. Land has developed the personal and social ethical implications of eschatology through orthopraxy, but he has not yet converted it into a fully-fledged political theology. Macchia articulates a social mission for Pentecostalism that is akin to Moltmann's, but which stems more from the social-political theology of Christoph Blumhardt and the resistance theology of Karl Barth. The similarity between Macchia and Moltmann stems more from their common theological sources in Blumhardt and Barth, though Macchia does claim that Moltmann's theology of creation has helped to shape his recent theology. The following will continue the dialogue between Moltmann and the Pentecostals on the relationship between eschatology and political theology.

Volf's political theology is influenced the most by Moltmann. Volf has continued to construct a political theology in his theology of work, and of embrace. The pneumatological theology of work is first of all a response to the alienation of work in the modern era. Volf claims: 'I believe that economic systems should be judged primarily by three normative principles: freedom of individuals, satisfaction of the basic needs of all people, and protection of nature from irreparable damage'.[86] These principles are judged by the new creation. In the first instance, Volf argues that the new creation protects individual dignity because each person is created in God's image and called to live in relationship with Christ and fellow human beings. In the second instance, the new creation forges community in solidarity, which mobilizes us to fulfil the basic human needs of all people, but especially through the 'preferential option for the poor'. In the third instance, new creation implies a responsibility to preserve the integrity of the natural environment. Nature has the basic right of protection from irreparable damage, because it has an eternal future within God's purposes.[87]

Volf further argues that political theology requires changes both in the life of the individual as social agent and social-structural systems as social arrangements, though he stresses the former.[88] Political theology cannot simply be a social-political call to society by the church, lest it become

---

86. Volf, *Work in the Spirit*, p. 15.
87. Volf, *Work in the Spirit*, pp. 15-16.
88. Volf, *Work in the Spirit*, pp. 20; 42; *idem*, *Exclusion and Embrace*, pp. 20-22.

reduced to a left-wing secular social critique,[89] but must include the dimension of faith. Volf argues:

> Justice is not simply the secular outworking of religious faith but an integral part of that faith…We should neither be so socially naive as to believe that when people have peace with God social arrangements will take care of themselves, nor so theologically blind as to assume that when people live in peace with one another they thereby live in peace with God.[90]

The implication is that an integration of belief and praxis is needed as the people of God wait and work for the kingdom. Moltmann's political theology, which argues for the same principles of protection of human dignity and rights, fulfilment of basic human needs and the protection of the rights of nature, underlies Volf's theology of work. Moltmann also insists that faith is an integral component of political theology. Work, as an outflowing of the Spirit of God, must be humanized and freed from alienating structures. This can be accomplished through a pneumatological view of work which looks for its transformation in the new creation.

Volf's theology of embrace is a significant, new development for political theology. The context is similar to Moltmann's: the social-political conflicts and divisions of Europe. However, whereas Moltmann is responding to the cold war divisions and nuclear build-up, Volf is responding to ethnic conflict in the Balkans. He argues that liberation is an inadequate category for promoting peace. In fact, it often risks producing more conflict. Both sides in conflict believe themselves oppressed. Both sides seek liberation. Thus 'liberation' can be used as an ideology to fuel further conflict.[91] Instead, the Christian's response to the social-political world must operate within the categories of exclusion and embrace. Exclusion is sin. It erects barriers to the other's distinctiveness and makes of another's otherness a symbol of hatred. It seeks to diminish another's humanity and cultural identity. Embrace, on the other hand, is a metaphor for the inclusion of the distinctiveness of the other. I embrace the other, not to absorb the other into my cultural identity, but to understand, respect and accept the other's distinctiveness. Volf's political theology reinterprets the ecclesial issue of unity in diversity within the social-political context. Embrace is a social understanding of reconciliation that hinges on the future, when God will include the diversity of creation with all its otherness within the unity of the triune God indwelling creation.

89. Volf, 'Church as a Prophetic Community', p. 14.
90. Volf, 'Church as a Prophetic Community', p. 23.
91. Volf, 'Vision of Embrace', p. 200.

Villafañe has constructed a pneumatological social ethic akin to political theology. Villafañe's ethic is similar to that of Moltmann and of liberation theology. Both emphasize the 'preferential option of the poor' and a praxis based in the contextualized situation of oppressed peoples. Villafañe's focus is on oppressed Hispanic Pentecostals in the urban centres of the United States, who have been socially and economically deprived by the 'powers-that-be'. He then constructs a pneumatology which seeks the liberation of Hispanic Pentecostals as a function of their faith. Moltmann criticizes liberation theology for not always incorporating a spirituality in its praxis, but Villafañe appears to have addressed this issue by synthesizing a Pentecostal Hispanic liberation theology with a pneumatic spirituality that leads to a pneumatic social ethic.

For Villafañe, social ethics is a function of pneumatology that is realized in history. 'Ethics as pneumatology', contextualized in a Hispanic Pentecostal social ethic, incorporates the two pillars of ethics: love and justice. Love corresponds to the nature of God and is the nature, content and motivation of our ethical response. Love is the basis for human rights and dignity. Love is also the basis of justice, for when there is justice there is also love.[92] For Villafañe, justice is 'love rationally distributed' in socio-political affairs. Instead of articulating the social political realm as negative reactions to government or as conservative appropriation of status quo political ideology, justice at the level of love liberates the oppressed. For Villafañe, justice is the outflow of divine love and the basis for human rights and dignity.[93]

Nevertheless, Villafañe's sources are primarily Hispanic and liberation theologians. He does, however, cite Moltmann's theology of the cross and employs its functional critique of society. Sin is both a personal and social reality that must be overcome through the power of the cross. Villafañe writes:

> Sin and its work is a social reality in all human experience. No area of personal and human history is left untouched by its destructive reality. It is ultimately and radically death/separation from God. The response to sin and death is the need for the loving initiative of the Spirit of God to convict sin, righteousness and judgement (John 16:8-11), based on the equally radical answer of 'The Crucified God'. [*sic*]...The power of sin and death is broken. In the Cross of Christ the believer has the resources to overcome domination.[94]

92. Villafañe, *Liberating Spirit*, pp. 212-13.
93. Villafañe, *Liberating Spirit*, pp. 214-15.
94. Villafañe, *Liberating Spirit*, p. 172.

The socio-critical function of the cross to overcome oppression and domination is a view held by both Villafañe and Moltmann.

Steven Land does not articulate a political theology as such, but his appropriation of Moltmann's eschatology suggests that he could easily construct one. Land's development of the concept of orthopraxy as a mode of sanctification would seem to imply a political theology. Land is typically within the Wesleyan Holiness tradition, believing that the initial moment of sanctification occurs simultaneously with justification and that entire sanctification is a subsequent moment when the perfect love of Christ fills the believer's heart. This moment is when the inner will of the believer is entirely harmonious with the will of God.[95] However, Land takes the doctrine of sanctification in a more social-critical direction. He argues:

> In justification, sanctification and Spirit baptism the believers were enabled to walk in the light, in perfect love, and in the power and demonstration of the Holy Spirit, respectively. This was the way of the kingdom. It was a journey into and with a righteous, holy, powerful God who was transforming them and the world by the power of the gospel in preparation and anticipation of the final apocalypse.[96]

World transformation will be the final revelation of God and the goal of all history. Believing in God is to be transformed through Christ in the Spirit.[97] Transformation of the believer is the first step in the transformation of the world, and although the inbreaking of the kingdom comes through the sovereign act of God, transformed believers can participate in the transformation of the social realm through political action and social ethics. 'Initially', claims Land, 'the realization of apocalyptic spirituality gave a sense of belonging, dignity and power to many who had seen themselves as victims'.[98]

We have seen that Macchia articulates a political theology which comes primarily through the social-critical theology of Christoph Blumhardt and the resistance theology of Karl Barth. Macchia notes, however, that Moltmann's theology is influenced by Christoph's message of integrating transcendent piety with social transformation.[99] Barth was also inspired by

---

95. Land, *Pentecostal Spirituality*, pp. 89-90.
96. Land, *Pentecostal Spirituality*, p. 93.
97. Land, *Pentecostal Spirituality*, pp. 93-94.
98. Land, *Pentecostal Spirituality*, p. 71.
99. Macchia, *Spirituality*, p. 1; cf. Moltmann, *Church in the Power of the Spirit*, pp. 283, 393-94; *idem, Coming of God*, pp. 199, 238-39.

the Blumhardts and appreciated Christoph's prophetic vision of seeking the dawning of the kingdom of God in the world without identifying it with the world. Barth praised Christoph's emphasis on 'waiting and hurrying' for the kingdom without succumbing to passivity.[100] Waiting and hurrying is the key concept Macchia himself uses to interpret the Blumhardts' kingdom eschatology.

Christoph Blumhardt is an important influence on Barth, Moltmann and Macchia himself. Christoph took his father's message that the poor and suffering were representative of the human condition under the bondage of sin[101] and contextualized it within the social conditions of his time as the alienation of the factory worker, the impoverishment of the farmer and the dying trees of a polluted creation. Christoph also believed that the outpouring of the Spirit stemmed from the incarnate and resurrected Christ who sought the transformation of creation. The Incarnation, cross and resurrection, was the focus for the universal unfolding of the kingdom in history.[102] The resurrection was already evident in creation through the incarnate Christ and outward moving in the care for the sick and suffering. The cross was the symbol of human participation in the Incarnation of God. It was a symbol of self-denial, but also a symbol that allowed us to participate in the liberation and redemption of the world.[103] Christoph's theology stressed the importance of human participation in the unfolding of the kingdom which led him into politics. He wanted to change the social conditions of the sick, the poor and the suffering.[104] Although Christoph was somewhat disillusioned by the political infighting of his party, and believed it lacked the christological focus of Jesus' help for the poor and oppressed, he remained a socialist until his death.[105] For Christoph, the liberation of humanity through the Incarnation of the crucified and resurrected Christ was one of the signs of the inbreaking of the kingdom.[106]

Macchia uses the Blumhardts' theology to criticize Pentecostalism. Healing must be interpreted as social liberation of the suffering of creation and a foretaste of the kingdom, not just a supernaturalistic or otherworldly alleviation of individual illness. The work of the Spirit must be interpreted as working throughout creation to liberate the world from social and sys-

100. Macchia, *Spirituality*, p. 163.
101. Macchia, *Spirituality*, p. 78.
102. Macchia, *Spirituality*, p. 116.
103. Macchia, 'Secular and the Religious', p. 67.
104. Macchia, *Spirituality*, p. 122.
105. Macchia, *Spirituality*, pp. 140-41.
106. Macchia, *Spirituality*, pp. 140-42.

temic evil and cannot be restricted solely to the church. The baptism of the Holy Spirit with the evidence of speaking in tongues cannot simply be viewed as the personal upwelling of the divine experience, but must be seen as the theophanic interruption of the Spirit of God. The person is so overwhelmed by the divine that language itself fails to express the encounter. Tongues is more than a sign of personal encounter with God, but the groaning for the liberation of creation from sin and suffering and a sign of the coming kingdom.

However, Macchia is also partially under the influence of Moltmann's political theology. Macchia himself claims that his recent articles 'The Secular and the Religious under the Shadow of the Cross', 'Spirit's Gifts—God's Reign', and his Society for Pentecostal Studies presidential address 'Justification through New Creation', 'reveal partial dependence on Moltmann'.[107] He maintains that social action and ecological measures must also be viewed, along with the baptism of the Holy Spirit and speaking in tongues, as signs of the inbreaking of God's presence and kingdom. He states:

> Not only preaching the gospel, but medical help, social action and ecological measures can also be signs of God's presence to make all things new. There has been a tendency in the West so to stress our historical destiny that nature is neglected, even exploited. A Pentecostal eschatology, if in line with the basic impulses of tongues and divine healing, will understand the role of liberation in history in the context of the new creation.[108]

Our participation in the social, political and ecological spheres are as much signs of the kingdom as speaking in tongues. Macchia's interest in social-political theology is further supported by his recent discussion of interfaith dialogue. Christian participation in interfaith dialogue cannot be orientated towards a common front against unbelief, declares Macchia, but a 'dialogue with the contemporary ideologies of the contemporary world. Together with them, it must ultimately be related to the people who are living, suffering, and dying in the world today.'[109] He specifically cites

---

107. Frank Macchia to Peter Althouse, letter, 1 September 2000; *idem*, 'Secular and the Religious', pp. 59-77; *idem*, 'Justification through New Creation: The Holy Spirit and the Doctrine by which the Church Stands or Falls', *Pneuma* 22.1 (2000), pp. 3-21; Yohan Hyun and Frank Macchia, 'Spirits Gifts—God's Reign', *Theology and Worship: Occasional Paper No. 11 Presbyterian Church (USA)* (1999), pp. 4-35.

108. Macchia, 'Sighs', p. 72; citing Moltmann, *God in Creation*, pp. 124-26.

109. Moltmann, *Church in the Power of the Spirit*, pp. 161-62, as quoted by Macchia, 'The Shadow of the Cross', p. 29.

Moltmann's revolutionary theodicy which defines 'divine omnipotence and freedom from the vantage point of the cross, namely, as God's limitedless capacity to suffer in redeeming the entire world from its condition of oppression, decay and death'.[110] Macchia's social critique comes primarily through the Blumhardts' Pietism, but it is a piety that Macchia also sees in Moltmann's pneumatology.[111] Thus Moltmann's work is having an increasing influence on Macchia's thought.

Dialogue on Cosmic Eschatology and the Transformation of Creation

Moltmann's cosmic eschatology as the transformation of creation is now having a considerable bearing upon Pentecostal scholarship. Early Pentecostalism generally did not articulate a cosmic eschatology per se. Admittedly, Seymour's theology envisioned the social integration of race and gender through the outpouring of the Spirit in the last days, but its cosmic implications were undeveloped. The early Pentecostal doctrine of healing may have implied a cosmic eschatology in that bodily existence as an aspect of creation was partially transformed in the present through healing, but early Pentecostals tended to articulate divine healing as an outflow of the atonement, rather than a prolepsis of the new creation. However, Land, Villafañe, Volf and Macchia have been inspired by Moltmann to develop a Pentecostal cosmic eschatology.

Although Land tends to use the terminology of apocalyptic and kingdom to refer to the inbreaking of the kingdom into history, he does argue that creation itself will be transformed into the new creation.[112] Land's use of apocalyptic also suggests a cosmic eschatology. His emphasis on the continuity and discontinuity of the present with the future kingdom suggests that he not only believes that the kingdom will be the fulfilment of history as the *telos* of history, but the kingdom will break into history from beyond to destroy the cosmic powers of sin.[113] This inbreaking will be

---

110. Macchia, 'Waiting and Hurrying', p. 21; cf. *idem*, 'Analogies of the Kingdom of God in Missions and Social Concern in the Message of Christoph Blumhardt' (unpublished paper), p. 9 n. 48; *idem*, 'Secular and the Religious', p. 73, where he claims that 'Later, in the Spirit of Blumhardt, Moltmann spoke of the cross as an "unreligious" act, since it cancels out all patterns of religious projections'. Also cf. Moltmann, *Crucified God*, p. 37.

111. Macchia, 'A Further Response', p. 127.

112. Land, *Pentecostal Spirituality*, p. 65.

113. Land, *Pentecostal Spirituality*, p. 65.

God's act of judgment upon sin and death. Pentecostals have 'a new hope and the awareness of being involved in a cosmic struggle with powers and principalities'.[114] Land claims that the Pentecostal apocalyptic follows what Moltmann calls 'good apocalyptic' or 'historifying of the world' and 'universalizing of history'.[115] Pentecostalism lapsed into social passivity, fatalism and the reduction of social, global and cosmic dimensions to a single focus on preaching the gospel to all nations in its adoption of the 'bad apocalyptic' of fundamentalism. This bad apocalyptic has displaced the positive social holiness heritage of the nineteenth-century Wesleyan Holiness ministry of soup kitchens, orphanages, rescue missions, and so on.[116] Land also argues that revisioning Pentecostal eschatology as the cosmic transformation of the world bears upon the church's mission. 'Defense of the weak and prophetic denunciation of sin and oppression are part of the church's mission to love the neighbour', argues Land. 'To seek to disciple only those who seem to be likely candidates for church membership is to deny the global care and providence of the Spirit.'[117] Land claims the personal, social and cosmic implications of the event of Pentecost are only now being grasped by Pentecostals.[118]

Similar to Moltmann's insistence that there is a correspondence between body and soul that requires the transformation of creation to bring about the resurrection of the dead in the eschaton, Land argues that Pentecostal spirituality reveals a strong correspondence between body and soul. He writes:

> The Pentecostal believer exists in the Spirit between creation and consummation—on the way to the end where there will be a spirit body in perfect correspondence with the Holy Spirit and free of all effects of the Fall. The body is dead because of sin, but it is the cleansed temple of the Holy Spirit. The cleansing of the blood makes possible the indwelling of the Spirit which constitutes Christian existence.[119]

For Land, both body and spirit will be transformed in the eschatological future. Yet there is also a 'total body life' now in Pentecostal worship which incorporates the whole body. The practice of hand-raising, clapping,

114. Land, *Pentecostal Spirituality*, p. 66.
115. Land, *Pentecostal Spirituality*, p. 70, citing Moltmann, *Theology of Hope*, pp. 124-38.
116. Land, *Pentecostal Spirituality*, pp. 70-71.
117. Land, *Pentecostal Spirituality*, p. 207.
118. Land, *Pentecostal Spirituality*, p. 207.
119. Land, *Pentecostal Spirituality*, p. 113.

swaying, tears and laughter, offering the right hand of fellowship, fasting which draws the whole person body and soul closer to God, eating and drinking at the Lord's Supper, footwashing, and so on, are not simply to discipline the human spirit for redemption, but include the whole body in the encounter with God.[120] What Land implies is that the transformation of the body is part of the fullness of salvation and necessitates the cosmic transformation of creation, for without the natural processes of creation the person cannot exist.

Land diverges from Moltmann, however, with regard to the evolution-ary element of his pantheistic theology of creation and eschatology, a theology many Pentecostals do not agree with. Moltmann argues that cre-ation is an act of theistic evolutionary development, albeit with recognition of evolution's disregard for suffering in the competition for survival. Cre-ation is a process which occurred in the beginning, which is occurring in the present and will be consummated in the *parousia*, when suffering and death will be no more. Such a theology sees creation as good but imper-fect. Eden was not a perfect state from which humanity fell, but a transfor-mation from one state to another. Thus the story of the Fall was not about humanity's fall from grace, but about coming to consciousness.[121] Accord-ing to this theology, Christ's Incarnation, death and resurrection were always intended, not merely a consequence of human sin. Moltmann com-ments that the problem with the traditional doctrine of creation is that it

> understands by creation only creation-in-the-beginning (*creatio originalis*) but not continuous creation (*creatio continua*) or the consummated new creation of all things (*nova creatio*). Creation and redemption then cleave apart and become two separate things. Creation is 'down-graded' into being a preparation of redemption, or redemption is reduced to the restoration of creation-in-the-beginning.[122]

The evolutionary component of Moltmann's cosmic eschatology is an area that Land and the other Pentecostal theologians need to address.

Villafañe's emphasis is more on social than on cosmic transformation. However, a cosmic eschatology could be developed from his definition of the human being as person-in-community. Villafañe refuses to define the human being as an isolated individual entity devoid of community, but as a person living in dynamic relation to community. The human being is

---

120. Land, *Pentecostal Spirituality*, pp. 113-15.
121. Moltmann, *God in Creation*, pp. 206-214; *idem*, *Way of Jesus Christ*, pp. 292-97.
122. Moltmann, *Way of Jesus Christ*, p. 286.

suspended in the webs of culture.[123] Villafañe's person-in-community does not yet imply a cosmic eschatology, but one need only extend person-in-community to person-in-community-in-creation. Not only is the human being dialectically related to culture, but to creation as well. One could even argue that culture and creation are dialectically related. The human being needs both community and creation to be constituted as person, suggesting with Moltmann an inseparability of body and soul, because they are embedded in nature.

Villafañe also discusses the relationship of the Christian to the world (*kosmos*). He notes that *kosmos* has both a positive and negative meaning in Scripture. Positively, it connotes all peoples as well as the physical and natural world and follows the classical Greek tradition as the ordering of human existence which protects human life and values. Negatively, it connotes human society organized on corrupt principles and follows the first-century apocalyptic tradition that critiques the corrupt values which threatened human life and values. When these are combined in Christian thought, we see that 'The *Kosmos*, as the legitimate ordering of social life, has itself been corrupted, and rather than protect values and life, it (the *Kosmos*, the order) "is the intruder bearing immorality" '.[124] According to Villafañe, *Kosmos* does not refer to the goodness of creation or human culture, but to the elements of the social realm which are corrupt, dehumanizing and oppositional to God's redemptive/ liberating purpose.[125] Villafañe is generally negative about 'world', believing that it represents the corruption of the 'principalities and powers', a world order which is evil and insinuated within human social organizations. He also adopts a pessimistic apocalyptic view which binds the world to evil and corruption. He would benefit from Moltmann's more positive view of cosmos as the future indwelling of God in creation. While sin and corruption will be separated from creation in the apocalypse, the cosmos itself will be transformed into the new creation. Villafañe asserts an apocalyptic eschatology as the struggle against personal and social powers and principalities to be eliminated by God's reign, but lacks a cosmic eschatology of the transformation of creation into the new creation.

Volf once again closely follows Moltmann's theological framework. Volf prefers the concept of new creation over kingdom of God because he believes that creation itself must be transformed. The belief in the

123. Villafañe, *Liberating Spirit*, pp. 134-35.
124. Villafañe, *Liberating Spirit*, p. 177.
125. Villafañe, *Liberating Spirit*, pp. 176-77.

resurrection of the dead mandates that body and soul must be included in transformation and that creation as the host of the body must also be transformed.[126] Volf follows Moltmann and the Eastern tradition to assert that the new creation will be a recapitulation of all creation. The fullness of salvation will be for all created reality in its entirety.[127] Volf also argues that a cosmic eschatology is implied in the Pentecostal doctrine of divine healing. Pentecostals stress the materiality of salvation in the doctrine of healing, as a partial realization of the reign of God in the present. Pentecostals stress 'bodily human existence' in salvation that comes through healing of the body.[128]

Volf's cosmic eschatology can also be seen in his insistence that the cumulative efforts of work will be recapitulated and transformed in the new creation and that the Christian is representative of the new creation by embodying it within through the indwelling of the Spirit of the new creation. Christians embody the Spirit of the new creation in their new life in God. Agreeing with Moltmann, Volf also argues that both body and soul must be transformed in the eschaton. There can be no personal salvation apart from creation, because the human personality is ensconced in the created orders of the body. To be devoid of the body is to be nothingness. Moltmann's tripartite schemata of creation that is fulfilled in the new creation is implied also in Volf's theology. Yet, though Volf argues that the social evolutionary view that assumes society is becoming progressively better is contrary to God's sovereignty to establish the kingdom as a gift, Volf too does not discuss the evolutionary assumptions of Moltmann's doctrine of creation. Volf needs to address how the mutability of creation in Moltmann's theology can be incorporated in an authentic Pentecostal theology.

The cosmic eschatology articulated by Macchia is influenced both by the Blumhardts and by Moltmann. The cosmic transformation of all things was an eschatological strain within Wuerttemberg Pietism. Macchia argues that the theosophically influenced cosmic transformation of all things was a significant strain in Johann Blumhardt's theology, but was converted to a concern for sociopolitical and humanitarian concerns by Christoph. Johann claimed that only through the redemption of all things as a whole can we secure our individual salvation. Sin and death will be eliminated from creation, and salvation will be universal as the resurrection life of Jesus

---

126. Volf, 'Loving with Hope', pp. 28-30.
127. Volf, *After our Likeness*, p. 267.
128. Volf, 'Materiality', p. 457.

permeates all of creation, so that nothing will be excluded from the all-encompassing grace of God.[129] Johann rejected the apocalyptic view of the end of history in favour of hope in the renewal of creation through the work of the Spirit. Creation is intended to glorify God, so the destruction of creation would disgrace God. Johann believed that the *parousia* will be both the inbreaking of the new creation and the fulfilment of present creation through the renewal of all things.[130] Christoph took up Johann's cosmic eschatology and reinterpreted it in terms of liberation in the socio-political sphere.[131] Although there was a concern for ecological responsibility in Christoph's theology, he moved from the more theosophical cosmic eschatology of his father to a social-ethical concern.

Macchia thinks that Pentecostalism embodies a cosmic eschatology in its theology of tongues. The expression of tongues is world transforming in its prayer 'groans' for the future revelation of Jesus Christ as universal Lord and *cosmocrator*. Tongues finds its strength in the suffering of the cross as representative of the suffering of creation and yearns for the future deliverance of creation and transformation of the world.[132] Tongues is a sign that Christ is transforming social relationships in history and allows us to participate in the cosmic transformation of the world through preaching, social action and ecological responsibility.[133] The groaning for the transformation of the world in the Blumhardts' theology is implied in the groaning of tongues in Pentecostalism. One may even argue that the overpowering presence of God in the expression of tongues is, to borrow Moltmann's terminology, the Spirit's 'shekinah' indwelling and a sign of the full indwelling of future cosmic glory when God's divine presence will be all in all through the full mutual indwelling of God in creation, and creation in God.

This dialogue reveals, then, an interesting influence of Moltmann's pneumatological eschatology on the contemporary Pentecostal theologians. Land, Villafañe, Volf and Macchia have all appropriated Moltmann's transformational eschatology in their own unique ways to recover the prophetic critique of the social world in early Pentecostalism and to critique the unfortunate infiltration of fundamentalist eschatology into mid-century Pentecostalism. Their apocalyptic is not the fundamentalist vision of world

---

129. Macchia, *Spirituality*, pp. 82-83.
130. Macchia, *Spirituality*, pp. 88-89.
131. Macchia, *Spirituality*, p. 138.
132. Macchia, 'Sighs', pp. 68-69.
133. Macchia, 'Sighs', pp. 71-72; cf. Moltmann, *God in Creation*, pp. 124-26.

destruction, but the separation of sin and death from the world at the moment of the eschatological transformation of the world into the new creation of the kingdom of God. They also show varying concerns for articulating an eschatology that is both continuous and discontinuous with the present world. For Moltmann, the kingdom is specifically the kingdom of Jesus Christ and the Spirit. Not only are Christ and the Spirit integral in the inbreaking of the kingdom through the eschatological event of the cross and resurrection and the indwelling of the Spirit of God in creation moving it to its fullness in God, but also the kingdom is formed through the outflowing fellowship of Christ and the Spirit in the triune God. Moltmann therefore articulates a Spirit-Christology that refuses to subordinate the Spirit to Christ. These themes are all at play in the work of the four Pentecostals, and with Moltmann, who generally wish to include a strengthened view of Pentecost as an eschatological event and tongues and healing as signs of the kingdom inbreaking.

Although the Pentecostal theologians see the cross as an important component in the revelation of God's kingdom, a further appropriation of Moltmann's theology of the cross as the point of solidarity with the suffering and oppression of creation would strengthen the social implications of Pentecostal theology. The eschatological kingdom has revolutionary impact on the present godforsaken sociopolitical structures and Moltmann constructs a political theology to reflect the righteousness of God's kingdom. The Pentecostals further develop this political theology, ranging from Land's orthopraxy and Macchia's insistence that social liberation is implicit in tongues and healing, to Villafañe's liberative social ethics and Volf's fully-fledged political theology that interprets atonement as embrace and work as pneumatological gifting.

Finally, Moltmann's cosmic eschatology with its integration of body and soul in the eschatological indwelling of creation finds resonance in all four Pentecostals, depicted in the charismata as a foretaste of the kingdom (Land), the integral connection between person and community (Villafañe), in the doctrine of healing, transformation of work and embrace as a proleptic recapitulation of the new creation (Volf) and the eschatological inbreaking and presence of the kingdom in history through the cross and the Spirit of Pentecost, but also a future that is longed for through the groaning of tongues as the groaning for creation's redemption (Macchia).

I proposed at the beginning of this book that a revisioning of Pentecostal theology is needed in order to recover prophetic elements of early Pentecostalism that invite responsible social engagement in the world. I have shown that this process has indeed begun in the work of a number of contemporary Pentecostal theologians who have been in dialogue with theology beyond Pentecostal circles. The pneumatological eschatology of Jürgen Moltmann has been particularly illuminating for the revisioning process which is now underway.

We have noted that, despite the diverse theological heritage of early Pentecostalism, the emphasis on the charismatic dimensions of the Spirit in Pentecostal worship and theology was of utmost importance. Tongues was a sign of the latter rain outpouring of the Spirit in preparation for the coming of the Lord. Seymour's prophetic message of social reconciliation envisioned a world where the personal and social prejudices of racism and gender division would be conquered through tongues and the baptism of the Holy Spirit. The Spirit's outpouring at Pentecost was a focus for the envisioned unity, reconciliation and justice in the church and the world. Seymour's vision was ultimately frustrated, however, by the social prejudices of competing voices. Nevertheless, his prophetic message of the kingdom contained the embryonic seeds for social-political protest. We have seen that, although Parham was insensitive to the issue of race, he was critical of certain social conventions of his day such as capitalism and unionism, and especially of church leaders who, in his opinion, were thwarting the supernatural manifestations of the Spirit. Though Parham's focus was on the missionary implications of speaking in tongues and the baptism of the Holy Spirit as divine help in preparation for the kingdom, the challenge to the dominant values demonstrates the prophetic thrust of his theology.

However, the social implications of the Pentecostal message were frustrated in part by the emerging voice of fundamentalist dispensationalism. The influence of fundamentalism shifted attention from the freedom of the Spirit to the illumination of Scripture and personal piety. The eschatological hope for the soon glorious return of Jesus Christ and his kingdom was supplanted by fear and passive withdrawal from the world in expectation of its destruction. The dynamic freedom of the Spirit breaking into the life of the believer, the church and creation in charismatic dimensions, faded. The social dimensions of the coming kingdom of God were curtailed.

The reaction of Pentecostal leaders to the Latter Rain Revival of 1948 reinforced the shift towards fundamentalism. The early Pentecostal doctrine of the latter rain, which connected the charismatic dimensions of the Spirit of the last days to the imminent return of Jesus Christ, was revised by the Latter Rain. As Pentecostalism institutionalized, the baptism of the Spirit with the evidence of speaking in tongues was emphasized as the distinctive doctrine of the movement. The Latter Rain Revival saw itself, however, as a continuation of the restoration of the apostolic church begun in early Pentecostalism, and insisted upon a heightened spirituality that shifted attention to the Pauline gifts of the Spirit, especially prophecy, healing and the ministry of apostles and prophets. This revival also criticized the Pentecostal movement for becoming too institutionalized and aggressively proselytized within mainline Pentecostal denominations. Classical Pentecostal leaders reacted to the Latter Rain Revival by suppressing the latter rain doctrine in favour of a fundamentalist eschatology with its emphasis upon premillennial dispensationalism and pre-tribulation Rapture. This shift was further reinforced by an invitation to Pentecostals in 1941 to be a founding partner in a coalition of Evangelicals and fundamentalists, eventually leading to Pentecostal participation in the National Association of Evangelicals. However, the latter rain doctrine did not disappear, but was transmuted and revitalized by the Charismatic Renewal and Independent Charismatic movements.

In recent years, there has been a renewed interest in the transformative vision of Seymour. Contemporary Pentecostal theologians, such as Steven Land, Eldin Villafañe, Miroslav Volf and Frank Macchia, have revisioned Pentecostal eschatology to recover the more prophetic, social-critical elements of the early movement. They reject fundamentalist eschatology, interpreting the Spirit of the last days as God's gracious presence and action to transform the person, society and creation itself into the eschatological new creation, a transformation that is already here through the person of Jesus Christ and the event of Pentecost, but awaiting the 'not yet' of the eschaton. This eschatological revisioning is better positioned to encourage contemporary Pentecostals to engage the world in a socially responsible manner.

I have placed these Pentecostal theologians in dialogue with the work of a major non-Pentecostal theologian, Jürgen Moltmann, whose voluminous

work is profoundly congenial to the original Pentecostal vision. Moltmann's theology is thoroughly eschatological, driven fundamentally by such
biblical concepts as the kingdom of God, the new creation, the millenarian
reign and the apocalyptic separation of good from evil. The kingdom of God
breaks into the present to transform history and create anticipatory hope for
the future. His work is also thoroughly pneumatological. His eschatology is
integrated with a christological pneumatology, in which the resurrection of
the crucified Christ grounds Christian hope for the future resurrection of
the dead and the transformation of creation. At the same time, the apocalyptic suffering of Christ on the cross is the point of God's solidarity with
the suffering of the poor and oppressed and the misery of all creation. As
well, the Spirit of God indwells creation in, with and through Christ, and
anticipates the future of the new creation, when God will indwell creation
fully and creation will dwell in God. Moltmann's christological pneumatology celebrates the charismatic indwelling of the Spirit in the people of
God, the church, and in creation itself. Moltmann's theology is also thoroughly political. The dehumanizing powers of the status quo are criticized
as contrary to God. We are called to live in solidarity with the poor and
oppressed and to resist the social-political powers of evil. Finally, Moltmann has developed a cosmic eschatology that envisions the future 'shekinah' indwelling of God in creation and creation in God, which will be the
sabbath rest of all creation. Important in Moltmann's eschatology is the
belief that God will not destroy the world in the eschaton, but will bring
creation to its final consummation. Moltmann's eschatology is therefore
thoroughly transformational.

All four Pentecostals reveal varying degrees of influence by Moltmann's
pneumatological eschatology. In their own unique ways, each Pentecostal
theologian has been in dialogue with Moltmann's theology to develop an
authentic Pentecostal theology that not only recovers the neglected socio-
critical elements of early Pentecostalism, but also seeks to broaden the
scope of Pentecostal eschatology to include the social and the cosmic as
well as the personal in eschatological transformation. Land articulates an
apocalyptic spirituality that emphasizes orthodoxy, orthopraxy and orthopathy that are correlative with the trinitarian being of God. Villafañe develops a pneumatological social ethic that hinges upon the future reign of
God, which has important implications for opposing the dehumanizing and
oppressing 'powers-that-be'. Villafañe, as a Hispanic American liberationist, is partially influenced by Moltmann's theology of the cross, in that
Christ's crucifixion functions as the point of God's solidarity with the poor

and suffering in humanity thereby instilling resistance to dominating political powers. However, the relationship is more one of resemblance than of influence. Volf constructs a political theology of human work and embrace that has its root in the eschatological new creation. Of the four Pentecostals, Volf is most influenced by Moltmann. Macchia argues for an eschatology rooted in Blumhardt Pietism, in which the kingdom of God is nascently present in history through the Incarnation, the event of Pentecost and ultimately in the future *parousia*. This eschatology allows Macchia to argue that a Pentecostal theology of tongues is sacramental, theophanic (divine appearance that is perceived by the human senses) and eschatological. Although Moltmann uses the term 'epiphanic' rather than theophanic to describe the appearance of the divine in the present, he rejects epiphanic theology because it confuses the presence of God for the eschatological promise. Macchia is thus partially influenced by, but is quite distinct from, Moltmann. The dialogue partners have one important point in common. They all argue for transformational eschatologies and thereby reject the fundamentalist vision of world destruction and passive resignation.

Throughout this book I have affirmed that a revisioning of Pentecostal eschatology is necessary to recover prophetic elements of the early movement that will allow Pentecostals to engage the world in a socially responsible manner. I have also argued that Pentecostals need to be critical of fundamentalist assumptions that have materialized within the Pentecostal movement, because passive resignation in the face of world destruction is dangerous, both theologically and politically. As well, the fundamentalist separation of the dispensation of Israel from the church is inconsistent with the Pentecostal emphasis upon the continuation of charismatic gifts of the Spirit from the time of the Old Testament prophets to the present age. All four Pentecostal theologians, in dialogue with Jürgen Moltmann, offer a Pentecostal eschatology that seeks to transform the world in the power of the Spirit of God.

These contemporary Pentecostal theologians are significant because they not only draw upon their early heritage for inspiration to plot a course for the Pentecostal movement in the twenty-first century, but they also broaden the scope of Pentecostal theology to dialogue with major theologians of other traditions. They engage Moltmann because his pneumatological eschatology with its transformational and liberationist tendencies resonates with currents within Pentecostalism. In dialogue with Moltmann, they gain a theology that is open to history and creation as an integral part of salvation, and consequently envision a Pentecostal ethic that is personal and social in breadth. Through theological engagement, they have moved Pentecostal theology from isolation to inclusion, from separation to ecumenism and from otherworldly preoccupation to transformation.

BIBLIOGRAPHY

Early Pentecostal Periodicals

Apostolic Faith (Topeka, KS; Houston, TX; Zion City, IL; Baxter Spring, KS [Parham] c. 1987–1909).
Apostolic Faith (Houston, TX [E.N. Bell and F.W. Carothers] c. 1907–1913).
Apostolic Faith (Azusa Street, California, CA, 1906–1908).
Apostolic Faith (Portland, OR [Florence Crawford] c. 1908–1909).
Apostolic Herald (Seattle, 1909).
Apostolic Messenger (Winnipeg, 1908).
Apostolic Witness and Missionary Herald (Dallas, OR, 1909).
Bible Friend (Minneapolis, 1921).
Bridal Call (Los Angeles, 1918–23).
Bridegroom Echo (Los Angeles, 1918).
Bridegroom's Messenger (Atlanta, 1907).
Christian Evangel (various places, 1913–15, 1918–19).
Christian Witness and Advocate of Bible Holiness (Chicago, 1916).
Church of God Evangel (title varies; Cleveland, TN, 1906–1929).
Elim Pentecostal Herald (Hornell, NY, 1935).
Evening Light and Church of God Evangel (see *Church of God Evangel*).
Foursquare Magazine (Los Angeles, 1944).
Glad Tidings Herald (title varies; New York, 1918–43).
God's Revivalist and Bible Advocate (Cincinnati, 1901, 1906–1908).
Gospel Witness (Los Angeles, 1914).
Gospel Witness (Louisville, KY, 1906).
Grace and Truth (Memphis, 1914–16, 1918).
Herald of Light (Indianapolis, 1905–1906, 1910).
Household of God (1909).
Latter Rain Evangel (Chicago, 1908–1912, 1915–16, 1925–34).
Living Truth (1907).
Los Angeles Times (Los Angeles, 1906, 1956).
The Midnight Cry (New York, 1911–18).
Missionary Review of the World (1904–1906, 1908).
Peniel Herald (Los Angeles, 1907–1909, 1911).
Pentecostal Evangel (Springfield, MO, 1919–32).
Pentecostal Herald (Chicago, 1917–18, 1920, 1922).
Pentecostal Herald (Louisville, 1915–20).
Pentecostal Herald (St Louis, 1967).
Pentecostal Holiness Advocate (Franklin Springs, GA, 1905–1906, 1916–25, 1937).
Pentecostal Testimony (Chicago).

Pentecostal Testimony (Winnipeg, 1928–30).
Upper Room (Los Angeles, 1909).
Victorious Gospel (Los Angeles, 1915).
Way of Faith (Columbia, SC, 1901, 1906, 1918, 1921).
Weekly Evangel (St Louis, 1915–18).
Word and Witness (Malvern, Ark, 1912–15).
Word and Work (Framington, MS, 1935).[1]

Primary Pentecostal Sources

Baker, Elizabeth V., *Chronicles of a Faith Life* (ed. Donald W. Dayton; HCL, 3; New York: Garland Publishing, 1985).
Barratt, Thomas Ball, *The Work of T.B. Barratt* (ed. Donald W. Dayton; HCL, 4; New York: Garland Publishing, 1985).
Bartleman, Frank, *Azusa Street* (S. Plainsfield, NJ: Bridge Publishing, 1980).
—*Witness to Pentecost: The Life of Frank Bartleman* (ed. Donald W. Dayton; HCL, 5; New York: Garland Publishing, 1985).
Corum, Fred T., and Rachel A. Harper Sizelove (eds.), *Like as of Fire: Newspapers from the Azusa Street World Wide Revival* (Washington, DC: Middle Atlantic Regional Press, 1991).
Davis, Clara, *Azusa Street Till Now: Eyewitness Accounts of the Move of God* (Tulsa, OK: Harrison House, 1983).
Dayton, Donald W. (ed.), *Holiness Tracts Defending the Ministry of Women* (HCL, 11; New York: Garland Publishing, 1985).
—*Seven 'Jesus Only' Tracts* (HCL, 13; New York: Garland Publishing, 1985).
—*Three Early Pentecostal Tracts* (HCL, 14; New York: Garland Publishing, 1985).
Durham, William H., 'Some Other Phases of Sanctification', *Pentecostal Testimony* in *Pentecostal Testimony File* (Assemblies of God Archives, Springfield, MO).
Ewart, Frank J., *The Phenomenon of Pentecost: 'A History of the Latter Rain'* (St Louis, MO: Pentecostal Publishing House, 1947).
Frodsham, Stanley Howard, *With Signs Following: The Story of the Pentecostal Revival in the Twentieth Century* (Springfield: Gospel Publishing House, 1926).
Gee, Donald, *Concerning Spiritual Gifts* (Springfield: Gospel Publishing House, rev. edn, 1949).
—*Pentecostal Experience: The Writings of Donald Gee. Settling the Question of Doctrine Versus Experience* (Springfield: Gospel Publishing House, 1993).
—*The Pentecostal Movement* (London: Elim Publishing Company, 1949).
—*Toward Pentecostal Unity* (Springfield: Gospel Publishing House, 1961).
Godbey, W.B., *Six Tracts by W.B. Godbey* (ed. Donald W. Dayton; HCL, 19; New York: Garland Publishing, 1985).
Goldee, Morris E., *The Life and Works of Bishop Garfield Thomas Haywood (1880–1931)* (Indianapolis: privately published, 1977).
Goss, Ethel E. (ed.), *The Winds of God: The Story of the Early Pentecostal Days (1901–1914) in the Life of Howard Goss* (New York: Comet Press, 1958).

---

1.   This list of early Pentecostal periodicals has been adapted from Anderson, *Vision of the Disinherited*, pp. 314-15.

Haywood, G.T., *The Life and Writings of Elder G.T. Haywood* (Portland, OR: Apostolic Book Publishers, 1984).

Hills, A.M., *Holiness and Power for the Church and the Ministry* (ed. Donald W. Dayton; HCL, 21; New York: Garland Publishing, 1985).

LaBerge, Agnes N.O., *What God Hath Wrought* (ed. Donald W. Dayton; HCL, 24; New York: Garland Publishing, 1985).

Martin, Larry, *The Topeka Outpouring of 1901: Eyewitness Accounts of the Revival that Birthed the 20th Century Pentecostal Charismatic Revival* (Joplin, MO: Christian Life Books, 1997).

Mason, Mary, *The History and Life Work of Elder C.H. Mason, Chief Apostle and his Co-Laborers* (Memphis, TN: Church of God in Christ, 1987).

McPherson, Aimee Semple, *This Is That: Personal Experiences, Sermons and Writings* (Los Angeles: Bridal Call Publishing House, 1918).

Montgomery, Carrie Judd, *The Life and Teaching of Carrie Judd Montgomery* (ed. Donald W. Dayton; HCL, 29; New York: Garland Publishing, 1985).

Parham, Charles F., *The Sermons of Charles F. Parham* (ed. Donald W. Dayton; HCL, 36; New York: Garland Publishing, 1985).

Parham, Sarah E., *The Life of Charles F. Parham, Founder of the Apostolic Faith Movement* (ed. Donald W. Dayton; HCL, 35; New York: Garland Publishing, 1985).

Seymour, William J., *Doctrine and Disciplines of the Azusa Street Apostolic Faith Mission of Los Angeles* (published by the author, 1915).

—*The Winds that Changed the World: Azusa Street Sermons* (Joplin, MO: Christian Life Books, 1999).

Tomlinson, A.J., *The Last Great Conflict* (ed. Donald W. Dayton; HCL, 46; New York: Garland Publishing, 1985).

Urshan, Andrew David, *The Life Story of Andrew D. Urshan* (Portland, OR: Apostolic Book Publishers, 1982).

Warner, Wayne E. (ed.), *Touched by the Fire: Eyewitness Accounts of the Early 20th Century Pentecostal Revival* (Plainsfield: Logos International, 1978).

Wigglesworth, Smith, *Cry of the Spirit* (ed. Roberts Liardon; Tulsa, OK: Harrison House, 1989).

—*On the Anointing* (New Kensington, PA: Whitaker House, 1999).

—*On Spirit-Filled Living* (New Kensington, PA: Whitaker House, 1998).

Woodworth-Etter, Maria, *The Holy Spirit* (New Kensington: Princeton University Press, 1998).

Secondary Pentecostal Sources

Alexander, Donald L. (ed.), *Christian Spirituality: Five Views of Sanctification* (Downers Grove, IL: InterVarsity Press, 1988).

Allen, David, *The Unfailing Stream: A Charismatic Church History in Outline* (Tonbridge: Sovereign World, 1994).

Anderson, Allan H., and Walter J. Hollenweger (eds.), *Pentecostals after a Century: Global Perspectives on a Movement in Transition* (JPTSup, 15; Sheffield: Sheffield Academic Press, 1999).

Anderson, Ray, *Ministry on the Fire Line: A Practical Theology for an Empowered Church* (Downers Grove, IL: InterVarsity Press, 1993).

Anderson, Robert Mapes, *Vision of the Disinherited: The Making of American Pentecostalism* (Oxford: Oxford University Press; Peabody, MA: Hendrickson, 1979).

Atter, Gordon F., *'The Third Force'* (Caledonia, ON: Acts Books, 3rd edn, 1970).

Baer, Hans A., 'The Social-Religious Development of the Church of God in Christ', in Hans A. Baer and Yvonne Jones (eds.), *African-Americans in the South: Issues of Race, Class and Gender* (SASP, 25; Athens: University of Georgia Press, 1992), pp. 111-22.

Baer, Hans A., and Merrill Singer, *African-American Religion in the Twentieth Century: Varieties of Pentecostal Accommodation* (Knoxville: University of Tennessee Press, 1992).

Baer, Richard, 'Quaker Silence, Catholic Liturgy, and Penetcostal Glossolalia: Some Functional Similarities', in Spittler (ed.), *Perspectives on the New Pentecostalism*, pp. 150-64.

Barfoot, Charles H., and Gerald T. Sheppard, 'Prophetic Vs. Priestly Religion: The Changing Role of Women Clergy in Classical Pentecostal Churches', *RevRR* 22 (1980), pp. 2-17.

Barron, Bruce, *The Health and Wealth Gospel: What's Going on Today in a Movement That Has Shaped the Faith of Millions?* (Downers Grove, IL: InterVarsity Press, 1987).

—*Heaven and Earth: The Political and Social Agenda of Dominion Theology* (Grand Rapids: Zondervan, 1992).

Bayes, Jonathan, 'The Significance of Restorationism: An Alternative View', *BQ* 32.7 (1988), pp. 341-47.

Bittlinger, Arnold (ed.), *The Church Is Charismatic: The World Council of Churches and the Charismatic Renewal* (Geneva: WCC, 1981).

Bloch-Hoell, Nils, *The Pentecostal Movement: Its Origins, Development and Distinctive Character* (Oslo: Universitetsforlaget, 1964).

Blumhofer, Edith L., *Aimee Semple McPherson: Everybody's Sister* (Grand Rapids: Eerdmans, 1993).

—*The Assemblies of God: A Chapter in the Story of American Pentecostalism.* I. *To 1941* (Springfield: Gospel Publishing House, 1989).

—*The Assemblies of God: A Chapter in the Story of American Pentecostalism.* II. *Since 1941* (Springfield: Gospel Publishing House, 1989).

—'For Pentecostals: A Move Toward Racial Reconciliation', *CC* 27 (1994), pp. 445-46.

—*Restoring the Faith: The Assemblies of God, Pentecostalism and American Culture* (Chicago: University of Chicago Press, 1993).

—'Women in Evangelicalism and Pentecostalism', in Melanie May (ed.), *Women and Church: The Challenge of Ecumenical Solidarity in the Age of Alienation* (Grand Rapids: Eerdmans, 1991), pp. 3-7.

Blumhofer, Edith L. (ed.), *'Pentecost in My Soul': Explorations in the Meaning of Pentecostal Experience in the Early Assemblies of God* (Springfield: Gospel Publishing House, 1989).

Blumhofer, Edith L., Russell P. Spittler and Grant A. Wacker (eds.), *Pentecostal Currents in American Protestantism* (Chicago: University of Illinois Press, 1999).

Boyd, Gregory A., *Oneness Pentecostals and the Trinity* (Grand Rapids: Baker Book House, 1992).

Brumback, Carl, *Suddenly from Heaven: A History of the Assemblies of God* (Springfield: Gospel Publishing House, 1961).

Bruner, F.D., *A Theology of the Holy Spirit: The Pentecostal Experience and the New Testament Witness* (London: Hodder & Stoughton, 1970).

Campbell, Joseph E., *The Pentecostal Holiness Church, 1898–1948* (Franklin Springs, GA: Publishing House of the Pentecostal Holiness Church, 1951).

Carpenter, Joel A. (ed.), *Fundamentalism in American Religion: 1800–1950* (New York: Garland Publishing, nd).

Cartledge, Mark J., 'The Future of Glossolalia: Fundamentalist or Experientialist?', *Religion* 28.3 (1998), pp. 223-44.

—'Interpreting Charismatic Experience: Hypnosis, Altered States of Consciousness and the Holy Spirit?', *JPT* 13 (1998), pp. 117-32.

Chan, Simon K.H., 'Evidential Glossolalia and the Doctrine of Subsequence', *AJPS* 2.2 (1999), pp. 195-211.

—*Pentecostal Theology and the Christian Spiritual Tradition* (JPTSup, 21; Sheffield: Sheffield Academic Press, 2000).

Clark, Matthew, Henry I. Lederle, *et al.*, *What is Distinctive about Pentecostal Theology?* (Pretoria: University of South Africa Press, 1989).

Clayton, Allan, 'The Significance of William H. Durham for Pentecostal Historiography', *Pneuma* 1 (1979), pp. 27-42.

Conn, Charles, *Like a Mighty Army Moves the Church of God, 1886–1955* (Cleveland, TN: Church of God Publishing House, 1955).

Cox, Harvey, *Fire from Heaven: The Rise of Pentecostal Spirituality and the Reshaping of Religion in the Twenty-first Century* (Reading: Addison-Wesley, 1995).

Darrand, Tom C., and Anson D. Shupe, *Metaphors of Social Control in a Pentecostal Sect* (SRS, 6; Lewiston, NY: Edwin Mellen Press, 1983).

Dayton, Donald W., 'The Doctrine of the Baptism of the Holy Spirit: Its Emergence and Significance', *WesTJ* 13 (1978), pp. 114-27.

—'The Holy Spirit and Christian Expansion in the Twentieth Century', *Missiology* 16.4 (1988), pp. 397-407.

—'Pneumtological Issues: The Holiness Movement', *GOTR* 31.3-4 (1986), pp. 361-67.

—*Theological Roots of Pentecostalism* (SE, 5; Metuchen: Scarecrow Press, 1987).

—'Yet Another Layer of the Onion, or Opening the Ecumenical Door to Let the Riffraff In', *ER* 40 (1988), pp. 87-110.

Dayton, Donald W., and Robert K. Johnston (eds.), *The Variety of American Evangelicalism* (Downers Grove, IL: InterVarsity Press, 1991).

Del Colle, Ralph, 'Oneness and Trinity: A Preliminary Proposal for Dialogue with Oneness Pentecostalism', *JPT* 10 (1997), pp. 85-110.

—'Pentecostalism and Apocalyptic Passion: A Review of Steven Land's *Pentecostal Spirituality: A Passion for the Kingdom*, A Catholic Response' (SPS response, Wycliffe College, Toronto, Ontario, March 9, 1996).

Dempster, Murray W., 'Christian Social Concern in Pentecostal Perspective: Reformulating Pentecostal Eschatology', *JPT* 2 (1993), pp. 51-64.

—'The Church's Moral Witness: A Study of Glossolalia in Luke's Theology of Acts', *Paraclete* 23 (1989), pp. 1-7.

—'Social Concern in the Context of Jesus' Kingdom, Mission and Ministry', *Transformation* 16.2 (1999), pp. 43-53.

Dempster, Murray W., Byron D. Klaus and Douglas Petersen (eds.), *Called and Empowered: Global Mission in Pentecostal Perspective* (Peabody, MA: Hendrickson, 1991).

Du Pree, Sherry S. (ed.), *Bibliographical Dictionary of African-American Holiness Pentecostals, 1880–1990* (New York: Garland Publishing, 1996).

Durasoff, Steve, *Bright Wind of the Spirit* (Englewood Cliffs, NJ: Prentice–Hall, 1972).

Dye, Colin, 'Are Pentecostals Pentecostal? A Revisit to the Doctrine of Pentecost', *EPTA* 19 (1999), pp. 56-80.

Elbert, Paul (ed.), *Essays on Apostolic Themes: Studies in Honor of Howard M. Ervin* (Festschrift Howard M. Ervin; Peabody, MA: Hendrickson, 1985).

—*Faces of Renewal: Studies in Honor of Stanley M. Horton on his 70th Birthday* (Festschrift Stanley M. Horton; Peabody, MA: Hendrickson, 1984).

Ervin, Howard, *Conversion-Initiation and the Baptism of the Holy Spirit: A Critique of James D.G. Dunn, Baptism in the Holy Spirit* (Peabody, MA: Hendrickson, 1984).

Faupel, D. William, *The American Pentecostal Movement: A Bibliographic Essay* (ed. Donald W. Dayton; HCL, 1; New York: Garland Publishing, 1985).

—'The Everlasting Gospel: The Significance of Eschatology in the Development of Pentecostal Thought' (PhD dissertation, University of Birmingham, 1989).

—*The Everlasting Gospel: The Significance of Eschatology in the Development of Pentecostal Thought* (JPTSup, 10; Sheffield: Sheffield Academic Press, 1996).

—'The Function of "Models" in the Interpretation of Pentecostal Thought', *Pneuma* 2.1 (1980), pp. 51-71.

—'Whither Pentecostalism? 22nd Presidential Address Society for Pentecostal Studies, November 7, 1992', *Pneuma* 15.1 (1993), pp. 9-27.

Fee, Gordon D., *God's Empowering Presence: The Holy Spirit in the Letters of Paul* (Peabody, MA: Hendrickson, 1978).

—*Gospel and Spirit: Issues in New Testament Hermeneutics* (Peabody, MA: Hendrickson, 1991).

Flokstra, Gerald J., 'Sources for the Initial Evidence Discussion: A Bibliographical Essay', *AJPS* 2.2 (1999), pp. 243-59.

Foster, Fred J., *'Think It Not Strange': A History of the Oneness Movement* (St Louis: Pentecostal Publishing House, 1965).

Gerlach, Luther P., and Virginia H. Hine, 'Five Factors Crucial to the Growth and Spread of a Modern Religious Movement', *JSSR* 7 (1968), pp. 23-40.

—*People, Power, Change: Movements of Social Transformation* (Indianapolis: Bobbs-Merrill, 1970).

Gill, Kenneth D., *Toward a Contextualized Theology for the Third World: The Emergence and Development of Jesus' Name Pentecostalism in Mexico* (IHC, 90; New York: Peter Lang, 1994).

Graham, Stephen, and Marcia W. Graham, *First the Kingdom: A Call to the Conservative Pentecostal/Charismatic and the Liberal Social Justice Advocates for Repentance and Reunification* (New York: University of America Press, 1994).

Goff, James R., *Fields White unto Harvest: Charles F. Parham and the Missionary Origins of Pentecostalism* (Fayetteville: University of Arkansas Press, 1988).

—'Charles F. Parham and his Role in the Development of the Pentecostal Movement: A Reevaluation', *Kansas History* 7 (1984), pp. 226-37.

—'Pentecostal Millenarianism: The Development of Premillennial Orthodoxy, 1909–1943', *Ozark Historical Review* 12 (1983), pp. 14-24.

Haight, Roger, 'The Case for Spirit Christology', *TS* 53 (1992), pp. 257-87.

Harper, George W., 'Renewal and Causality: Some Thoughts on a Conceptual Framework for a Charismatic Theology', *JES* 24.1 (1987), pp. 93-103.

Harrell, David Edwin, Jr, *All Things Are Possible: The Healing and Charismatic Revivals in Modern America* (Bloomington: Indiana University Press, 1975).

Hathaway, Brian, 'The Kingdom Manifesto', *Transformation* 7.3 (1990), pp. 6-11.

Hauerwas, Stanley, and Scott Sage, 'Domesticating the Spirit: Eldin Villafañe's *The Liberating Spirit: Towards an Hispanic American Pentecostal Social Ethic*', *JPT* 7 (1995), pp. 5-10.

Hellstern, Mark, 'The "Me Gospel": An Examination of the Historical Roots of the Prosperity Emphasis within Current Charismatic Theology', *FH* 21.3 (1989), pp. 78-92.

Hereford, Marie J., and Corrine Thomas, *A New Babel, A New Pentecost: Communicating the Gospel in a Mass Culture* (Boston: Pauline Books and Media, 1997).

Hocken, Peter D., 'A Survey of Independent Charismatic Churches', *Pneuma* 18.1 (1996), pp. 93-105.

—'Charismatic Movement', in DPCM, pp. 130-60.

—'Dialogue Extraodinary', *OC* 24.3 (1988), pp. 202-13.

—'Ecumenical Dialogue: The Importance of Dialogue with Evangelicals and Pentecostals', *OC* 30.1 (1994), pp. 101-123.

—'The Challenge of Non-Denominational Charismatic Christianity', in Jongeneel (ed.), *Experiences of the Spirit*, pp. 221-38.

—'The Pentecostal-Charismatic Movement as Revival and Renewal', *Pneuma* 3.1 (1981), pp. 31-47.

Holdcraft, Thomas, *The Holy Spirit: A Pentecostal Interpretation* (Springfield: Gospel Publishing House, 1979).

—'The New Order of the Latter Rain', *Pneuma* 2.2 (1970), pp. 46-58.

Hollenweger, Walter J., 'After Twenty Years Research on Pentecostalism', *Theology* 87.720 (1984), pp. 403-12 (reprinted in *IRM* 75.297 [1986], pp. 3-12).

—'All Creatures Great and Small: Toward a Pneumatology of Life', in David Martin and Peter Muller (eds.), *Strange Gifts: A Guide to Charismatic Renewal* (Oxford: Basil Blackwell, 1984), pp. 41-53.

—'Creator Spiritus: The Challenge of Pentecostal Experience to Pentecostal Theology', *Theology* 81 (1978), pp. 32-40.

—'The Critical Tradition of Pentecostalism', *JPT* 1 (1992), pp. 7-17.

—'The House Church Movement in Great Britain', *ExpTim* 92 (1980), pp. 45-47.

—*Pentecost Between Black and White: Five Case Studies on Pentecost and Politics* (Belfast: Christian Journals, 1974).

—*Pentecostalism: Origins and Developments Worldwide* (Chicago: University of Chicago Press, 1997).

—'Pentecostalism and Academic Theology: From Confrontation to Cooperation', *EPTA* 10.1-2 (1992), pp. 42-49.

—*The Pentecostals* (trans. R.A. Wilson; Chicago: University of Chicago Press, 1972).

—'The Social and Ecumenical Significance of Pentecostal Liturgy', *SL* 8.4 (1969), pp. 207-15.

—'Syncretism and Capitalism', *AJPS* 2.1 (January 1999), pp. 47-61.

Horton, Stanley, *What the Bible Says about the Holy Spirit* (Springfield: Gospel Publishing House, 1976).

Horton, Stanley (ed.), *Systematic Theology: A Pentecostal Perspective* (Springfield: Gospel Publishing House, 1994).

Horton, Wade H., *Pentecost Yesterday, Today and Forever* (Cleveland: Pathway Press, 1972).

House, H. Wayne, and Thomas Ice, *Dominion Theology: Blessing or Curse?* (Portland, OR: Multnomah Press, 1988).

Howard, Ronald, *Charismania: When Christian Fundamentalism Goes Wrong* (London: Mowbray, 1997).

Howell, Joseph H., 'The People of the Name: Oneness Pentecostalism in the U.S' (PhD dissertation, Florida State University, 1985).

Hubbard, Daniel Allan, *The Holy Spirit in Today's World* (Waco, TX: Word Books, 1986).

Hummel, Charles E., *Fire in the Fireplace: Charismatic Renewal in the Nineties* (Downers Grove, IL: InterVarsity Press, 2nd edn, 1993).

Hunt, Stephen, 'Magical Moments: An Intellectualist Approach to the Neo-Pentecostal Faith Ministries', *Religion* 28.3 (1998), pp. 271-80.

Hunt, Stephen, Malcolm Hamilton and Tony Walter (eds.), *Charismatic Christianity: Sociological Perspectives* (New York: St Martin's Press, 1997).

Hunter, Harold D., 'Reflections by a Pentecostalist on Aspects of BEM', *JES* 24.3-4 (1992), pp. 317-45.

—*Spirit-Baptism: A Pentecostal Perspective* (Lanham, MD: University Press of America, 1983).

Hunter, Harold, and Peter D. Hocken (eds.), *All Together in One Place: Theological Papers from the Brighton Conference on World Evangelization* (JPTSup, 4; Sheffield: Sheffield Academic Press, 1993).

Hywel-Davies, Jack, *Baptized by Fire: The Story of Smith Wigglesworth* (London: Hodder & Stoughton, 1987).

Hyatt, Eddie L., *2000 Years of Charismatic Christianity: A 20th Century Look at Church History from a Pentecostal/Charismatic Perspective* (Tulsa, OK: Hyatt International Ministries, 1997).

Irving, Dale T., 'Drawing All Together in One Bond of Love: The Ecumenical Vision of William J. Seymour and the Azusa Street Revival', *JPT* 6 (1995), pp. 25-53.

Jackson, Robert, 'Prosperity Theology and the Faith Movement', *Themelois* 15.1 (1989), pp. 16-24.

Jacobsen, D., 'Knowing the Doctrines of Pentecostals: The Scholastic Theology of the Assemblies of God, 1930–55', in Blumhofer, Spittler and Wacker (eds.), *Pentecostal Currents in American Protestantism*, pp. 90-107.

Johannesen, Stanley, 'Remembering and Observing: Modes of Interpreting Pentecostal Experience and Language' (SPS; Dallas, TX; 8–10 Nov. 1990).

Jones, Charles Edwin, 'The Color Line Washed away in Blood: The Holiness Church at Azusa Street and Afterwards', *WesTJ* 34.2 (1999), pp. 252-65.

—*A Guide to the Study of the Pentecostal Movement* (ATLA Bibliography Series, 6; Metuchen: Scarecrow Press, 1979).

—*Black Holiness: A Guide to the Study of Black Participation in Wesleyan, Perfectionist and Glossolalic Pentecostal Movements* (ATLA Bibliography Series, 18; Metuchen: Scarecrow Press, 1987).

Jongeneel, Jan A.B. (ed.), *Experiences of the Spirit: Conference on Pentecostal and Charismatic Research in Europe at Utrecht University, 1989* (IHC, 68; New York: Peter Lang, 1991).

Jongeneel, Jan A.B., *et al.* (eds.), *Pentecost, Mission and Ecumenism: Essays on Intercultural Theology* (Festschrift Walter J. Hollenweger; IHC, 75; New York: Peter Lang, 1992).

Johns, Cheryl Bridges, 'Partners in Scandal: Wesleyan and Pentecostal Scholarship', *WesTJ* 34.1 (1999), pp. 7-23.

Johnson, Luke Timothy, 'Glossolalia and the Embarrassments of Experience', *PSB* 18.2 (1997), pp. 113-34.

Kärkkäinen, Veli-Matti, 'Mission, Spirit and Eschatology: An Outline of a Pentecostal-Charismatic Theology of Mission', *MS* 15 (1999), pp. 73-94.

—'Pentecostal Hermeneutics in the Making: On the Way from Fundamentalism to Postmodernism', *EPTA* 18 (1998), pp. 76-115.

—'Pentecostal Missiology in Ecumenical Perspective: Contributions, Challenges, Controversies', *IRM* 88 (1999), pp. 207-25.

—'Towards a Theology and Ecclesiology of the Spirit: Marquette University's 1998 Symposium, "An Advent of the Spirit: Orientations in Pneumatology"', *JPT* 14 (1999), pp. 65-80.

Kelsey, Morton T., *Encounter with God: A Theology of Christian Experience* (Minneapolis: Bethany Fellowship, 1972).

—*Tongues Speaking: A Experiment in Spiritual Experience* (Garden City, NY: Doubleday, 1964).

Kendrick, Klaude, *The Promise Fulfilled: A History of the Modern Pentecostal Movement* (Springfield: Gospel Publishing House, 1961).

Kenyon, Howard N., 'An Analysis of Ethical Issues in the History of the Assemblies of God' (PhD dissertation, Baylor University, 1988).

Kuzmic, Peter, 'The Spirit, the Kingdom, the Church: An Evangelical Way Forward', in Bruce J. Nicholls and Bong Rin Ro (eds.), *Beyond Canberra: Evangelical Responses to Contemporary Ecumenical Issues* (Oxford: Regnum Books, 1993), pp. 139-44.

Land, Steven, J., 'A Passion for the Kingdom: Revisioning Pentecostal Spirituality', *JPT* 1 (1992), pp. 19-46.

—'A Stewardship Manifesto for a Discipling Church', in Donald Bowdle (ed.), *The Power and the Promise* (Cleveland: Pathway Press, 1980), pp. 289-317.

—'Be Filled with the Spirit: The Nature and Evidences of Spiritual Fullness', *Ex Auditu* 12 (1996), pp. 108-120.

—'The Local Church and the Poor', *The Pentecostal Minister* 5.3 (1986), pp. 6-10.

—*Pentecostal Spirituality: A Passion for the Kingdom* (JPTSup, 1; Sheffield: Sheffield Academic Press, 1993).

—'Pentecostal Spirituality: Living in the Spirit', in Louis Dupuis and Don E. Saliers (eds.), *Christian Spirituality: Post-Reformational and Modern* (New York: Crossroad, 1989; London: SCM Press, 1990), pp. 479-99.

—'Praying in the Spirit: A Pentecostal Perspective', in Jürgen Moltmann and Karl-Josef Kuschel (eds.), *Pentecostal Movements as an Ecumenical Challenge* (Concilium, 3; London: SCM Press, 1996), pp. 85-103.

—'Response to Professor Harvey Cox', *JPT* 5 (1994), pp. 13-16.

—'The Triune Center: Wesleyans and Pentecostals Together in Mission', *WesTJ* 34.1 (1999), pp. 83-100 (repr. in *Pneuma* 21.2 [1999], pp. 199-214).

Land, Steven J., and Cheryl Bridges Johns, 'Pentecostal Ministerial Formation', *Ministerial Formation* 70 (July 1995), p. 34.

Lanooy, Rienk (ed.), *For Us and our Salvation: Seven Perspectives on Christian Soteriology* (Utrecht-Leider: Interuniverstein Institute voor Missiologie en Oecumenica, 1994).

Larden, Robert A., *Our Apostolic Heritage: An Official History of the Apostolic Church of Pentecost* (Calgary, AB: Kyle Printing & Stationary, 1971).

Lederle, Henry I., 'An Ecumenical Investigation into the Proprium or Distinctive Element of Pentecostal Theology', *TE* 21.2 (1988), pp. 34-41.

—'The Charismatic Movement: The Ambiguous Challenge', *Missionalia* 14 (1986), pp. 61-75.

—'The Spirit of Unity: A Discomforting Comforter: Some Reflections on the Holy Spirit, Ecumenism and the Pentecostal-Charismatic Movements', *ER* 42.3-4 (1990), pp. 279-87.

—*Treasures Old and New: Interpretations of 'Spirit Baptism' in the Charismatic Renewal Movement* (Peabody, MA: Hendrickson, 1988).

Lee, Paul D., 'Pneumatological Ecclesiology in the Roman Catholic–Pentecostal Dialogue: A Catholic Reading of the Third Quinquennium (1985–1989)' (PhD dissertation, Pontificiam Universitatem S. Thomae in Urbe, 1994).

Lewis, Paul W., 'Value Formation and the Holy Spirit in the Theologies of Thomas C. Ogden, Jürgen Moltmann and J. Rodman Williams' (PhD dissertation, Baylor University, 1985).

Lincoln, C. Eric, and Lawrence H. Maniya, *The Black Church in the African American Experience* (Durham, NC: Duke University Press, 1990).

Ling, Tay May, 'A Response to Frank Macchia's "Groans too Deep for Words" ', *AJPS* 1.2 (1998), pp. 175-83.

Lord, Andrew M., 'Mission Eschatology: A Framework for Mission in the Spirit', *JPT* 11 (1997), pp. 111-23.

Lovelace, Richard, 'Baptism in the Holy Spirit and the Evangelical Tradition', *Pneuma* 7.2 (1985), pp. 101-124.

Lovett, Leonard, 'Aspects of the Spiritual Legacy of the Church of God in Christ', *Mid-Stream* 24.4 (1985), pp. 389-97.

—'Black Holiness Pentecostalism: Implications for Ethics and Social Transformation (PhD dissertation, Emory University, 1979).

—'Perspective on the Black Origins of the Contemporary Pentecostal Movement', *JITC* 1 (1973), pp. 36-49.

—'The Spiritual Legacy and Role of Black Holiness Pentecostalism in the Development of American Culture', *OC* 1–2 (1987), pp. 144-56.

Macchia, Frank D., 'A North American Response', *JPT* 4 (1994), pp. 25-33.

—'Analogies of the Kingdom of God in Missions and Social Concern in the Message of Christoph Blumhardt' (Unpublished Paper).

—'The Challenge of Liberation Theology to Pentecostal Piety' (SPS; Tulsa, OK; 13–15 November 1980).

—'The Church as an End-Time Missionary Fellowship of the Spirit: A Pentecostal Perspective on the Significance of Pneumatology for Ecclesiology' (Pentecostal/National Council of Churches in Dialogue, Oakland, California, 12 March 1997), pp. 1-32.

—'Discerning the Spirit in Life: A Review of '*God the Spirit*' by Michael Welker', *JPT* 10 (1997), pp. 3-28.

—'Discerning the Truth of Tongues Speech: A Response to Amos Yong', *JPT* 1.2 (1998), pp. 67-71.

—'From Azusa Street to Memphis: Evaluating the Racial Reconciliation Dialogue among Pentecostals', *Pneuma* 17.2 (1995), pp. 203-18.

—'God Present in a Confused Situation: The Mixed Influence of the Charismatic Movement on Classical Pentecostalism', *Pneuma* 18.1 (1996), pp. 33-54.

—'Groans Too Deep for Words: Towards a Theology of Tongues as Initial Evidence', *AJPS* 1.2 (1998), pp. 149-73.

—'Guest Editorial: "The Toronto Blessing": No Laughing Matter', *JPT* 8 (1996), pp. 3-6.

—'Is Footwashing the Neglected Sacrament? A Theological Response to John Christopher Thomas', *Pneuma* 19.2 (1997), pp. 239-49.

—'Justification through New Creation: The Holy Spirit and the Doctrine by which the Church Stands or Falls', *Pneuma* 22.1 (2000), pp. 3-21.

—'A North American Response', *JPT* 4 (1994), pp. 25-33.

—'The Question of Tongues as Initial Evidence: A Review of *Initial Evidence*, Edited by Gary B. McGee', *JPT* 2 (1993), pp. 117-27.

—'Revitalizing Theological Categories: A Classical Pentecostal Response to J. Rodman Williams' Renewal Theology', *Pneuma* 16.2 (1994), pp. 293-304.

—'Sighs Too Deep for Words: Toward a Theology of Glossolalia', *JPT* 1 (1992), pp. 47-73.

—'The Secular and the Religious under the Shadow of the Cross: Implications in Christoph Blumhardt's Kingdom Spirituality for a Christian Response to World Religions', in Arvind Sharma (ed.), *Religion in a Secular City: Essays in Honor of Harvey Cox* (Festschrift Harvey Cox; Harrisburg, PA: Trinity Press International, 2001), pp. 59-77.

—'The Spirit and Life: A Further Response to Jürgen Moltmann', *JPT* 5 (1994), pp. 121-27.

—'The Spirit and the Kingdom: Implications in the Message of the Blumhardts for a Pentecostal Social Spirituality', *Transformation* 33 (1994), pp. 1-5.

—*Spirituality and Social Liberation: The Message of the Blumhardts in the Light of Wuerttemberg Pietism* (PWS, 4; Metuchen: Scarecrow Press, 1993).

—'Spirituality and Social Liberation: The Message of the Blumhardts in the Light of Württemberg Pietism, with Implications for Pentecostal Theology', in A.B. Jongeneel (ed.), *Experiences of the Spirit: Conference on Pentecostal and Charismatic Research in Europe at Utrecht University, 1989* (IHC, 68; New York: Peter Lang, 1991), pp. 65-84.

—'The Struggle for Global Witness: Shifting Paradigms of Pentecostal Theology', in Murray W. Dempster, *et al.* (eds.), *The Globalization of Pentecostalism: A Religion Made to Travel* (Oxford: Regnum Books International, 1999), pp. 8-29.

—'Tongues and Prophecy: A Pentecostal Perspective', in Jürgen Moltmann and Karl-Josef Kuschel (eds.), *Pentecostal Movements as an Ecumenical Challenge* (Concilium, 3; London: SCM Press, 1996), pp. 63-83.

—'Tongues as a Sign: Towards a Sacramental Understanding of Pentecostal Experience', *Pneuma* 15.1 (1993), pp. 61-76.

—'The Tongues of Pentecost: A Pentecostal Perspective on the Promise and Challenge of Pentecostal/Roman Catholic Dialogue', *JES* 35.1 (1998), pp. 1-18.

—'Tradition and the *Novum* of the Spirit: A Review of Clark Pinnock's *Flame of Love*', *JPT* 13 (1998), pp. 31-48.

—'Waiting and Hurrying for the Healing of Creation: Implications in the Message of the Blumhardts for a Pentecostal Theology of Divine Healing' (SPS and EPTA, Mattersey, England, July 10-14, 1995), pp. 1-30.

Macchia, Frank D., and Yohan Hyun, 'Spirit's Gifts —God's Reign', *Theology and Worship: Occasional Paper No. 11. Presbyterian Church (USA)* (1999), pp. 4-35.

MacRobert, Iain, *The Black Roots and White Racism of Early Pentecostalism in the USA* (New York: St Martin's Press, 1988).

Malony, H. Newton, and A. Adams Lovekin, *Glossolalia: Behavioral Science Perspectives on Speaking in Tongues* (Oxford: Oxford University Press, 1985).

Martin, David, and Peter Mullen (eds.), *Strange Gifts: A Guide to Charismatic Renewal* (Oxford: Basil Blackwell, 1984).

Martin, Larry, *In the Beginning: Readings on the Origins of the 20th Century Pentecostal Revival and the Birth of the Pentecostal Church of God* (Joplin, MO: Christian Life Books, 1997).

McConnel, D.R., *The Promise of Health and Wealth: Historical and Biblical Analysis of the Modern Faith Movement* (Toronto: Hodder & Stoughton, 1990; repr. in *idem*, *A Different Gospel: Updated Edition* [Peabody, MA: Hendrickson, 2nd edn, 1995]).

McDonnell, Kilian, 'A Trinitarian Theology of the Spirit?', *TS* 46 (1985), pp. 191-227.

—'Catholic Charismatic Renewal and Classical Pentecostalism: Growth and the Critique of Systematic Suspicion', *OC* 23 (1987), pp. 36-61.

—'The Death of Mythologies: The Classical Pentecostal/Roman Catholic Dialogue', *America* 172 (1995), pp. 14-19.

—'The Determinative Doctrine of the Holy Spirit', *TTod* 39 (1982), pp. 142-61.

—'The Distinguishing Characteristics of the Charismatic-Pentecostal Spirituality', *OC* 10.2 (1974), pp. 117-28.

—'The Ecumenical Significance of the Pentecostal Movement', *Worship* 40.10 (1966), pp. 608-29.

—'The Experiential and Social: New Models from Pentecostal/Roman Catholic Dialogue', *OC* 9.1 (1972), pp. 43-58.

—'Five Defining Issues: The International Pentecostal/ Roman Catholic Dialogue', *OC* 31.2 (1995), pp. 110-21.

—'I Believe That I Might Experience', *Continuum* 5 (1967–68), pp. 637-85.

McDonnell, Kilian (ed.), *Presence, Power and Praise: Documents on the Charismatic Renewal* (Collegeville, MN: Liturgical Press, 1980).

McDonnell, Kilian, and Arnold Bittlinger, *The Baptism in the Holy Spirit as an Ecumenical Problem* (Notre Dame: Charismatic Renewal Service, 1972).

McGee, Gary B. (ed.), *Initial Evidence: Historical and Biblical Perspectives on the Pentecostal Doctrine of Spirit Baptism* (Peabody, MA: Hendrickson, 1991).

McNamee, J.J., 'The Role of the Spirit in Pentecostalism: A Comparative Study' (PhD dissertation, Eberhard Karld University, 1974).

Menzies, Robert P., *The Development of Early Christian Pneumatology* (JSNTSup, 54; Sheffield: Sheffield Academic Press, 1991).

—*Empowered for Witness: The Spirit in Luke–Acts* (JPTSup, 6; Sheffield: Sheffield Academic Press, 1994).

—'Evidential Tongues: An Essay on Theological Method', *AJPS* 1.2 (1998), pp. 111-23.

—'Paul and the Universality of Tongues: A Response to Max Turner', *AJPS* 2.2 (1999), pp. 283-95.

—'The Spirit of Prophecy, Luke–Acts and Pentecostal Theology: A Response to Max Turner', *JPT* 15 (1999), pp. 49-74.

Menzies, William M., *Anointed to Serve: The Story of the Assemblies of God* (Springfield: Gospel Publishing House, 1971).

—'The Holy Spirit in Christian Theology', in Kenneth Kantzer (ed.), *Perspectives in Evangelical Theology* (Grand Rapids: Baker Book House, 1979), pp. 67-79.

Michael, David, *Telling the Story: Black Pentecostals in the Church of God* (Cleveland: Pathway Press, 2000).

Mills, Watson M., *Speaking in Tongues: A Guide to Research on Glossolalia* (Grand Rapids: Eerdmans, 1986).

Moo, Douglas, 'Divine Healing in the Health and Wealth Gospel', *TJ* 9.2 (1988), pp. 191-209.

Moriarty, Michael, *The New Charismatics: A Concerned Voice Responds to Dangerous New Trends* (Grand Rapids: Zondervan, 1992).

Mour, Richard J., 'Humility, Hope and the Divine Slowness', *CC* 107 (1990), pp. 364-68.

—'Life in the Spirit in an Unjust World', *Pneuma* 9.2 (1987), pp. 109-28.

Nelson, Douglas J., 'For Such a Time as This: The Story of Bishop William J. Seymour and the Azusa Street Revival: A Search for Pentecostal-Charismatic Roots' (PhD dissertation, University of Birmingham, England, 1981).

Nelson, R.J., 'International Theology Congress on Pneumatology', *JES* 19 (1982), pp. 675-98.

Nicol, John Thomas. *Pentecostalism* (New York: Harper & Row, 1966).

Noble, John, *House Churches: Will They Survive?* (Eastbourne: Kingswood Publications, 1988).

Noel, Bradley T., 'From Wesley to Azusa: The Historical Journey of the "Second Work" Doctrine', in Scott A. Durham (ed.), *Full of the Holy Spirit and Faith: Essays Presented in Honor of Dr Allison A. Trites* (Wolfville, NS: Gaspereau Press, 1997), pp. 41-62.

Palma, Marta, 'A Pentecostal Church in the Ecumenical Movement', *ER* 37 (1985), pp. 223-29.

Paris, Arthur Ernest, *Black Pentecostalism: Southern Religion in an Urban World* (Amherst: University of Massachussetts, 1982).

Penny, John Michael, *The Missionary Emphasis of Lukan Pneumatology* (JPTSup, 12; Sheffield: Sheffield Academic Press, 1997).

Percy, Martyn, 'Fundamentalism: A Problem for Phenomenology?', *JCR* 10.1 (1995), pp. 83-91.

—'The City on the Beach: Future Prospects for Charismatic Movements at the End of the Twentieth Century', in Hunt, Hamilton and Walter (eds.), *Charismatic Christianity*, pp. 205-228.

Petersen, Douglas, *Not by Might Nor by Power: A Pentecostal Theology of Social Concern in Latin America* (Irving, CA: Regnum Books International, 1996).

Petrella, Lidia Suzana Vaccaro de, 'The Tension between Evangelicalism and Social Action in the Pentecostal Movement', *IRM* 75 (1986), pp. 34-38.

Pettegrew, Larry D., 'Dispensationalists and Spirit Baptism', *MSJ* 8 (1997), pp. 29-46.

Petts, David, *The Holy Spirit: An Introduction* (Mattersey, England: Mattersey Hall, 1998).

Pillay, Gerald J., 'The Antithetical Structure of Pentecostal Theology', *JTSA* 50 (1985), pp. 27-36.

Pinnock, Clark H., 'A Bridge and Some Points of Growth: A Reply to Cross and Macchia', *JPT* 13 (1998), pp. 49-54.

Plüss, Jean-Daniel, 'Azusa and Other Myths: The Long and Winding Road from Experience to Stated Belief and Back Again', *Pneuma* 15.2 (1993), pp. 189-201.

—'Initial Evidence or Evident Initials? A European Point of View on a Pentecostal Distinctive', *AJPS* 2.2 (1999), pp. 213-22.

Poewa, Karla (ed.), *Charismatic Christianity as a Global Culture* (Columbia: University of South Carolina Press, 1994).

Poloma, Margaret M., *The Assemblies of God at the Crossroads: Charism and Institutional Dilemmas* (Knoxville: University of Tennessee Press, 1989).

—*The Charismatic Movement: Is There a New Pentecost?* (Boston: Twayne Publishers, 1982).

Poloma, Margaret M., and Brian F. Pendleton, 'Religious Experiences, Evangelism and Institutional Growth with the Assemblies of God', *JSSR* 28.4 (1989), pp. 415-31.

Pomerville, Paul A., *The Third Force in Missions: A Pentecostal Contribution to Contemporary Mission Theology* (Peabody, MA: Hendrickson, 1985).

Prosser, Peter E., *Dispensational Eschatology and its Influence on American and British Religious Movements* (TSR, 82; Queenston, ON: Edwin Mellen Press, 1999).

Randall, Claire, 'The Importance of the Pentecostal and Holiness Churches in the Ecumenical Movement', *Pneuma* 9.1 (1987), pp. 50-60.

Reed, David A., 'Oneness Pentecostalism', in *DPCM*, pp. 644-51.

—'Origin and Development of the Theology of Oneness Pentecostalism in the United States' (PhD dissertation, Boston University, 1978).

Riss, Richard M., *A Survey of 20th-Century Revival Movements in North America* (Peabody, MA: Hendrickson, 1988).

—*Latter Rain: The Latter Rain Movement of 1948 and the Mid-Twentieth Century Evangelical Awakening* (Mississauga, ON: Honeycomb Visual Productions, 1987).

—'Latter Rain Movement', in DPCM, pp. 532-34.

—'The Latter Rain Movement of 1948', *Pneuma* 4.1 (1982), pp. 32-45.

Robeck, Cecil M., Jr, 'Discerning the Spirit in the Life of the Church', in William Barr and Rena Yocum (eds.), *The Church in the Movement of the Spirit* (Grand Rapids: Eerdmans, 1994), pp. 29-49.

—'Pentecostals and Social Ethics', *Pneuma* 5.2 (1987), pp. 103-107.

—'Pentecostals and the Apostolic Faith: Perspectives for Ecumenism', *Pneuma* 9.1 (1987), pp. 61-84.

—'William J. Seymour and "The Bible Evidence"', in McGee (ed.), *Initial Evidence*, pp. 72-95.

Robeck, Cecil M., Jr (ed.), *Charismatic Experiences in History* (Peabody, MA: Hendrickson, 1985).

Rusch, William G., 'The Theology of the Holy Spirit and the Pentecostal Churches in the Ecumenical Movement', *Pneuma* 9.1 (1987), pp. 19-30.

Ruthven, John, *On the Cessation of the Charismata: A Critique of the Protestant Polemic on Postbiblical Miracles* (JPTSup, 3; Sheffield: Sheffield Academic Press, 1993).

Rybarczyk, Edmund J., 'Beyond Salvation: An Analysis of the Doctrine of Transformation Comparing Eastern Orthodoxy with Classical Pentecostalism' (PhD dissertation, Fuller Theological Seminary, 1999).

Sahlberg, Carl E., 'From Esctasy to Enthusiasm: Some Trends in the Scientific Attitude to the Pentecostal Movement', *ERT* 9.1 (1985), pp. 70-77.

Saunders, Cheryl J., *Saints in Exile: The Holiness-Pentecostal Experience on African American Religion and Culture* (New York: Oxford University Press, 1999).

Scotland, Nigel, *Charismatics and the Next Millennium: Do They Have a Future?* (London: Hodder & Stoughton, 1995).

Sepúlveda, Juan, 'Pentecostalism as Popular Religiosity', *IRM* 78 (1989), pp. 80-88.

Shaull, Richard, and Waldo Caesar, *Pentecostalism and the Future of the Christian Churches: Problems, Limitations, Challenges* (Grand Rapids: Eerdmanns, 2000).

Shelton, James B., *Mighty in Word and Deed: The Role of the Holy Spirit in Luke–Acts* (Peabody, MA: Hendrickson, 1991).

Sheppard, Gerald T., 'The Nicene Creed, *Filoque*, and the Pentecostal Movements in the United States: Ecumenical Perspective on the Holy Spirit', *GOTR* 31.3-4 (1986), pp. 401-18.

—'Pentecostalism and the Hermeneutics of Dispensationalism: The Anatomy of an Uneasy Relationship', *Pneuma* 2.2 (1984), pp. 5-34.

—'The Seduction of Pentecostals within the Politics of Exegesis: The Nicene Creed, *Filioque*, and Pentecostal Ambivalence regarding the Ecumenical Challenge of a Common Confession of Apostolic Faith' (SPS; Gaithensburg, MD, 1985).

—'Word and Spirit: Scripture in the Pentecostal Tradition', *Agora* 1.4 (1978), pp. 14-19.

Sheppard, Gerald T., and Frank Macchia, 'The Gospel that Speaks to Blackness: An Interview with Herbert Daughtry', *Agora* (1980), pp. 14-17, 9.

Simmons, Dale H., *E.W. Kenyon and the Postbellum Pursuit of Peace, Power and Plenty* (SE, 13; Lanham: Scarecrow Press, 1997).

Smail, Thomas, Andrew Walker and Nigel Wright, *Charismatic Renewal: The Search for a Theology* (London: SPCK, 1993).

Smith, Harold B. (ed.), *Pentecostals from the Inside Out* (Wheaton: Victor Books, 1990).

Snyder, Howard A., and Daniel V. Runyon, *The Divided Flame: Wesleyan and Charismatic Renewal* (Grand Rapids: Francis Asbury Press, 1986).

Solivan, Samuel, *The Spirit, Pathos and Liberation: Toward an Hispanic Pentecostal Theology* (JPTSup, 14; Sheffield: Sheffield Academic Press, 1998).

Spittler, Russell P., 'How are Pentecostalism and Fundamentalism Related? In What Way are Pentecostals Fundamentalists?' ('Global Culture' Pentecostal/Charismatic Worldwide, 9–11 May 1991, University of Calgary, Canada).

—'Theological Style among Pentecostals and Charismatics', in John D. Woodbridge and Thomas E. McComskey (eds.), *Doing Theology in Today's World* (Grand Rapids: Zondervan, 1991), pp. 291-318.

Spittler, Russell P. (ed.), *Perspectives on the New Pentecostalism* (Grand Rapids: Baker Book House, 1976).

Stonstadt, Roger, 'Affirming Diversity: God's People as a Community of Prophets', *Pneuma* 17 (1995), pp. 145-57.

—*The Charismatic Theology of St Luke* (Peabody, MA: Hendrickson, 1984).

—*The Prophethood of All Believers: A Study in Luke's Charismatic Theology* (JPTSup, 16; Sheffield: Sheffield Academic Press, 1999).

—*Spirit, Scripture and Theology: A Pentecostal Perspective* (Baguio City, Philippines: Asia Pacific Theological Press, 1995).

Strong, Douglas M., 'William Seymour (1870–1922), Pentecostal Leader at the Azusa Street Revival: Empowered to Bring All Races into One Common Family', in *idem*, *They Walked in the Spirit: Personal Faith and Social Action in America* (Louisville, KY: Westminster/ John Knox Press, 1997), pp. 33-47.

Suurmond, Jean-Jacques, 'A Fresh Look at Spirit Baptism and the Charisms', *ExpTim* 109 (1998), pp. 103-106.

—'Christ King: A Charismatic Appeal for Ecological Lifestyle', *Pneuma* 10.1 (1988), pp. 26-35.

—*Word and Spirit at Play: Towards a Charismatic Theology* (Grand Rapids: Eerdmans, 1994).

Synan, Vinson, *The Holiness-Pentecostal Movement in the United States* (Grand Rapids: Eerdmans, 1971; rev. edn, 1997).

—*In the Latter Days: The Outpouring of the Holy Spirit in the Twentieth Century* (Ann Arbor, MI: Servant, 1984).

—*The Old-Time Power* (Franklin Springs, GA: Advocate, rev. edn, 1986).

—'Pentecostalism: Varieties and Contributions', *Pneuma* 5.1 (1987), pp. 31-49.

—*The Spirit Said 'Grow': The Astounding Worldwide Expansion of Pentecostal and Charismatic Churches* (Monrovia, CA: MARC, 1992).

—'Theological Boundaries: The Arminian Tradition', *Pneuma* 3.2 (1982), pp. 38-53.

—*The Twentieth-Century Pentecostal Explosion: The Exciting Growth of Pentecostal Churches and Charismatic Renewal Movements* (Altamonte Springs, FL: Creation House, 1987).

Synan, Vinson (ed.), *Aspects of Pentecostal-Charismatic Origins* (Plainsfield, NJ: Logos International, 1975).

Thurman, Joyce V., *New Wineskins: A Study of the House Church Movement* (IHC, 30; Bern: Peter Lang, 1982).

Tinney, James, 'The Blackness of Pentecostalism', *Spirit* 3.2 (1979), pp. 27-36.

—'Exclusivist Tendencies in Pentecostal Self Definition' (SPS; Valley Forge, PA, 1978).

—'William J. Seymour: Father of Modern Day Pentecostalism', *JITC* 4 (1976), pp. 33-44.

Turner, Max, 'Eccesiology in the Major "Apostolic" Restoration Churches in the United Kingdom', *VE* 19 (1989), pp. 83-108.

—*Power from on High: The Spirit in Israel's Restoration and Witness in Luke–Acts* (JPTSup, 9; Sheffield: Sheffield Academic Press, 1996).

—'Tongues: An Experience for All in the Pauline Churches?', *AJPS* 1.2 (1998), pp. 231-53.

Turner, William Clair, Jr, 'The United Holy Church of America: A Study in Black Holiness Pentecostalism' (PhD dissertation, Duke University, 1984).

Villfañe, Eldin, 'A Pentecostal Call to Social Spirituality: Confronting Evil in Urban Society' (SPS; Dallas, TX, 1990).

—'The Contours of a Pentecostal Social Ethic: A North American Hispanic Perspective', *Transformation* 33 (1994), pp. 6-10.

—'The Jeremiah Paradigm for the City', *ChrCr* 52 (1992), pp. 374-75.

—'Latino Religion in the United States', in Patrick Allit (ed.), *Major Problems in American Religious History* (Boston: Houghton Mifflin & Company, 2000), pp. 448-52.

—*The Liberating Spirit: Toward an Hispanic American Pentecostal Social Ethic* (Grand Rapids: Eerdmans, 1993).

—'*Mañana* Is Today: A Socio-theological Reflection on the Latino Journey', in Arvind

Sharma (ed.), *Religion in a Secular City: Essays in Honor of Harvey Cox* (Festschrift Harvey Cox; Harrisburg, PA: Trinity Press International, 2001), pp. 105-15.

—'The Politics of the Spirit: Reflections on a Theology of Social Transformation for the Twenty-First Century', *Pneuma* 18.2 (1996), pp. 161-70.

—*Seek Peace in the City: Reflections on Urban Ministry* (Grand Rapids: Eerdmans, 1995).

Volf, Miroslav, *A Passion for God's Reign: Theology, Christian Learning, and the Christian Self* (Grand Rapids: Eerdmans, 1998).

—'A Rhythm of Adoration and Action: A Response to Jürgen Moltmann', in Harold Hunter and Peter Hocken (eds.) *All Together in One Place: Theological Papers from the Brighton Conference on World Evangelization* (JPTSup, 4; Sheffield: Sheffield Academic Press, 1993), pp. 38-45.

—'A Theology of Embrace in a World of Exclusion', in *Reconciliation: A Theology of Embrace in an Age of Exclusion* (Federal Way: World Vision, 1997), pp. 89-100.

—'A Vision of Embrace: Theological Perspectives on Cultural Identity and Conflict', *ERI* 47.2 (1995), pp. 195-205.

—'After Moltmann: Reflections on the Future of Eschatology', in Richard Bauckham (ed.), *God Will Be All in All: The Eschatology of Jürgen Moltmann* (Edinburgh: T. & T. Clark, 1999), pp. 233-57.

—*After our Likeness: The Church as the Image of the Trinity* (Grand Rapids: Eerdmans, 1998).

—'Catholicity of "Two or Three": Free Church Reflections on the Catholicity of the Local Church', *Jurist* 52.1 (1992), pp. 525-46.

—'The Challenge of Protestant Fundamentalism', in Hans Küng and Jürgen Moltmann (eds.), *Fundamentalism as an Ecumenical Challenge* (Concilium, 28; London: SCM Press, 1992).

—'Christian Faith and Human Enmity', in *idem, Steps toward Reconciliation: Ecumenical Conference on Christian Faith and Human Enmity* (Budapest: Ecumenical Council of Churches in Hungary, 1996), pp. 61-78.

—'The Church as a Prophetic Community and a Sign of Hope', *EJT* 2.1 (1993), pp. 9-30.

—'Church, State and Society: Reflections on the Life of the Church in Contemporary Yugoslavia', *Transformation* 6.1 (1989), pp. 24-32.

—'Democracy and Charisma: Reflections on the Democratization of the Church', in James Provost and Knut Walf (eds.), *The Tabu of Democracy within the Church* (Concilium, 5; London: SCM Press, 1992), pp. 114-20.

—'Democracy and Crisis of the Socialist Project: Toward a Post-Revolutionary Theology of Liberation', *Transformation* 7.4 (1990), pp. 11-17.

—'Doing and Interpreting: An Examination of the Relation between Theory and Practice in Latin American Liberation Theology', *Themolios* 8.3 (April 1983), pp. 11-19.

—'Enter into Joy! Sin, Death, and the Life of the World to Come', in John Polkinghorne and Michael Welker (eds.), *The End of the World and the Ends of God: Science and Technology on Eschatology* (Harrisburg, PA: Trinity Press International, 2000), pp. 256-78.

—'Eschaton, Creation, and Social Ethics', *CTJ* 30 (1995), pp. 130-43.

—*Exclusion and Embrace: A Theological Exploration of Identity, Otherness, and Reconciliation* (Nashville: Abingdon Press, 1996).

—'Exclusion and Embrace: Theological Reflections in the Wake of "Ethnic Cleansing" ', *JES* 29.2 (1992), pp. 230-48.

—'The Final Reconciliation: Reflections on a Social Dimension of the Eschatological Transition', *MT* 16.1 (2000), pp. 91-113.

—'Fishing in the Neighbor's Pond: Mission and Proselytism in Eastern Europe', *IBMR* 20.1 (1996), pp. 26-31.

—'God, Freedom, and Grace: Reflections on the Essentiality of Atheism for Marx and Marxism', *Occasional Papers on Religion in Eastern Europe* 10.4 (1990), pp. 15-31.

—'Human Work, Divine Spirit, and New Creation: Toward a Pneumatological Understanding of Work', *Pneuma* 9.2 (1987), pp. 173-93.

—' "It Is Like Yeast": How the Gospel Should Relate to Culture', *TNN* 41.3 (1994), pp. 12-15.

—'In the Cage of Vanities: Christian Faith and the Dynamics of Economic Progress', in Robert Wuthnow (ed.), *Rethinking Materialism: Perspectives on the Spiritual Dimensions of Economic Behavior* (Grand Rapids: Eerdmans, 1995), pp. 169-91.

—'Justice, Exclusion, and Difference', *SP* 9 (1994), pp. 455-76.

—'Market, Central Planning and Participatory Economy: A Response to Robert Goudzwaard', *Transformation* 4 (1987), pp. 60-63.

—'Materiality of Salvation: An Investigation in the Soteriologies of Liberation and Pentecostal Theologies', *JES* 26.3 (1989), pp. 447-67.

—'New Congregationalism: A Protestant Response', in Jürgen Moltmann and Karl-Josef Kuschel (eds.), *Pentecostal Movements as an Ecumenical Challenge* (Concilium, 3; London: SCM Press 1996), pp. 37-43.

—'On Human Work: An Examination of the Key Ideas of the Encyclical *Laborem Exercens*', *SJT* 37 (1984), pp. 65-79.

—'On Loving with Hope: Eschatology and Social Responsibility', *Transformation* 7.3 (1990), pp. 28-31.

—'The Social Meaning of Reconciliation', *Interpretation* 54.1 (2000), pp. 158-72.

—'Soft Difference: Theological Reflections on the Relation between Church and Culture in I Peter', *Ex Auditu* 10 (1994), pp. 15-30.

—'Theology, Meaning, and Power', in Carmen Krieg and Thomas Kucharz (eds.), *The Future of Theology: Essays in Honor of Jürgen Moltmann* (Grand Rapids: Eerdmans, 1996), pp. 98-113.

—' "The Trinity Is Our Social Program": The Doctrine of the Trinity and the Shape of Social Engagement', *MT* 14.3 (1998), pp. 403-23.

—'Trinity, Unity, Primacy: On the Trinitarian Nature of Unity and its Implications for the Question of Primacy', in James F. Puglisi (ed.), *Petrine Ministry and the Unity of the Church: Toward a Patient and Fraternal Dialogue* (Collegeville, MN: Liturgical Press, 1999), pp. 171-84.

—'Truth, Freedom, Violence', in A. Hoekema and Boby Fong (eds.), *Christianity and Culture in the Crossfire* (Grand Rapids: Eerdmans, 1997), pp. 28-50.

—'When the Gospel and Culture Intersect: Notes on the Nature of Christian Difference', in Wonsuk Ma and Robert P. Menzies (eds.), *Pentecostalism in Context: Essays in Honor of William P. Menzies* (Festschrift William W. Menzies; JPTSup, 11; Sheffield: Sheffield Academic Press, 1997), pp. 223-36.

—'When the Unclean Spirit Leaves', *EJT* 1.1 (1992), pp. 15-24.

—'Work', in Michael D. Palmer (ed.), *Elements of a Christian Worldview* (Springfield: Logion Press, 1998), pp. 219-39.

—'Work and the Gifts of the Spirit', in Herbert Schlossberg, Vinay Samuel and Ronard J. Sider (eds.), *Christianity and Economics in the Post-Cold War Era: The Oxford Declaration and Beyond* (Grand Rapids: Eerdmans, 1994), pp. 33-44.

—*Work in the Spirit: Toward a Theology of Work* (New York: Oxford University Press, 1991).

—'Worship as Adoration and Action: Reflections on Christian Way of Being-in-the-World', in D.A. Carson (ed.), *Worship, Adoration and Action* (Grand Rapids: Baker Book House, 1993), pp. 203-11.

Volf, Miroslav, Carmen Krieg and Thomas Kucharz (eds.), *The Future of Theology: Essays in Honor of Jürgen Moltmann* (Grand Rapids: Eerdmans, 1996).

Volf, Miroslav, and Gordon Preece, 'Work', in Adrian Hastings, Alistair Mason and Hugh Pyper (eds.), *The Oxford Companion to Christian Thought* (Oxford: Oxford University Press, 2000), pp. 759-61.

Volf, Miroslav, and Judith M. Gundry, *A Spacious Heart: Essays on Identity and Togetherness* (Harrisburg, PA: Trinity Press International, 1997).

—'Paul and the Politics of Identity: A Review of *Daniel Boyarin, A Radical Jew: Paul and the Politics of Identity*', *Books and Culture* 3.4 (1997), pp. 16-18.

Wacker, Grant A., 'Character and the Modernization of North American Pentecostalism' (SPS; Lakeland, FL, 1991).

—'The Functions of Faith in Primitive Pentecostalism', *HTR* 77 (1984), pp. 353-75.

—'The Holy Spirit and the Spirit of the Age in American Protestantism, 1880–1910', *JAH* 72.1 (1985), pp. 45-62.

—'Pentecostalism', in Charles H. Lippy and Peter W. Williams (eds.), *Encyclopedia of American Religious Experience*, II (New York: Charles Scribner's Sons, 1988), pp. 933-45.

—'Playing for Keeps: The Primitivist Impulse in Early Pentecostalism', in Richard T. Hughes (ed.), *The American Quest for the Primitivist Church* (Urbana: University of Illinois Press, 1988), pp. 196-219.

—'Taking a Look at the *Vision of the Disinherited*', *RelSRev* 8 (1982), pp. 15-22.

—'Travail of a Broken Family: Radical Evangelical Responses to the Emergence of Pentecostalism in America, 1906–16', in Blumhofer, Spittler and Wacker (eds.), *Pentecostal Currents in American Protestantism*, pp. 23-49.

Waldvogel, Edith L., 'The Overcoming Life: A Study in the Evangelical Origins of Pentecostalism' (PhD dissertation, Harvard University, 1977).

Walker, Andrew, *Restoring the Kingdom: The Radical Christianity of the House Church Movement* (London: Hodder & Stoughton, 1985).

—'Thoroughly Modern: Sociological Reflections on the Charismatic Movement from the End of the Twentieth Century', in Hunt, Hamilton and Walter (eds.), *Charismatic Christianity*, pp. 17-42.

Wallis, Arthur, 'Springs of Restoration: Part I', *Restoration* (July–August 1980), pp. 21-24.

—'Springs of Restoration: Part II', *Restoration* (September–October 1980), pp. 6-9.

Walter, Tony, and Steven Hunt, 'The Charismatic Movement and Contemporary Change', *Religion* 28.3 (1998), pp. 219-21.

Ware, Steven, 'Restorationism in the Holiness Movement: Late Nineteenth and Early Twentieth Centuries', *WesTJ* 34.1 (1999), pp. 200-19.

Warner, Wayne E., *The Woman Evangelist: The Life and Times of Charismatic Evangelist Maria B. Woodsworth-Etter* (SE, 8; Metuchen: Scarecrow Press, 1986).

Warnock, George H., *The Feast of Tabernacles: The Hope of the Church* (North Battleford, Sask: Sharon Publishers, 1951).

Warrington, Keith (ed.), *Pentecostal Perspectives* (London: Paternoster Press, 1998).

Washington, Joseph R., Jr, *Black Sects and Cults* (Garden City, NY: Doubleday, 1972).

—'The Black Holiness and Pentecostal Sects', in C. Eric Lincoln (ed.), *The Black Experience in Religion* (Garden City, NY: Anchor Press, 1974), pp. 196-212.

Watson, David, *I Believe in the Church: The Revolutionary Potential of the Family of God* (London: Hodder & Stoughton, 2nd edn, 1983).

Welker, Michael, 'Spirit Topics: Trinity, Personhood, Mystery and Tongues', *JPT* 10 (1997), pp. 29-43.

Whittaker, Colin C. (ed.), *Seven Pentecostal Pioneers* (Springfield: Gospel Publishing House, 1983).

Williams, Derek, 'Denominations the End of the Road? An Investigation into "House Churches" ', *Crusade* (January 1981), pp. 22-26.

Williams, Melvin D., *Community in a Black Pentecostal Church* (Pittsburgh: University of Pittsburgh Press, 1974).

Williams, Rodman J., *The Era of the Spirit* (Plainsfield: Logos International, 1971).

—'The Holy Spirit and Eschatology', *Pneuma* 3.2 (1981), pp. 54-58.

—*The Pentecostal Reality* (Plainsfield: Logos International, 1972).

—*Renewal Theology: Systematic Theology from a Charismatic Perspective* (Grand Rapids: Zondervan, 1996).

Willmer, Haddon, 'The Significance of Restoration', *BQ* (March 1987), pp. 19-27.

Wilson, John, and Harvey K. Chow, 'Themes of Power and Control in a Pentecostal Assembly', *JSSR* 20 (1981), pp. 241-50.

Womack, David A., *The Wellspring of the Pentecostal Movement* (Springfield: Gospel Publishing House, 1968).

Wonsuk, Ma, and Robert P. Menzies (eds.), *Pentecostalism in Context: Essays in Honor of William W. Menzies* (JPTSup, 11; Sheffield: Sheffield Academic Press, 1997).

Wood, Dillard L., and William H. Preskitt, Jr, *Baptized with Fire: A History of the Fire Baptized Holiness Church* (Franklin Springs, GA: Advocate Press, 1983).

Wright, Nigel G., 'The Kansas City Prophets: An Assessment', *Themelios* 17.1 (1991), pp. 20-21.

—'The Nature and Variety of Restorationism and the "House Church" Movement', in Hunt, Hamilton and Walter (eds.), *Charismatic Christianity*, pp. 60-76.

Wright, John H., 'The Church: Community of the Holy Spirit', *TS* 48 (1987), pp. 25-44.

Yong, Amos, *Discerning the Spirit(s): A Pentecostal-Charismatic Contribution to the Christian Theology of Religion* (JPTSup, 20; Sheffield: Sheffield Academic Press, 2000).

—' "Not Knowing Where the Wind Blows…": On Envisioning a Pentecostal-Charismatic Theology of Religion', *JPT* 14 (1999), pp. 81-112.

—' "Tongues of Fire" in the Pentecostal Imagination: The Truth of Glossolalia in Light of R.C. Neville's Theory of Religious Symbolism', *JPT* 12 (1998), pp. 39-65.

—'The Truth of Tongues Speech: A Rejoinder to Frank Macchia', *JPT* 13 (1998), pp. 107-15.

Zeegaart, Huibert, 'Apocalyptic Eschatology and Pentecostalism: The Relevance of John's Millennium for Today', *Pneuma* 10.1 (1988), pp. 3-25.

Zimmerman, Thomas F., 'The Reason for the Rise of the Pentecostal Movement', in Synan (ed.), *Aspects of Pentecostal-Charismatic Origins*, pp. 5-13.

General Theology

Barth, Karl, *Church Dogmatics* (ed. G.W. Bromiley and T.F. Torrance; trans. G.W. Bromiley; Edinburgh: T. & T. Clark, 2nd edn, 1975).

—*Prayer* (ed. D.E. Saliers; trans. S. Terrien; Philadelphia: Westminster Press, 1985), pp. 17-19.

—*The Epistle to the Romans* (trans. Edwyn C. Hoskyns; London: Oxford University Press, 6th edn, 1993).

Bassett, William W., and Peter Huizing (eds.), *Experience of the Spirit* (Concilium, 9; New York: Seabury Press, 1974).

Bebbington, D.W., *Evangelicalism in Modern Britain: A History from the 1730s to the 1980s* (London: Unwin Hyman, 1989).

Berger, Peter L., and Thomas Luckmann, *The Social Reality of Religion* (New York: Anchor Books, 1967).

Brummett, Barry, *Contemporary Apocalyptic Rhetoric* (New York: Praeger Publishers, 1991).

Costas, Orlando, *The Integrity of Mission: The Inner Life and Outreach of the Church* (New York: Harper & Row, 1979).

Del Colle, Ralph, *Christ and the Spirit: Spirit-Christology in Trinitarian Perspective* (New York: Oxford University Press, 1994.

—'The Experience of the Divine', *CS* 31.3 (1992), pp. 290-300.

Dillenberger, John (ed.), *Martin Luther: Selections from his Writing* (New York: Anchors Books, 1961).

Dunn, James D.G., *Baptism of the Holy Spirit: A Re-Examination of the New Testament Teaching on the Gift of the Holy Spirit in Relation to Pentecostalism Today* (London: SCM Press, 1970).

—'The Baptism of the Holy Spirit... Yet Once More', *EPTA* 18 (1998), pp. 3-25.

—*Jesus and the Spirit: A Study of the Religious and Charismatic Experience of Jesus and the First Christians as Reflected in the New Testament* (Philadelphia: Westminster Press, 1975).

Erickson, Millard J., *Contemporary Options in Eschatology: A Study of the Millennium* (Grand Rapids: Baker Book House, 1977).

Frei, Hans W., *Types of Christian Theology* (eds. George Hunsinger and William C. Placher; New Haven: Yale University Press, 1992).

Gaybba, Brian, *The Spirit of Love: Theology of the Holy Spirit* (London: Geoffrey Chapman, 1987).

Geertz, Clifford, *The Interpretation of Cultures: Selected Essays* (New York: Basic Books, 1973).

Gorringe, T.J., *Discerning Spirit: A Theology of Revelation* (London: SCM Press, 1990).

Gresham, John L. Jr, 'Three Trinitarian Spiritualities', *JSF* 15.1 (1994), pp. 21-33.

Hadden, Jeffrey and Anson Shupe (eds.), *Prophetic Religions and Politics* (New York: Paragon House, 1986).

Hanson, Paul D., *The Dawn of the Apocalyptic* (Philadelphia: Fortress Press, 1979).

Heron, Alasdair I.C., *The Holy Spirit: The Holy Spirit in the Bible, the History of Christian Thought, and Recent Theology* (Philadelphia: Westminster Press, 1983).

Hill, William J., *The Three-Person God* (Washington: Catholic University of America Press, 1982).

Inch, Morris A., *Saga of the Spirit: A Biblical and Historical Theology of the Spirit* (Grand Rapids: Baker Book House, 1985).

Kierkegaard, Søren, *Concluding Unscientific Postscript* (trans. David F. Swenson and Walter Lowrie; Princeton, NJ: Princeton University Press, 1968).

Lampe, G.W.H., *The Seal of the Spirit: A Study of the Doctrine of Baptism and Confirmation in the New Testament and the Fathers* (London: Longmans, Green, 1951).

Maddox, Randy L., *Responsible Grace: John Wesley's Practical Theology* (Nashville: Abingdon Press, 1994).

Marsden, George M., *Fundamentalism and American Culture: The Shaping of Twentieth-Century Evangelicalism 1870–1925* (New York: Oxford University Press, 1980).

—*Understanding Fundamentalism and Evangelicalism* (Grand Rapids: Eerdmans, 1991).

Marsden, George M. (ed.), *Evangelicalism and Modern America* (Grand Rapids: Eerdmans, 1984).

Marshal, I. Howard (ed.), *Christian Experience in Theology and Life: Papers Read at the 1994 Conference of the European Evangelical Theologians* (Edinburgh: Rutherford House, 1988).

Niebuhr, H. Richard, *Christ and Culture* (New York: Harper Torchbooks, 1951).

Oden, Thomas C., *Life in the Spirit: Systematic Theology* (San Francisco: HarperCollins, 1992).

Opsahl, Paul D. (ed.), *The Holy Spirit in the Life of the Church: From Biblical Times to the Present* (Minneapolis: Augsburg, 1978).

Pinnock, Clark H., *Flame of Love: A Theology of the Holy Spirit* (Downers Grove, IL: Inter-Varsity Press, 1996).

Ragaz, L., 'Der Kampft um das Reich Gottes', in C. Blumhardt, *Vater und Sohn- und weiter* (Zürich: Rotapfel Verlag, 1923).

Sandeen, Ernest R., *The Roots of Fundamentalism: British and American Millenarianism, 1800–1930* (Chicago: University of Chicago Press, 1970).

Schalzmann, Siegfried, *A Pauline Theology of Charismata* (Peabody, MA: Hendrickson, 1987).

Stackhouse, Reginald, *The End of the World? A New Look at an Old Belief* (New York: Paulist Press, 1997).

Thorsen, Donald A.D., *The Wesleyan Quadrilateral: Scripture, Tradition, Reason and Experience as Model of Evangelical Theology* (Grand Rapids: Zondervan, 1990).

Weber, Timothy P., *Living in the Shadow of the Second Coming: American Premillennialism, 1875–1925* (New York: Oxford University Press, 1979).

Wells, Harold, 'The Holy Spirit and Theology of the Cross: Significance for Dalogue', *TS* 53 (1992), pp. 476-92.

Wesley, John, *John Wesley* (ed. Albert Outler; New York: Oxford University Press, 1964).

—*The Works of John Wesley: Complete and Unabridged* (Grand Rapids: Baker Book House, 3rd edn, 1984).

Wood, Laurence W., 'Pentecostal Sanctification in John Wesley and Early Methodism', *WesTJ* 34.1 (1999), pp. 24-63.

Moltmann

Ansell, Nik, review of *The Coming of God: Christian Eschatology* (trans. Margaret Kohl; Minneapolis: Fortress Press, 1996), by Jürgen Moltmann, in *Themolios* 24 (1999), pp. 75-76.

Aung, Salai Hla, *The Doctrine of Creation in the Theology of Barth, Moltmann and Pannenberg* (Regensburg: Roderer, 1998).

Bauckham, Richard J., 'Bibliography: Jürgen Moltmann', *ModC* 28.2 (1986), pp. 55-60.

—*Moltmann: Messianic Theology in the Making* (London: Marshall Pickering, 1987).

—*The Theology of Jürgen Moltmann* (Edinburgh: T. & T. Clark, 1995).

Bauckham, Richard J. (ed.), *God Will Be All in All: The Eschatology of Jürgen Moltmann* (Edinburgh: T. & T. Clark, 1999).

Bentley, James, 'Christoph Blumhardt: Preacher of Hope', *Theology* 78 (1975), pp. 577-82.

Bouma, Prediger Steven, 'Creation as the Home of God: The Doctrine of Creation in the Theology of Jürgen Moltmann', *CTJ* 32 (1997), pp. 72-90.

—*The Greening of Theology: The Ecological Models of Rosemary Radford Ruether, Joseph Sittler and Jürgen Moltmann* (Atlanta: Scholars Press, 1995).

Burnham, Frederick B., Charles S. McCoy and M. Douglas Meeks, *Love: The Foundation of*

Hope. The Theology of Jürgen Moltmann and Elisabeth Moltmann-Wendel (San Francisco: Harper & Row, 1988).

Byran, G. McLeod (ed.), *Communities of Faith and Radical Discipleship: Jürgen Moltmann and Others* (Macon, GA: Mercer University Press, 1986).

Cabestrero, Teofilo (ed.), *Faith: Conversations with Contemporary Theologians* (trans. Donald D. Walsh; Maryknoll, NY: Orbis Books, 1980).

Callen, Barry L., 'Wesleyan Theology and Eschatology', *WesTJ* 29 (1994), pp. 5-164.

Capps, Walter H., *Hope against Hope: Moltmann to Merton in One Decade* (Philadelphia: Fortress Press, 1976).

Chapman, G. Clarke, 'Jürgen Moltmann and the Christian Dialogue with Marxism', *JES* 18 (1981), pp. 435-50.

Clutterbuck, Richard, 'Jürgen Moltmann as Doctrinal Theologian: The Nature of Doctrine and the Possibilities for its Development', *SJT* 48.4 (1995), pp. 489-505.

Conyers, A.J., *God, Hope and History: Jürgen Moltmann and the Christian Concept of History* (Macon, GA: Mercer University Press, 1988).

Cornelison, Robert Thomas, *The Christian Realism of Reinhold Niebuhr and the Political Theology of Jürgen Moltmann in Dialogue* (San Francisco: Mellen Research University Press, 1992).

Cousins, Evert H. (ed.), *Hope and the Future of Man* (Philadelphia: Fortress Press, 1972).

Dabney, D. Lyle, 'The Advent of the Spirit: The Turn to Pneumatology in the Theology of Jürgen Moltmann', *ATJ* 48 (1993), pp. 81-107.

—'Jürgen Moltmann and John Wesley's Third Article Theology', *WesTJ* 29 (1994), pp. 140-48.

Davis, Joe, 'The Eschatology of Jürgen Moltmann', *SWJT* 36 (1994), pp. 26-27.

Deane-Drummond, Alia, *Ecology in Jürgen Moltmann's Theology* (Lewiston, NY: Edwin Mellen Press, 1997).

Dillistone, Frederick W., 'Theology of Jürgen Moltmann', *ModC* 18 (1975), pp. 145-50.

Ford, David, *The Modern Theologians: An Introduction to Christian Theology in the Twentieth Century* (Oxford: Basil Blackwell, 1989).

Gorringe, Timothy, 'Eschatology and Political Radicalism: The Example of Karl Barth and Jürgen Moltmann', in Bauckham (ed.), *All in All*, pp. 87-114.

Gunton, Colin E. (ed.), *The Doctrine of Creation: Essays in Dogmatics, History and Philosophy* (Edinburgh: T. & T. Clark, 1997).

Hatt, Harold, 'Baptism as a Liberating Event: The Witness of C.C. Morrison, Jürgen Moltmann and BEM', *Mid-Stream* 26 (1987), pp. 22-30.

Haynes, Stephen R., *Prospects for Post-Holocaust Theology* (Atlanta: Scholars Press, 1992).

Herzog, Frederick (ed.), *The Future of Hope: Theology as Eschatology* (New York: Herder & Herder, 1970).

Jaeger, John David, 'Abraham Heschel and the Theology of Jürgen Moltmann', *PRS* 24 (1997), pp. 167-79.

—'Jürgen Moltmann and the Problem of Evil', *ATS* 53 (1998), pp. 5-14.

Küng, Hans, and David Tracy (eds.), *Paradigm Change in Theology: A Symposium for the Future* (New York: Crossroad, 1989).

Küng, Hans, and Jürgen Moltmann (eds.), *A Council for Peace* (Concilium, 1; Edinburgh: T. & T. Clark, 1988).

—*An Ecumenical Confession of Faith?* (Concilium, 118; New York: Seabury, 1979).

—*Christianity among the World Religions* (Concilium, 1; Edinburgh: T. & T. Clark, 1986).

—*Conflicting Ways of Interpreting the Bible* (Concilium, 138; Edinburgh: T. & T. Clark, 1980).

—*Conflicts about the Holy Spirit* (Concilium, 128; New York: Seabury, 1979).

—*The Ethics of World Religions and Human Rights* (Concilium, 2; London: SCM Press, 1990).

—*Islam: A Challenge for Christianity* (Concilium, 3; London: SCM Press, 1994).

—*Mary in the Churches* (Concilium, 8; Edinburgh: T. & T. Clark, 1983).

—*The Right to Dissent* (Concilium, 8; New York: Seabury, 1982).

—*Who Has a Say in the Church* (Concilium, 8; Edinburgh: T. & T. Clark, 1981).

—*Why Did God Make Me?* (Concilium, 108; New York: Seabury, 1978).

Lapide, Pinchas, and Jürgen Moltmann, *Jewish Monotheism and Christian Trinitarianism: A Dialogue* (Philadelphia: Fortress Press, 1981).

MacLeon, Donald, 'The Christology of Jürgen Moltmann', *Themolios* 24.2 (1999), pp. 35-47.

MacQuarrie, John, review of *The Theology of Jürgen Moltmann* (Edinburgh: T. & T. Clark, 1995), by Richard J. Bauckham, in *ExpTim* 107 (1995), p. 89.

March, W. Eugene, 'A Theology of Hope: Grateful Reflections on the Work of Jürgen Moltmann', *ASBFE* 84 (1969), pp. 40-56.

McSwain, Larry L., 'Foundations for a Ministry of Transformation', *RevExp* 77 (1980), pp. 253-70.

McWilliam, Warren, 'Christic Paradigm and Cosmic Christ: Ecological Christology in the Theologies of Sallie McFague and Jürgen Moltmann', *PRS* 25 (1998), pp. 341-55.

—'Trinitarian Doxology: Jürgen Moltmann the Relation of the Economic and Immanent Trinity', *PRS* 23 (1996), pp. 25-38.

—'Why All the Fuss about Filioque? Karl Barth and Jürgen Moltmann on the Procession of the Spirit', *PRS* 22 (1995), pp. 167-81.

Meeks, M. Douglas, *Origins of the Theology of Hope* (Philadelphia: Fortress Press, 1974).

Metz, Johannes B. (ed.), *New Questions on God* (New York: Herder & Herder, 1972).

Metz, Johannes Baptist, and Jürgen Moltmann, *Faith and the Future: Essays on Theology, Solidarity and Modernity* (Concilium, 6; Maryknoll, NY: Orbis Books, 1995).

Min, Anschen Kyengsuk, 'Liberation, the Other and Hegel in Recent Pneumatologies', *RelSRev* 22 (1996), pp. 28-33.

Moltmann, Jürgen, 'The Alienation and Liberation of Nature', in Leroy S. Rouner (ed.), *On Nature* (Notre Dame: University of Notre Dame Press, 1984), pp. 133-44.

—'All Things New: Invited to God's Future Evangelism and Eschatology', *ATJ* 48 (1993), pp. 29-38.

—'American Dream: Dreamed by a Non-American', *MoravianTSB* (1972–77), pp. 91-99.

—'The Challenge of Religions in the '80s: How my Mind Has Changed', *CC* 97 (1980), pp. 465-68.

—'Christ in Cosmic Context', in Hilary Regan, Alan J. Torrance and Antony Wood (eds.), *Christ in Context* (Edinburgh: T. & T. Clark, 1993), pp. 205-209.

—'Christian Hope: Messianic or Transcendent: A Theological Discussion with Joachim of Fiori and Thomas Aquinas', *Horizons* 12 (1985), pp. 328-48.

—'Christian Theology and its Problem Today', *RW* 32 (1972), pp. 5-16.

—'Christian Theology and Political Religion', in Leroy S. Rouner (ed.), *Civil Religion and Political Theology* (BUSPR, 8; Notre Dame: University of Notre Dame Press, 1986), pp. 41-58.

—'Christianity in the Third Millennium', *TTod* 51 (1994), pp. 75-89.

—'Christology in the Jewish–Christian Dialogue', in Val Ambrose McInnes (ed.), *New Visions* (New York: Crossroad, 1993), pp. 77-93.

—*The Church in the Power of the Spirit: A Contribution to Messianic Ecclesiology* (trans. Margaret Kohl; London: SCM Press, 1977).

—*The Coming of God: Christian Eschatology* (trans. Margaret Kohl; Minneapolis: Fortress Press, 1996).

—'Communities of Faith and Radical Discipleship: Interview by Miroslav Volf', *CC* 100 (1983), pp. 246-49.

—'The Confession of Jesus Christ: A Biblical Theological Consideration', in Hans Küng and Jürgen Moltmann (eds.), *An Ecumenical Confession of Faith?* (Concilium, 118; New York: Seabury, 1979), pp. 13-19.

—'The Cosmic Community: A New Ecological Concept of Reality in Science and Religion', *Ching-Feng* 29.2-3 (1986), pp. 93-105.

—'Covenant or Leviathan? Political Theology for Modern Times', *SJT* 47.1 (1994), pp. 19-41.

—*Creating a Just Future: The Politics of Peace and the Ethics of Creation in a Threatened World* (London: SCM Press, 1989).

—'Creation and Redemption', in Richard W.A. McKinney (ed.), *Creation, Christ and Culture* (Edinburgh: T. & T. Clark, 1976), pp. 119-34.

—'The Cross and Civil Religion', in Institute of Christian Thought (ed.), *Religion and Political Society* (trans. Institute of Christian Thought; New York: Harper & Row, 1970), pp. 14-47.

—*The Crucified God: The Cross of Christ as the Foundation and Criticism of Christian Theology* (trans. R.A. Wilson and John Bowden; London: SCM Press, 1974).

—'Descent into Hell', *DukeR* 33 (1968), pp. 115-19.

—'Die einladende Einheit des dreieinigen Gottes', in *In der Geschichte des dreieinigen Gottes: Beitrage zur trinitarischen Theologie* (Munich: Kaiser, 1991), pp. 117-28.

—'The Ecological Crisis: Peace with Nature', *ScotJRS* 9 (1988), pp. 5-18.

—'The End of Everything Is God: Has Belief in Hell Had its Day?', *ExpTim* 108 (January 1997), pp. 263-64.

—*Ethics of World Religions and Human Rights* (Philadelphia: Trinity Press International, 1990).

—'The Expectation of his Coming', *Theology* 88 (1985), pp. 425-28.

—*Experiences in Theology: Ways and Forms of Christian Theology* (trans. Margaret Kohl; London: SCM Press, 2000).

—*Experiences of God* (trans. Margaret Kohl; London: SCM Press, 1980).

—*The Experiment Hope* (ed. M. Douglas Meeks; trans. M. Douglas Meeks; Philadelphia: Fortress Press, 1975).

—'Fellowship in a Divided World', *ER* 24 (1972), pp. 436-46.

—'The Fellowship of the Holy Spirit: Trinitarian Pneumatology', *SJT* 37.3 (1984), pp. 287-300.

—'First the Kingdom of God', *Tripod* 63 (1991), pp. 6-27.

—*Following Jesus Christ in the World: Responsibility for the World and Christian Discipleship* (Eckhart, IN: Institute of Mennonite Studies, 1983).

—'The Future as a New Paradigm of Transcendence', *Concurrence* 1 (1969), pp. 334-45.

—*The Future of Creation* (trans. Margaret Kohl; San Franscisco: SCM Press, 1979).

—'God and the Nuclear Catastrophe', *Pacifica* (1988), pp. 157-70.

—*God for a Secular Society: The Public Relevance of Theology* (trans. Margaret Kohl; London: SCM Press, 1999).

—*God in Creation: An Ecological Doctrine of Creation* (trans. Margaret Kohl; London: SCM Press, 1985).

—'God in the Revolution', *Student World* 61.3 (1968), pp. 241-52.

—'God Is Unselfish Love', in John B. Cobb, Jr, and Christopher Ives (eds.), *Emptying God: A Buddhist-Jewish-Christian Conversation* (Faith Meets Faith Series; Maryknoll, NY: Orbis Books, 1990), pp. 116-24.

—'God Means Freedom', in Henry James Young (ed.), *God and Human Freedom: A Festschrift in Honor of Howard Thurman* (Festschrift Howard Thurman; Richmond, IN: Friends United Press, 1983), pp. 10-22.

—'God Reconciles and Makes Free', *RPW* 31 (September–December 1970), pp. 105-18.

—*The Gospel of Liberation* (Waco, TX: Word Books, 1973).

—'Has Modern Society Any Future', in *On the Threshhold of the Third Millennium* (Concilium, 1990/1; Philadelphia: Trinity Press International, 1990), pp. 10-22.

—'Henriette Visser't Hooft and Karl Barth', *TTod* 55 (1999), pp. 524-31.

—*History and the Triune God: Contributions to Trinitarian Theology* (New York: Crossword, 1991).

—'The Holy Spirit and the Theology of Life: Seven Theses', in Arvind Sharma (ed.), *Religion in a Secular City: Essays in Honor of Harvey Cox* (Festschrift Harvey Cox; Harrisburg, PA: Trinity International Press, 2001), pp. 116-20.

—'Homecoming for Abraham's and Sarah's Children and Augustine's Lonely Soul', *Dialog* 35 (1998), pp. 277-81.

—'Hope and Confidence: A Conversation with Ernst Bloch', *Dialogue* 7 (1968), pp. 42-55.

—'Hope and History', *TTod* 25 (1968), pp. 369-86.

—*Hope and Planning* (New York: Harper & Row, 1971).

—'Hope Beyond History', *DukeR* 33 (1968), pp. 109-14.

—*How I Have Changed: Reflections on 30 Years of Theology* (Harrisburg, PA: Trinity Press International, 1997).

—'I Believe in God the Father: Patriarchal or Non-Patriarchal Reference', *Drew-Gateway* 59 (1990), pp. 3-25.

—'In the End, All Is God's: Is Belief in Hell Obsolete?', *SewTR* 40 (1997), pp. 232-34.

—'The Inviting Unity of the Triune God', in Claude Geffré and Jean-Pierre Jossua (eds.), *Monotheism* (Concilium, 177; trans. Robert Nowell; Edinburgh: T. & T. Clark, 1985), pp. 50-58.

—'Is "Pluralistic Theology" Useful for the Dialogue of World Religions', in Gavin D'Costa (ed.), *Christian Uniqueness Reconsidered: The Myth of a Pluralistic Theology of Religion* (FFS; Maryknoll, NY: Orbis Books, 1990), pp. 149-56.

—'Is Protestantism the "Religion of Freedom" ', in Leroy S. Rouner (ed.), *On Freedom* (Notre Dame: University of Notre Dame Press, 1989), pp. 30-45.

—*Is There Life After Death?* (Milwaukee: Marquette University Press, 1998).

—'Jesus and the Kingdom of God', *ATJ* 48 (1993), pp. 5-17.

—'Jesus between Jews and Christians', *ARC* 24 (1996), pp. 61-76.

—*Jesus Christ for Today's World* (London: SCM Press, 1994).

—'Justice for Victims and Perpetrators', *RW* 44 (1994), pp. 2-12.

—'Knowing and Community', in Leroy S. Rouner (ed.), *On Community* (BUSPR, 12; Notre Dame: University of Notre Dame Press, 1991), pp. 162-76.

—'The Liberating Feast', in Herman Schmidt and David Power (eds.), *Politics and Liturgy* (New York: Herder & Herder, 1974), pp. 74-84.

—'Liberating Yourselves and Accepting One Another', in Nancy L. Eiesland and Don E. Saliers (eds.), *Human Disability and the Service of God* (Nashville: Abingdon Press, 1998), pp. 105-122.

—'Liberation in the Light of Hope', in Alexander L. McKelway and David E. Willis (eds.), *Contexts of Contemporary Theology: Essays in Honor of Paul Lehmann* (Festschrift Paul Lehmann; trans. M. Douglas Meeks; Atlanta: John Knox Press, 1974), pp. 127-46.

—*Man: Christian Anthropology in the Conflicts of the Present* (trans. John Sturdy; London: SPCK, 1974).

—'Man and the Son of Man', in J. Robert Nelson (ed.), *No Man Is Alien: Essays on the Unity of Mankind* (Leiden: E.J. Brill, 1971), pp. 203-24.

—'Messianic Atheism', in Leroy S. Rouner (ed.), *Knowing Religiously* (BUSPR, 7; Notre Dame: University of Notre Dame Press, 1985), pp. 192-205.

—'Messianic Hope in Christianity', in Hans Küng and Walter Kasper (eds.), *Christians and Jews* (Concilium, 5; New York: Seabury, 1974), pp. 61-67.

—'New Boundaries in Christendom', *Dialogue* 7 (1968), pp. 283-93.

—*The Open Church: Invitation to Messianic Lifestyle* (London: SCM Press, 1978).

—'Original Study Paper', in Allen O. Miller (ed.), *Christian Declaration on Human Rights: Theological Studies of the World Alliance of Reformed Churches* (Grand Rapids: Eerdmans, 1977), pp. 25-38.

—*A Passion for God's Reign: Theology, Christian Learning and the Christian Life* (Grand Rapids: Eerdmans, 1998).

—*A Passion for Life: A Messianic Lifestyle* (trans. M. Douglas Meeks; Philadelphia: Fortress Press, 1978).

—'The Passion of Christ and the Suffering of God', *ATJ* 49 (1993), pp. 19-28.

—'The Passion of Life', *CurTM* 4 (1977), pp. 3-9.

—'A Pentecostal Theology of Life' (trans. Frank D. Macchia), *JPT* 9 (1996), pp. 3-15.

—'Political Discipleship of Christ Today', in G. McLeod Bryan (ed.), *Communities of Faith and Radical Discipleship* (Macon, GA: Mercer University Press, 1986), pp. 15-31.

—'Political Reconciliation', in Leroy S. Rouner (ed.), *Religion, Politics and Peace* (BUSPR, 20; Notre Dame: University of Notre Dame Press, 1999), pp. 17-31.

—'Political Theology and Liberation Theology', *USQR* 45.3-4 (1991), pp. 205-17.

—'Political Theology', *TTod* 28 (1971), pp. 6-23.

—'Political Theology and the Ethics of Peace', in Leroy S. Rouner (ed.), *Celebrating Peace* (BUSPR, 11; Notre Dame, University of Notre Dame Press, 1990), pp. 102-17.

—'Political Theology and the Ethics of Peace', in Theodore Runyon (ed.), *Theology, Politics and Peace* (Maryknoll, NY: Orbis Books, 1989), pp. 31-42.

—'Political Theology and the Theology of Liberation', in Joerg Rieger (ed.), *Liberating the Future: God, Mammon and Theology* (Minneapolis: Fortress Press, 1998), pp. 60-80.

—'Politics and the Practice of Hope', *CC* (March 11, 1970), pp. 288-91.

—'The Possible Nuclear Catastrophe and Where Is God?', *ScotJRS* 9 (1988), pp. 71-88.

—*The Power of the Powerless* (San Francisco: Harper & Row, 1983).

—'Racism and the Right to Resist', *Study Encounter* 8.1 (1972), pp. 1-10.

—'Realism of Hope: The Feast of the Resurrection and the Transformation of the Present Reality', *CTM* 40 (1969), pp. 149-55.

—'Reconciliation with Nature: Ecological Crisis as Religious Crisis', *WW* 11 (spring 1991), pp. 117-23 (repr. in *Pacifica* 5 [1992], pp. 301-313).

—'Reformation and Revolution', in Manfred Hoffman (ed.), *Martin Luther and the Modern Mind* (Toronto: Edwin Mellen Press, 1985), pp. 163-89.

—*Religion, Revolution and the Future* (trans. M. Douglas Meeks; New York: Charles Scribner's Sons, 1969).

—'A Response to my Pentecostal Dialogue Partners', *JPT* 4 (1994), pp. 59-70.

—'Resurrection as Hope', *HTR* 61 (1968), pp. 129-47.

—'The Resurrection of Christ: Hope of the World', in Gavin D'Costa (ed.), *Resurrection Reconsidered* (Oxford: Oneworld Publications, 1996), pp. 73-86.

—'Revolution as an Issue in Theology: Jürgen Moltmann', *ResQ* 26.2 (1983), pp. 105-20.

—'The Scope of Renewal in the Spirit', *ER* 42 (1990), pp. 98-106 (repr. in *Perspectives* 6 [1991], pp. 14-17).

—'Shekinah: The Home of the Homeless God', in Leroy S. Rouner (ed.), *Longing for Home* (BUSPR, 17; Notre Dame: University of Notre Dame Press, 1996), pp. 170-83.

—'Some Reflections on the Social Doctrine of the Trinity', in James M. Byrne (ed.), *Christian Understanding of God Today* (Dublin: Columbia Press, 1993), pp. 104-11.

—*The Source of Life: The Holy Spirit and the Theology of Life* (trans. Margaret Kohl; Minnesota: Fortress Press, 1997).

—'Special Column: The Church as Communion', in Wim Beuken, Seán Freyne and Anton Weiler (eds.), *Messianism through History* (Concilium, 1; London: SCM Press, 1993), pp. 136-38.

—'Special Column: End of Utopia —End of History?', in Norbert Grienacker and Norbert Mette (eds.), *Christianity and Cultures* (Concilium, 2; Maryknoll, NY: Orbis Books, 1994), pp. 134-36.

—'The Spirit Gives Life: Spirituality and Vitality', in Harold Hunter and Peter Hocken (eds.), *All Together in One Place: Theological Papers from the Brighton Conference on World Evangelization* (JPTSup, 4; Sheffield: Sheffield Academic Press, 1993), pp. 22-37.

—*The Spirit of Life: A Universal Affirmation* (trans. Margaret Kohl; Minneapolis: Fortress Press, 1992).

—'Stubborn Hope: Interview by C.A. Hall', *CT* 37 (1993), pp. 30-33.

—'Talk Back Session with Jürgen Moltmann', *ATJ* 48 (1993), pp. 39-47.

—'Teresa of Avila and Martin Luther: The Turn to the Mysticism of the Cross', *SR* 13.3 (1984), pp. 265-78.

—'Theologia Reformata et Semper Reformanda', in David Willis and Michael Welker (eds.), *Toward the Future of Reformed Theology: Tasks, Topics, Traditions* (London: SCM Press; Grand Rapids: Eerdmans, 1999), pp. 120-35.

—'Theological Basis of Human Rights and the Liberation of Man', *RW* 31 (1971), pp. 348-57.

—'Theological Proposal towards the Resolution of the Filioque Controversy', in Lukas Vischer (ed.), *Spirit of God, Spirit of Christ: Ecumenical Reflections on the Filioque Controversy* (Faith and Order Paper, 103; Geneva: WCC, 1981), pp. 164-73.

—*Theology and Joy* (trans. Reinhard Ulrich; London: SCM Press, 1973).

—'Theology in Germany Today', in Jürgen Habermas (ed.), *Observations on 'the Spiritual Situation of the Age'* (trans. Andrew Buchwalter; Cambridge, MA: MIT Press, 1984), pp. 181-205.

—*Theology of Hope: On the Ground and the Implications of a Christian Eschatology* (trans. James W. Leitch; London: SCM Press, 1967).

—'Theology of Mystical Experience', *SJT* 32.6 (1979), pp. 501-20.

—*Theology Today: Two Contributions towards Making Theology Present* (London: SCM Press, 1988).

—*There Is Enough for Everyone: A Sermon Given at Ryerson United Church, Vancouver, February 26, 1989* (Vancouver: Vancouver School of Theology, 1989).

—'Toward a Political Hermeneutics of the Gospel', *USQR* 23 (1968), pp. 303-23.

—*The Trinity and the Kingdom* (trans. Margaret Kohl; Minneapolis: Fortress Press, 1991).

—'Trinitarian History of God?', *Theology* 78 (1975), pp. 632-46.

—*Two Studies in the Theology of Bonhoeffer* (New York: Charles Scribner's Sons, 1967).

—'Unity of the Triune God', *StVTQ* 28.3 (1984), pp. 157-71.

—*The Way of Jesus Christ* (trans. Margaret Kohl; London: SCM Press, 1990).

—'The Wealth of Gifts of the Spirit and their Christian Identity', in Christopher Theobald (ed.), *Unanswered Questions* (Concilium, 1; London: SCM Press, 1999), pp. 30-35.

—'What Kind of Unity: The Dialogue Between the Traditions of East and West', in Emilio Castro (ed.), *Lausanne 77* (Geneva: WCC, 1977), pp. 38-47.

—'Wrestling with God: A Personal Meditation', *CC* 114 (1997), pp. 726-29.

Moltmann, Jürgen (ed.), *Hope for the Church: Moltmann in Dialogue with Practical Theology* (Nashville: Abingdon Press, 1979).

—*Religion and Political Society* (New York: Harper & Row, 1974).

Moltmann, Jürgen, and Karl-Josef Kuschel (eds.), *Pentecostal Movements as an Ecumenical Challenge* (Concilium, 3; London: SCM Press, 1996).

Moltmann-Wendel, Elisabeth, and Jürgen Moltmann, 'Becoming Human in New Community', in Constance F. Parvey (ed.), *Community of Women and Men in the Church* (Philadelphia: Fortress Press, 1983), pp. 29-42.

—*God—His and Hers* (trans. John Bowden; New York: Crossroad, 1991).

—*Humanity in God* (Cleveland, OH: Pilgrim Press, 1983).

Mondin, Battista, 'The Pneumatic Structure of the Church: Charisms and Evangelical Counsels', in Hermann Deuser, *et al.* (eds.), *Gottes Zukunft-zukunft der Welt: Festschrift für Jürgen Moltmann zum 60 Geburtstag* (Festschrift Jürgen Moltmann; Munich: Chr. Kaiser Verlag, 1986), pp. 190-98.

Morse, Christopher, *The Logic of Promise in Moltmann's Theology* (Philadelphia: Fortress Press, 1979).

O'Donnell, John J., *Trinity and Temporality: The Christian Doctrine of God in the Light of Process Theology* (Oxford: Oxford University Press, 1983).

Olson, Robert, 'Trinity and Eschatology: The Historical Being of God in Jürgen Moltmann and Wolfhart Pannenberg', *SJT* 36.2 (1983), pp. 213-27.

O' Malley, J. Steven, 'Pietist Influences in Eschatological Thought of John Wesley and Jürgen Moltmann', *WesTJ* 29 (1994), pp. 127-39.

—'The Role of Pietism in the Theology of Jürgen Moltmann', *ATJ* 48 (1993), pp. 121-27.

Otto, Randall E., 'God and History in Jürgen Moltmann', *JETS* 35.3 (1992), pp. 375-88.

—'Resurrection in Jürgen Moltmann', *JETS* 35 (1992), pp. 81-90.

Pinnock, Clark H., review of *The Source of Life: The Holy Spirit and the Theology of Life* (trans. Margaret Kohl; Minnesota: Fortress Press, 1997), by Jürgen Moltmann, in *PSB* 20.2 (1999), pp. 227-28.

Preece, Gordon R., *The Viability of the Vocational Tradition in Trinitarian Creedal and Reformed Perspectives* (Lewiston, NY: Edwin Mellen Press, 1998).

Rasmusson, Arne, *The Church as Polis: From Political Theology to Religious Politics as Exemplified by Jürgen Moltmann and Stanley Hauerwas* (Notre Dame: University of Notre Dame Press, 1995).

Rhodes, J. Stephen, 'Jürgen Moltmann: The Comfort and Challenge of Open Friendship', *ATJ* 49 (1994), pp. 63-69.

Robinson, James McConkey, *The Beginnings of Dialectic Theology* (Richmond, VA: John Knox Press, 1968).

Scaer, David P., 'Jürgen Moltmann and his "Theology of Hope" ', *JETS* 13 (1970), pp. 69-79.

Schuurman, Douglas J., 'Creation, Eschaton and Ethics: An Analysis of Theology and Ethics in Jürgen Moltmann', *CTJ* 22 (1987), pp. 42-67.

—*Creation, Eschaton and Ethics: The Ethical Significance of the Creation-Eschaton Relation in the Thought of Emil Brunner and Jürgen Moltmann* (TR, 86; New York: Peter Lang, 1991).

Schweitzer, Don, 'Contrasting Approaches to Social Analysis in the Theologies of Douglas Hall and Jürgen Moltmann', *RST* 16 (1997), pp. 37-54.

Scott, Mark Allen, *Theodicy: Failure and Promise within the Theology of Karl Barth, David R. Griffin and Jürgen Moltmann* (Grand Rapids: UMI Dissertation Services, 1987).

Tang, Sui-Kwong, *God's History in the Theology of Jürgen Moltmann* (New York: Peter Lang, 1976).

Taylor, Michael J. (ed.), *The Mystery of Suffering and Death* (New York: Alba House, 1973).

Toon, Peter, and James D. Spiceland (eds.), *One God in Trinity* (Westchester, IL: Cornerstone Books, 1980).

Torrance, Alan J., 'Creatio ex Nihilo and the Spatial-Temporal Dimension, with Special Reference to Jürgen Moltmann', in Colin E. Gunton (ed.), *Doctrine of Creation* (Edinburgh: T. & T. Clark, 1997), pp. 83-103.

—'An Interview with Jürgen Moltmann', in Bryan (ed.), *Communities of Faith and Radical Discipleship*, pp. 5-12.

Volf, Miroslav (ed.), *The Future of Theology* (Grand Rapids: Eerdmans, 1996).

Wagner, C. Peter, 'Mission and Hope: Some Missiological Implications of the Theology of Jürgen Moltmann', *Missiology* 2 (1974), pp. 455-74.

Walsh, Brian J., 'Theology of Hope and the Doctrine of Creation: An Appraisal of Jürgen Moltmann', *EvQ* 59 (1987), pp. 53-76.

Wiebe, Don, 'Interpretation and Historical Criticism: Jürgen Moltmann', *ResQ* 24.3 (1981), pp. 155-66.

Willis, W. Waite, *Theism, Atheism and the Doctrine of the Trinity: The Trinitarian Theologies of Karl Barth and Jürgen Moltmann* (Atlanta: Scholars Press, 1987).

Wood, Laurence W., 'From Barth's Trinitarian Christology to Moltmann's Trinitarian Pneumatology: A Methodist Perspective', *ATJ* 48.1 (1993), pp. 49-79.

—'Theology of Jürgen Moltmann', *ATJ* 48 (1993), pp. 5-127.

INDEXES

INDEX OF REFERENCES

BIBLE